South Asian Perspectives in Mental Health and Psychology

This series of books is an endeavor to gather and present a comprehensive understanding of the various aspects of mental health that are relevant to people living in South Asia. The books aim to provide in-depth guidance and practical solutions to the mental health challenges that are unique to these areas. The content covers a wide range of topics, including but not limited to, climate change and its impact, prison mental health, perinatal mental health, social psychiatry, mental health and disorder among the elderly population, psychiatry education and training, suicide, SDGs and mental health, trauma, addiction, and social isolation. The books also emphasize the importance of early intervention and provide resources for seeking help. The ultimate goal of this series is to empower individuals and communities to take proactive steps toward enhancing their mental wellbeing. The proposed books will fill the existing unmet need in the region with huge populations in low and middle-income country (LMIC) settings.

South Asia, home to about 2 billion people, is a region of diverse cultures, languages, and religions. It caters to about 25% of the global population. This densely populated region faces a myriad of challenges, both natural and man-made. The frequent occurrence of natural disasters, such as earthquakes, floods, and landslides, threaten the lives and livelihoods of millions of people. War, terrorism, and political instability have caused significant disruptions to the region's socio-political fabric. Poverty, migration, and tropical infectious diseases remain major challenges that hinder progress towards sustainable development. Climate change exacerbates these challenges, causing widespread environmental degradation, food insecurity, and water scarcity. Despite these obstacles, South Asian people have shown remarkable resilience and strength in the face of adversity.

Mental health issues in the South Asian region significantly contribute to the global burden of mental illnesses. However, the region faces plenty of challenges such as high stigma, low mental health literacy, poor budgetary allocation, high out-of-pocket expense for mental health services, lack of adequate infrastructure, and limited human resources are significant barriers in mental healthcare. The majority of research on mental health issues is produced by the western countries which may not fit all in the South Asian culture, albeit evidence is needed to test. There is a paucity of research and evidence-based strategies that are region-specific. This series of books is an attempt to compile the important dimensions of mental health that will benefit the regional people.

Arpit Parmar • Sujita Kumar Kar
S. M. Yasir Arafat
Editors

Forensic Psychiatry and Prison Mental Health in South Asia

Springer

Editors
Arpit Parmar
All India Institute of Medical Sciences
Bhubaneswar, Odisha, India

S. M. Yasir Arafat
Bangladesh Specialized Hospital
Dhaka, Bangladesh

Sujita Kumar Kar
Department of Psychiatry
King George's Medical University
Lucknow, Uttar Pradesh, India

ISSN 3059-3646 ISSN 3059-3522 (electronic)
South Asian Perspectives in Mental Health and Psychology
ISBN 978-981-96-7205-9 ISBN 978-981-96-7206-6 (eBook)
https://doi.org/10.1007/978-981-96-7206-6

This Springer imprint is published by the registered company Springer Nature Singapore Pte Ltd.
The registered company address is: 152 Beach Road, #21-01/04 Gateway East, Singapore 189721, Singapore

Foreword

People with mental health issues often find themselves in the crosshairs of law, for a variety of reasons. Mental health professionals—partly owing to their training, which invariably inculcates an empathetic attitude and partly because of inadequate understanding of legal matters—often find themselves on crossroads while encountering such patients. Practitioners of forensic sciences, on the other hand, often lack optimum understanding of mental health issues. Consequently, mental health of people living in prisons or the forensic psychiatry in general remains an under-researched discipline. With the mounting realization of the importance of human rights of incarcerated individuals, it is high time that the academic discipline of psychiatry shifts its gaze toward this relatively neglected area. This is especially true for the lower- and middle-income countries, where forensic psychiatry continues to be a growing discipline still trying to find its feet. Given this background, I was delighted to find that a book dedicated to Forensic Psychiatry and Prison Mental Health is being published. Authored by a group of expert mental health professionals from all the major South Asian countries, the carefully curated chapters delve into a variety of issues related to the central theme of the book.

While there are individual chapters exclusively dedicated to forensic psychiatry and prison mental health from each of the major South Asian Countries (Bangladesh, India, Nepal, Pakistan, Sri Lanka), in the very first chapter, Parmar and colleagues provide a comprehensive, bird's eye view of the South Asian region as a whole and point out the subtle similarities and differences in the countries of the region. It is fascinating to see how the authors in this chapter (as well as in those chapters dedicated to the individual countries) examine the myriad social and public policy issues through the prism of forensic psychiatry. After these "national" chapters, the book contains dedicated chapters on each of the four important themes of: Mental health of people in prisons, Suicide, Substance use, and Child sexual abuse. Notably, each of these thematic chapters does maintain a "South Asia" perspective. Most of the chapters—while still being shining examples of good "academic" text—have the lucid flow and narrative to keep the reader engaged.

This book would be an invaluable addition to the growing literature on forensic psychiatry in South Asia. Indeed, considering that countries in the Indian sub-continent share a variety of social, economic, political characteristics with other developing countries of the global south, I am certain that scholars from other parts of the world would also find this book useful. Despite its title it would be an injustice to see this book as only meant for psychiatrists or forensic medicine specialists. Anyone interested in the interface of mental health with criminology, sociology, public policy, political science will find this book engaging and enlightening.

If you are holding this book, in all probability you have made a correct choice.

National Drug Dependence Treatment Centre
All India Institute of Medical Sciences, New Delhi,
New Delhi, India

Atul Ambekar

Preface

The intersection between mental illnesses and the legal system represents one of the most complex areas for psychiatrists, psychologists, and legal professionals. Unique issues such as cultural factors, overpopulation, limited infrastructure and resources, and varying (and, at times, outdated) legal frameworks make it more complex in South Asian countries. Due to limited infrastructure and resources and limited attention from policymakers and health professionals working in the psychiatry, psychology, and legal fields, forensic psychiatry as a specialty is relatively underdeveloped in this region. In addition, prisons in South Asia have several issues, including overcrowding, poor infrastructure, limited healthcare resources, stigma, and other cultural issues. Colonial-era laws that some of these countries still follow further complicate the issue, leading to under-identification of these conditions.

The idea for this book stemmed from the recognition of this critical gap in the academic literature. It, *Forensic Psychiatry and Prison Mental Health in South Asia*, is the first attempt to comprehensively document the aspects of forensic psychiatry relevant to South Asian countries. With the help of expert academicians working in this field, we provide a detailed and nuanced view of the forensic psychiatry practice, service delivery, and research in the region.

Within this book, the readers will find comprehensive insights into the development of forensic psychiatry services in each of the South Asian nations, service delivery in prison settings and community rehabilitation, laws in relation to mental and substance use disorders (MSUDs), disability, sexual abuse, and other related aspects and legal provisions for insanity defense and psychiatric admissions. The book covers certain critical areas, such as the prevalence of MSUD conditions; the inadequacy of services in prison settings with limited aftercare and rehabilitation; child sexual abuse in the region and aspects related to the assessment and legal requirements; suicide and self-harm in prison populations, and substance use, international conventions, and related regional/national legal provisions. We also highlight the emerging success stories about service delivery innovations even in such challenging environments.

The book is intended for a diverse group of professionals, including psychiatrists, psychologists, forensic psychiatrists, addiction psychiatrists, social workers, trainees in psychiatry and psychology, legal professionals, policymakers, prison administrators, researchers, and students interested in understanding the forensic psychiatry aspects of the region. Professionals from other medical fields, such as forensic medicine and pediatrics, and students of these fields may find many aspects of this book beneficial in their practice.

The book primarily focuses on the academic aspects of forensic psychiatry and prison mental health in the region. The book serves as a foundation for call for more attention to this aspect in clinical, research, and advocacy areas of the psychiatry and psychology fields. We hope that the book will contribute to raising awareness and stimulate future research in forensic psychiatry aspects in the region. Finally, we hope that the book shall help improve the lives of at least some of the most marginalized and vulnerable sections of society, i.e., prison populations with MSUD conditions.

We are incredibly grateful to all the contributors who have contributed chapters to the book and have made this volume possible with their knowledge, experience, and insights based on the available evidence and expertise. However, our contributors mostly have psychiatry, psychology, and medical expertise. We hope criticism and suggestions from other fields of expertise will be helpful for the healthy growth of the book in the coming editions. We consider that this is the foundation of a long journey on Forensic Psychiatry in South Asia, which will be enriched in the future with upcoming evidence, changes in legal structure over time, comments, and criticisms from readers and experts in various fields.

Odisha, India — Arpit Parmar
Lucknow, Uttar Pradesh, India — Sujia Kumar Kar
Dhaka, Bangladesh — S. M. Yasir Arafat

Contents

About the Editors

S. M. Yasir Arafat is currently working as an Associate Consultant of Psychiatry at Bangladesh Specialized Hospital, Dhaka, Bangladesh. He is affiliated with Frontier University Garowe, Somalia as an Associate Professor, Dnet as an Honorary Research Fellow and with the Biomedical Research Foundation, Bangladesh as a Senior Research Fellow. He was affiliated with the University of Bristol, UK as a Visiting Senior Research Associate (August 2021–2023). He completed his MD in Psychiatry, an MPH in Health Economics, an MBA in Marketing, and an MBBS. Dr. Arafat has (co)authored more than 350 peer-reviewed articles and 50 book chapters and (co)edited more than ten books with Springer. He has been included in the global 2% researcher list in 2021, 2022, and 2023. He is an editorial member of more than 10 leading journals in mental health, published by Elsevier, Wiley, Springer, and Taylor and Francis. His research focused on mental health, suicidal behavior, psychometrics, panic buying, and psycho-sexual disorders.

Sujita Kumar Kar is currently working as an Additional Professor of Psychiatry at King George's Medical University, Lucknow, Uttar Pradesh, India. He is the editor-in-chief of Indian Journal of Health, Sexuality and Culture. He is also the editorial board member and reviewer of various national and international journals. He had written 74 book chapters and more than 500 articles in various national & international journals and made 70 presentations at various national and international conferences. He has been included in the global 2% researcher list released by Stanford University in 2021, 2022, 2023, and 2024. His research interests include brain stimulation, neuropsychiatry, and suicide prevention.

Arpit Parmar is currently working as an Associate Professor of Psychiatry at All India Institute of Medical Sciences Bhubaneswar, Odisha, India. He has completed an MD in Psychiatry and a DM in Addiction Psychiatry from All India Institute of Medical Sciences New Delhi. He has written more than 90 research articles and 10 book chapters. He has made more than 40 presentations at national and international prestigious conferences. His research interests include addiction psychiatry, social psychiatry, and public mental health. He is a peer reviewer of many national and international psychiatry journals and is a section editor of the Indian Journal of Psychological Medicine.

List of Figures

List of Tables

Chapter 1
Forensic Psychiatry in South Asia: An Overview

Arpit Parmar, Sujita Kumar Kar, and S. M. Yasir Arafat

Abstract Although forensic psychiatric services are an integral part of the mental health services component, they are largely under development and neglected in South Asian countries due to various reasons like low priority and budget for mental health, lack of trained human resources, inadequate collaboration between law and mental health professionals, poor human rights conditions, and outdated legal structures. Along with regular issues, prison mental health services, child sexual abuse, and domestic violence are largely neglected despite a high burden and demand for mental healthcare. This chapter discusses the enduring status and challenges of forensic psychiatric aspects, including law and mental health, substance abuse, child sexual abuse, domestic violence, and prison mental health. There is a need for a multipronged approach to expand forensic psychiatry services in the South Asian region, including increasing government spending on healthcare, developing dedicated programs for forensic psychiatry training, and updating the legislation over time.

Keywords Forensic psychiatry · South Asia · Prison psychiatry · Law and psychiatry · Mental health

---

A. Parmar (✉)
Department of Psychiatry, All India Institute of Medical Sciences, Bhubaneswar, Odisha, India

S. K. Kar
Department of Psychiatry, King George's Medical University, Lucknow, Uttar Pradesh, India

S. M. Y. Arafat
Department of Psychiatry, Bangladesh Specialized Hospital, Dhaka, Bangladesh

A. Parmar et al. (eds.), *Forensic Psychiatry and Prison Mental Health in South Asia*, South Asian Perspectives in Mental Health and Psychology,
https://doi.org/10.1007/978-981-96-7206-6_1

1 History of Forensic Psychiatry

Forensic psychiatry is a subspecialty that involves the interface between law, the criminal justice system, and psychiatry. As a specialized field of psychiatry, forensic psychiatry applies scientific and clinical experience in legal contexts (such as civil, criminal, correctional, regulatory, and legislative matters). Even though the medical field of psychiatry did not exist before the eighteenth century, the issues involving legal and social problems related to psychiatric issues go back many centuries (Gold & Frierson, 2018). For example, the Code of Hammurabi in the ancient Babylonian system considered the importance of intention in judging actions. Similar provisions also existed in the ancient Hebrew laws. However, the Jewish Talmud recommended capital punishment for murder committed under the intoxication of alcohol. Under Islamic law, murder by a person with mental illness (PwMI) was considered to be an involuntary homicide requiring only compensation and not punishment. India also provided special considerations for children and retarded individuals around 880 BC.

During medieval times, supernatural beliefs about the PwMI dominated the globe, including South Asia. Mental illnesses were attributed to witchcraft and demonic possession, and PwMI were called names such as "insane," "crazy," and "mad." By the fourteenth century, English courts started recognizing the defense of insanity. In the eighteenth century, Immanuel Kant emphasized accountability, freedom, and proper mental faculties and differentiated between various forms of psychosis as relevant to forensic psychiatry. He advocated utilizing psychologists, not physicians, to assess criminal responsibility in court matters. The landmark case of M'Naughten in 1843 AD established the principles of the insanity defense across the globe, including in South Asian countries (Asokan, 2016). In South Asian countries, especially India, Pakistan, Nepal, Bangladesh, and Sri Lanka, forensic psychiatry was developed within the colonial framework of the legal system and evolved through the lunatic asylum. However, it has further evolved to incorporate the respective countries' local social, religious, and social contexts.

2 Overview of South Asian Countries

2.1 *Demographic Profile*

The South Asian region, comprising Afghanistan, Bangladesh, Bhutan, India, Maldives, Nepal, Pakistan, and Sri Lanka, is one of the most densely populated regions of the world, housing approximately 2 billion (almost 25%) of the global population (*World Bank Open Data | Data*, n.d.). As per the recent World Bank data, India is the largest country in South Asia, with a population of more than 1.4 billion people. Countries like Pakistan (more than 240 million people) and Bangladesh (approximately 170 million) also have a sizeable population. In contrast, other

South Asian countries like Nepal (approximately 29 million), Afghanistan (almost 41 million), Sri Lanka (around 22 million), Bhutan (approximately 0.8 million), and Maldives (around 0.5 million) are relatively less populated (Arafat & Kar, 2024).

2.2 Healthcare Profile

Healthcare, particularly mental healthcare, in South Asian nations faces many issues and challenges. Countries allocate less than 4% of their GDP to healthcare, which is considerably lower than that of many Western developed countries. As per the latest Global Health Expenditure Database of the WHO, India spends around 3.8% of its GDP on healthcare (*Global Health Expenditure Database*, 2025). On the other hand, despite having a robust healthcare system, Sri Lanka allocates around 4.07% of the GDP.

The healthcare infrastructure also varies significantly between countries. For example, countries like India, Sri Lanka, and Bangladesh have an established network of medical colleges, hospitals, and primary healthcare facilities. These countries have a varied mix of public and privately funded healthcare models. It is important to note that even in different countries, there is a rural-urban divide for seeking healthcare for various illnesses. Traditional healing practices are common in this region, with many choosing conventional healthcare as an initial health contact. Mental healthcare is heavily stigmatized in the area.

2.3 Mental Healthcare in South Asia

Mental healthcare is relatively poorly developed compared to general healthcare in the region. Of the total healthcare expenditure, South Asian countries allocate a much lesser amount to mental healthcare than developed countries in the Western world. For example, 0.5% of Bangladesh's total government health expenditure was allocated to mental healthcare (*Global Health Expenditure Database*, n.d.). Countries like Pakistan, Nepal, and Bhutan allocate 0.04%, 0.2%, and 0.2% of their total government health expenditure to mental healthcare, respectively (Hossain et al., 2020; Parmar et al., 2023).

On the other hand, mental and substance use disorders (MSUDs) are quite prevalent in the region. For example, as per the recent national survey in India, one in ten persons suffers from any mental illness (Murthy, 2017). Depression, anxiety, and substance use disorders (especially tobacco, betel nut, and alcohol use) are common across the region (Hossain et al., 2020; Naveed et al., 2020). The burden related to these conditions is huge. In Sri Lanka, the burden of mental disorders is 1379.4 disability-adjusted life years (DALYs) per 100,000 population, as per the recent WHO Mental Health Atlas 2020 (World Health Organization, 2021). A similar burden has also been reported from other South Asian countries.

Trained human resources in mental healthcare are also an important issue in the service delivery for mental illnesses. As per the recent WHO Mental Health Atlas 2020, the number of total mental health professionals in South Asian countries ranges from 0.55 per 100,000 population in Pakistan to 5.46 per 100,000 population in Sri Lanka (Arafat and Kar, 2024; World Health Organization, 2021). The number of trained psychiatrists is even lower. For example, India‘s number of psychiatrists per 100,000 population stands at 0.75, suggesting a shortage of qualified mental health professionals (Garg et al., 2019).

Other issues are also prevalent besides a shortage of trained human resources. PwMI is highly stigmatized in the region (Parmar, Mohanty, et al., 2024; Vaishnav et al., 2023). The medical model is poorly understood, and superstitious beliefs are often attributed to its occurrence. Owing to this, PwMI and their family members frequently seek help through traditional methods or with faith healers. This culminates in poor rates of treatment seeking for mental ailments. For example, only one or two out of ten PwMI receive any treatment for mental illness in India (Murthy, 2017). Finally, the availability of MSUD medications in essential drug lists of South Asian countries is also limited (Parmar, Nath, et al., 2022).

2.4 *Legal Frameworks*

The following sections will discuss various aspects related to mental healthcare acts, substance use-related acts, and other legislation. Table 1.1 provides an overview of some of these legislation.

The laws related to MSUD in South Asian countries are inherited from the legal systems in place during the British colonial era. However, significant reforms have occurred during recent decades, keeping in mind the cultural and social influences and modernization.

In India, the Mental Healthcare Act was enacted in 2017, a paradigm shift from the previous Indian Lunacy Act of 1912—a law passed during the British colonial era (Namboodiri et al., 2019). The newer legislature focuses on the human rights of PwMI, with the provision of treatment access to those suffering from MSUD. The act also decriminalized suicide in the country. The act tries to address the need for treatment of prisoners suffering from MSUDs. Finally, the act also provides for the nominated representative for PwMI with limited decision-making capacity.

Bangladesh also passed a new Mental Health Act in 2018, replacing the Lunacy Act 1912 (Mental Health Act, 2018). The act mentions various aspects related to mental healthcare in the country, such as assessment and hospitalization for MSUDs, capacity assessment, forceful hospitalization, guardianship, and establishment of psychiatric hospitals. The act also emphasizes the rights of PwMI in terms of their clinical assessment, treatment, property, and legal proceedings.

Nepal has not yet adopted a national mental healthcare act. However, other acts, such as the Act Relating to the Rights of Persons with Disabilities 2017, and policies, such as the National Mental Health Strategy and Action Plan 2020, address

Table 1.1 Laws related to mental health in South Asia

Country	Act/Legislation
Afghanistan	• Mental Health Act, 1997 • Tobacco Control Law, 2015 • Counter Narcotics Law, 2005 • Elimination of Violence Against Women law, 2009 • Juvenile Law (Juvenile Code), 2005 • Law on Protection of Child Rights, 2019 • Afghan Penal Code—Article 67 (Insanity Defense)
Bangladesh	• Mental Health Act, 2018 • Rights and Protection of Persons with Disabilities Act, 2013 • Narcotics Control Act of 1990 • Domestic Violence (Prevention and Protection) Act, 2010 • Section 84 of the Penal Code (Insanity Defense) • Children Act of 2013 • Smoking and Tobacco Products Usage (Control) Act of 2005 • Penal Code 1860 and Code of Criminal Procedure 1898 • Various acts related to marriage
Bhutan	• Narcotic Drugs, Psychotropic Substances and Substance Abuse Act of Bhutan, 2015 • Tobacco Control Act of Bhutan, 2010 (amended in 2021) • Child Care and Protection Act of Bhutan (CCPA) of 2011 • Domestic Violence Prevention Act of Bhutan, 2013 • Penal Code (Amendment) Act of Bhutan, 2021 • Marriage (Amendment) Act of Bhutan 2009
India	• Mental Healthcare Act, 2017 • Rights of Persons with Disabilities Act, 2016 • National Trust Act, 1999 • Bharatiya Nyaya Samhita Act, 2023 (various sections such as Section 22 deal with insanity defense) • Protection of Children from Sexual Offences (POCSO) Act, 2012 • Narcotic Drugs and Psychotropic Substances Act, 1985 • Cigarettes and Other Tobacco Products (Prohibition of Advertisement and Regulation of Trade and Commerce, Production, Supply, and Distribution) Act 2003 • Drugs and Cosmetics Act 1940 • Various acts related to marriage • Protection of Women from Domestic Violence Act, 2005 • Juvenile Justice (Care and Protection of Children) Act, 2015
Maldives	• Disability Act, 2010 (Law Number 8/2010) • Law No 17/77—The Law on Drugs • Tobacco Control Act, 2010 (Law no 15/2010) • Juvenile Justice Act, 2019 (Act No 18/2019) • Domestic Violence Prevention Act, 2012 (Act No 3/2012) • Child Rights Protection Act (CRC), 2019 (Act No. 2019-19) • Maldives Family Act, 2000 (Act No. 4/2000)

(continued)

Table 1.1 (continued)

Country	Act/Legislation
Nepal	• The Act Relating to Rights of Persons with Disabilities, 2074 (2017) • Public Health Service Act, 2075 (2018) • National Penal Code, 2074 (2017) • National Civil Code, 2074 (2017) • Tobacco Product (Control and Regulatory) Act, 2068 (2011) • Narcotic Drugs Control Act, 2033 (1976) • The Act Relating to Children, 2075 (2018) • Domestic Violence (Crime and Punishment) Act, 2066 (2009) • Various acts related to marriage
Pakistan	• Mental Health Ordinance, 2001 • Rights of Persons with Disability Act, 2020 • Juvenile Justice System Act (JJSA), 2018 • Prohibition of Smoking and Protection of Non-smokers Health Ordinance No. LXXIV, 2002 • The Cigarette (Printing of Warning) (Amendment) Ordinance No.LXXV, 2002 • Control of Narcotic Substances Act, 1997 • Domestic Violence (Prevention and Protection) Act, 2010 • Marriage acts • Penal Code, 1898 (Section 84—Insanity defense) • Child Protection and Welfare Act, 2010
Sri Lanka	• Mental Diseases Ordinance, 1956 • Conventions Against Illicit Traffic in Narcotic Drugs and Psychotropic Substances. Act, No. 1 of 2008 • Poisons, Opium, and Dangerous Drugs (Amendment) Act, No. 41 of 2022 • Children and Young Persons Ordinance, No. 48 of 1939 • Youthful Offenders (Training Schools) Act, No. 42 of 1944 • Probation of Offenders Act, No. 10 of 1948 • National Authority on Tobacco and Alcohol (NATA) Act, 2006 • Tobacco Tax Act, 1999 • Protection of Women from Domestic Violence Act, 2005 • Penal Code of Sri Lanka, 1883 and Penal Code (Amendment) Act, No. 25 of 2021 (Section 77—Insanity Defense) • Marriage related acts

mental healthcare issues (Adhikari et al., 2024). Pakistan has also enacted regional acts (such as the Punjab Mental Health Act 2014) that were subsequently amended in 2018 as the Mental Health Act (Javed et al., 2020). Like in other South Asian countries like India and Bangladesh, this act emphasizes the human rights of PwMI. However, it provides very little guidance on its overall implementation. Pakistan also recently decriminalized suicide attempts in 2022 (Khan, 2024; Kline & Sabri, 2023). In Sri Lanka, the Mental Diseases Ordinance of 1956 governs the aspects of mental healthcare (Kathriarachchi et al., 2019). The ordinance replaced the previous British colonial-era lunacy ordinance of 1873. The act provides for the treatment of severe mental illnesses in mental hospitals through courts. Sri Lanka, in fact, was the first country in the region to decriminalize suicide in 1998 (Mukherjee & Bhandarkar, 2014). In Afghanistan, the first mental health act was ratified in 1987. On the other hand, Maldives has no mental health policy or law.

Apart from the specific acts related to mental health, other acts also govern mental healthcare in the region. For example, issues related to the insanity defense are dealt with under India's Bharatiya Nyaya Samhita Act 2023 (Hegde et al., 2024). The same is covered under section 77 of the Penal Code of Sri Lanka and Nepal's National Penal (Code) Act, 2017. Disability-related acts, such as the Rights of Persons with Disabilities Act 2016 in India and the Act Relating to Rights of Persons with Disabilities, 2017 of Nepal, also identify mental disability and ensure their rights.

2.5 Substance Use and Drug Trafficking

Substance use (especially tobacco, alcohol, betel nut, cannabis, and opioids) is a major concern in the region (Vashney et al., 2020; *World Drug Report 2024*, n.d.). South Asia is sandwiched between two important areas, which are the top illicit opioid producers in the world: the "Golden Triangle" and the "Golden Crescent." Narcotic trades begin from the areas of the "Golden Crescent" and then travel via India to other parts of the world. Thus, drug control is an important international concern in the region.

Three UN conventions govern the current regulatory framework in South Asian countries: the Single Convention on Narcotic Drugs 1961, the Convention on Psychotropic Substances 1971, and the Convention against Illicit Trafficking in Narcotic Drugs and Psychotropic Substances 1988. Apart from this, a regional convention—SAARC Convention on Narcotic Drugs and Psychotropic Substances—was also signed by the countries in 1993. The laws of South Asian countries primarily follow a criminal justice approach to the substance use problem and not a public health approach. These acts criminalize drug use, possession, and other drug-related aspects. The policies in the region vary from strict punitive measures to the decriminalization of certain drug use to harm reduction approaches. For example, certain exceptions to the drug use ban, such as the legalization of cannabis leaves (*bhang*) in India, also exist (Balhara et al., 2022). The Indian Narcotic Drugs and Psychotropic Substances Act of 1985 not only criminalizes drug use but also includes provisions for treatment and rehabilitation (Parmar, Narasimha, et al., 2024). Apart from this, countries like India and Bangladesh also have provisions for capital punishment for certain drug-related offenses.

On the other hand, tobacco-related laws in the region are predominantly based on the WHO Framework Convention on Tobacco Control (FCTC) 2003. Most countries ratified it between 2003 and 2006. India regulates the various aspects related to tobacco use under the Cigarettes and Other Tobacco Products (Prohibition of Advertisement and Regulation of Trade and Commerce, Production, Supply, and Distribution) Act 2003 (Gupta et al., 2025). The act prohibits the advertisement of tobacco-related products, among many other tobacco-related provisions. India also banned the use of e-cigarettes in 2019 (Chakma et al., 2020). Bhutan enacted the Tobacco Control Act of 2010 to ban the sale and smoking of tobacco products in public spaces (Chakma et al., 2020). The act prohibited the production and sale of tobacco, along with a 100% sales tax on imported products. The ban was relaxed in 2021, with permission to sell tobacco products in shops. In Nepal, the Tobacco Product (Control and Regulatory) Act of 2011 is the primary act that governs tobacco use (Bhatta et al., 2020). The law covers various aspects related to tobacco use, such as advertising, labeling, and smoking in public places. Bangladesh also follows the WHO FCTC. Tobacco and alcohol use in Sri Lanka is governed by the National Authority on Tobacco and Alcohol (NATA) under the National Authority on Tobacco and Alcohol Act 2006 (Rajapaksa et al., 2021).

The majority of the countries in South Asia have no separate national policies about alcohol use. However, there is a complete ban on using alcohol in the Maldives, Bangladesh, and Afghanistan. Alcohol is banned in some Indian states, like Gujarat and Bihar (Parmar et al., 2023a, b).

2.6 *Child Sexual Abuse*

Child sexual abuse (CSA) is an important public health issue in the South Asian countries. These countries account for the world's 36% of children's population. The prevalence of CSA in the region ranges from 3.3% to as high as 60% (Selengia et al., 2020). The issue is prevalent among both male and female children, with a slightly higher prevalence among females. Multiple interconnected factors in the individual, familial, and social domains are identified as risk factors, including poverty, non-availability of caregivers, societal patriarchal norms, and poor law enforcement (Choudhry et al., 2018). Various impacts on the psychological health of children have also been recorded in the literature concerning South Asia, including depression, PTSD, and personality issues (Papalia et al., 2020). On the other hand, the healthcare professionals in the region face unique challenges when it comes to CSA due to cultural stigma, family dynamics, balancing mandatory reporting with therapeutic relationships, and limited mental health services for children and adolescents (Jiloha et al., 2019). Limited research on culturally appropriate, child-friendly interventions for such psychiatric issues also complicates the issue further (Kuttala et al., 2025).

The UN Convention on the Rights of the Child (UNCRC), an important, legally binding agreement, has been signed by all the South Asian nations (*UN Convention on Rights of a Child (UNCRC)—UNICEF UK*, 2025). The UNCRC covers all the aspects related to the rights of children and applies to all children, i.e., it is universal in nature. Various rights included under the convention include civil, economic, social, and cultural rights. Article 34 of the UNCRC pertains to the protection of children from all forms of sexual exploitation and abuse, while Article 19 pertains to protection from violence, abuse, and neglect. Apart from this, Article 33 ensures the protection of children from the use of illegal drugs and their involvement in the drug trade.

South Asian countries have attempted to build legislation based on the UNCRC. For example, India has a very comprehensive legislation, the Protection of Children from Sexual Offenses (POCSO) Act, 2012, which covers various aspects related to CSA, such as sexual abuse, harassment, and pornography (Jatchavala et al., 2024). The Act is gender-neutral in nature and provides for mandatory recording and reporting of the CSA, along with the establishment of special courts for trials in such matters. Nepal covers CSA-related aspects in its special act, "The Act Relating to Children, 2075," and Nepal Penal Code chapter 18 (Bakhadyo, 2021). In Bangladesh, the Prevention of Oppression against Women and Children Act, 2000, the Pornography Control Act, 2012, and Penal Code Section 366-A deal with the CSA-related aspects (Alam & Bari, 2014). Other countries also have specific laws about CSA. However, some common regional challenges, such as limited enforcement of the CSA-related provisions in the laws, cultural barriers in the reporting of CSA, and poor coordination between the legal and health systems, hamper the overall effectiveness of the legal provisions.

2.7 *Domestic Violence*

Domestic violence is another pervasive issue across the South Asian countries. The studies indicate that up to half of the married females in the region suffer from domestic violence from their husbands, with most of the violence starting during the early period of their marital relationships (Sabri et al., 2014). Alcohol and other substance use among spouses is one of the commonly associated factors with domestic violence (Singh et al., 2024). Physical and sexual violence in marital relationships is related to many adverse mental health outcomes, apart from injuries, unwanted pregnancies, adverse obstetric outcomes, poor neonatal health, and pregnancy loss, among many others (*Violence Against Women Prevalence Estimates*, 2025).

From a legal perspective, there are laws in all South Asian countries mandating support for domestic violence victims in need. For example, the Protection of Women from Domestic Violence Act, 2005, of India requires that protection officers ensure the medical examination of a victim of domestic violence who has "sustained bodily injuries" (Jejeebhoy et al., 2014). It also has other provisions like custody of the child, fast judgments, recognition of verbal as well as emotional abuse, and the right to residence. Similar provisions also exist in the laws of other countries, such as the Domestic Violence (Offense and Punishment) Act 2009 of Nepal, the Domestic Violence (Prevention and Protection) Act 2010 of Bangladesh, the Domestic Violence (Prevention and Protection) Act 2010 of Pakistan, the Domestic Violence Act 2012 of Maldives, and the Protection of Women from Domestic Violence Act 2005 of Sri Lanka (Jejeebhoy et al., 2014).

Despite this, there is very little help-seeking in South Asian women due to egalitarian norms about gender prevalent in the region. The usual reaction to the violence among females is toleration and silence. Even when help is sought, it is overwhelmingly from family members and friends and not from authorities or healthcare providers. The countries lack any screening system in place at the healthcare facility level for such victims. The healthcare providers also lack specific training in handling such issues. Finally, they may also consider domestic violence a private matter or may share societal attitudes that may normalize such violence.

2.8 Mental Illness and Nullity of Marriage

Marital life is significantly affected by mental illness. Marriage is a social contract, and at times, mental illness can stand as a basis for the nullity of marriage. Several Indian laws mention "unsoundness of mind" as grounds for the nullity of marriage (Nambi and Sarkar, 2015; Nambi, 2005; Pathare et al., 2015; Narayan et al., 2015; Sharma et al., 2015; Bhugra et al., 2016). The nature and severity of mental illness, the decision-taking ability of the person with mental illness, the ability to lead a married life, and the ability to procreate are considered important domains in a marriage contract. Often, legal issues arise due to conflict in any of these domains among the persons with mental illnesses. Different countries follow different legal standards with respect to marriage in persons with mental illness. There is a gross variation in the laws among the countries. There is a lack of clarity in the laws in several countries (Bhugra et al., 2016).

3 Criminal Responsibility and Insanity Defense

The concept of the insanity defense has been used for more than two centuries and is generally related to cases of criminal prosecutions. It assumes that if a person, while committing the crime, suffers from such severe mental illness that they are incapable of appreciating the nature of the crime and what is right and wrong, then the person is not accountable for the crimes committed in such a state. This is primarily a legal concept. However, the term "insanity" does not have any precise definition, i.e., it can have different meanings in different contexts.

Most South Asian countries' legal systems regarding the insanity defense were strongly influenced by the British colonial era, particularly the famous McNaughten Rules. The Bharatiya Nyaya Samhita Act 2023 in Section 22 states that "Nothing is an offense which is done by a person who, at the time of doing it, by reason of unsoundness of mind, is incapable of knowing the nature of the act or that he is doing what is either wrong or contrary to law." (Hegde et al., 2024) Similar to India, countries of South Asia (particularly Sri Lanka, Bangladesh, Pakistan, and Nepal) also recognize the insanity defense as a result of an unsound mind. The onus of proving the "unsoundness of mind" while committing the act is on the accused. Though the term "person of unsound mind" is considered to be stigmatizing and is replaced by many countries across the world with more appropriate, alternative terms like "defense of a person with mental impairment," the term continues to be utilized in legal systems of most of the South Asian countries.

4 Prison Mental Health

Mental health in the prison setting is a neglected domain in South Asian countries. In general, the prevalence of MSUDs is higher in prison populations as compared to the general population. A previous review that covered India, Bangladesh, Sri Lanka, and Nepal reported that overcrowding (131% to 215%) is a major issue in the prisons of these countries (Arafat et al., 2024). Females constitute a minor proportion of prisoners in these countries. Overcrowding in the prisons leads to environmental conditions that may cause or exacerbate MSUDs. This is evident from the alarmingly high rates of MSUDs in the prison population of these countries. A review reported that the prevalence of MSUDs in the prison population was up to 100% in some studies (Arafat et al., 2024). Among these countries, Bangladesh has the highest rates of MSUD in prisons. It is important to note that there is a dearth of nationwide data on MSUDs and suicide in these countries, and most of the studies are conducted in a limited sample of single prison facilities. Additionally, mental health services are scarce in South Asian countries, where even some countries like Bangladesh do not have provisions for visits to prisons by mental health professionals. There is a very limited number of beds for forensic psychiatry in the region (Arafat et al., 2024). Very little is known about self-harm and suicide among prisoners in South Asian countries. Among the eight countries, the rate of suicide in prison has been noted only in India.

All South Asian countries have criminalized the use of drugs. On the other hand, the use of alcohol is also prohibited in countries like the Maldives and Afghanistan. In India, alcohol use is prohibited in certain large states like Gujarat and Bihar (Parmar, Balhara, et al., 2023a). The arrests related to the use of substances have been shown to impede healthcare-seeking and exacerbate the stigma related to SUDs. It is also seen that many drug-related arrests are related to personal use and not trafficking of drugs.

5 Current Practices and Service Delivery

Despite this huge issue of high MSUD in the prison population, mental healthcare in prisons or correctional facilities is largely inadequate (Arafat et al., 2024). Specialized services for substance use treatment are largely unavailable in the prisons, except for a few prisons in India. For example, Opioid Agonist Treatment for opioid use disorder is not available in most of the prisons of these countries (Parmar, Mohanty, et al., 2024).

Some promising interventions have been piloted in limited prison settings. For example, Tihar prison in India launched rehabilitation programs incorporating psychological counseling and vocational training (Kaur & Roy, 2022). The jail administration initiated a pilot project of the first-ever OAT in a prison setting in the region. In partnership with Sankalp Rehabilitation Trust, the Arthur Road jail administration started a rehabilitation program to provide counseling, medications, and treatment. Vocational training and rehabilitation initiatives have been started in Pakistan's Sindh region's correctional facilities (Ahmed et al., 2022). Telepsychiatry services for prison mental health have been tested in India, which could be further helpful in reducing the mental healthcare gap in correctional facilities in the region (Arafat et al., 2024).

In Sri Lanka, forensic psychiatry services are concentrated in the major cities, though limited in number. These services operate in collaboration between prison mental health services, forensic units, and general psychiatry setups. However, like in other South Asian countries, prison mental healthcare services are only available in a few prisons.

Besides limited-service availability during prison, aftercare and rehabilitation services are almost nonexistent in the region. For example, some prisons, like Tihar Prison in India, provide some reintegration services through continued care for substance use-related issues. On the other hand, the double whammy of stigma related to incarceration, along with the presence of mental illness, creates a significant barrier to seeking community-based care for MSUD. There is limited collaboration and coordination between the legal and health systems.

6 Forensic Psychiatry Training in South Asia

In South Asian countries, there is very little training in forensic psychiatry aspects. Countries like the UK, Australia, and the USA provide specific training in forensic psychiatry, including 3-year dedicated programs in forensic psychiatry (Ellis, 2020; Harkavy-friedman et al., 2012; Sebastian, 2012). On the other hand, very few such courses exist in South Asia. For example, the National Institute of Mental Health and Neurosciences (NIMHANS), Bengaluru, offers a 3-year super-specialty course and a 1-year Postdoctoral Fellowship course in forensic psychiatry. However, apart from NIMHANS, no other institutions in India provide forensic psychiatry training (Malathesh & Das, 2017). The psychiatrists have to depend on the training received as part of their general psychiatry training during the three-year MD course, which is grossly insufficient. In Bangladesh, forensic psychiatry training is provided as part of general psychiatry training, and there are no specialized degrees or training programs on forensic psychiatry in the country (Ahmed et al., 2024). Sri Lanka offers a board certification in forensic psychiatry for MD graduates at the University of Colombo. Other. South Asian countries also have a limited scope of training in forensic psychiatry.

7 Systemic Challenges

South Asian countries suffer from many interconnected issues and challenges when it comes to forensic psychiatry and service delivery in prison settings.

1. As discussed, most of these countries allocate less than 4% of their GDP to healthcare, with an even lesser percentage to mental healthcare. This results in severe resource and infrastructure constraints. Hence, there are no specifically designated forensic psychiatry services in the region.
2. The prisons in the region are generally overcrowded, leading to the onset of new mental illnesses or exacerbation of existing conditions (Arafat et al., 2024). Criminalization of drug use (and, in some countries, prohibition of alcohol use) also leads to overcrowding in prisons. Most of these prisons do not have services for mental healthcare and substance use treatment. Systematic screening protocols for prison populations are largely unavailable, with an absence of standardized forensic assessments. This further exacerbates the grim situation.
3. There is an acute shortage of qualified mental health professionals, especially psychiatrists, in most of these countries (Garg et al., 2019). The treatment gap in the general population for mental healthcare is as high as 90% in these countries (Arafat and Kar, 2024).
4. Apart from the shortage of qualified mental health professionals, the lack of focus on forensic psychiatry in general psychiatry training is another contemporary issue. Only some centers provide specialized training in the field, which is grossly inadequate for the vast population of South Asia.
5. There is generally poor coordination between the region's legal and healthcare systems. Due to this, there are limited aftercare services and rehabilitation for MSUD patients after release from prison.
6. Cultural barriers are also significant barriers to seeking care, especially in forensic populations. MSUD conditions are highly stigmatized in the region (Balhara et al., 2016). Apart from the stigma related to illness, the stigma of incarceration further complicates the situation, leading to a further decline in treatment-seeking. On the other hand, less stigma is reported among those who use drugs like cannabis and opium, which have some social sanction in the region (Gupta et al., 2019; Parmar, Gupta, et al., 2022).
7. Many of the laws in the region are still outdated, with many countries still following British Colonial era legislation. Even when the legislation has been amended as per modern requirements, countries face significant challenges in implementing the same. Laws still utilize outdated and potentially stigmatizing terminologies (for example, "unsoundness of mind"), which are sometimes poorly defined in the legislation (Hegde et al., 2024).
8. Despite human rights concerns over the death penalty for substance use-related cases, there are still provisions for death penalties in the drug acts of some countries in the region.
9. Faith-healing practices, along with traditional medicine, are still the initial contact for help-seeking in the region for many (Parmar et al., 2020; Parmar, Gupta,

et al., 2022; Sarkar et al., 2020). This further leads to delays in the treatment of MSUD conditions.

10. Finally, there is very little research emphasis on the research aspects related to forensic psychiatry in the region. For example, there are no large-scale nation-wide surveys from the region to assess the overall burden of MSUD in prison populations. Interventions for dealing with MSUD conditions are relatively less studied for the prison populations.

8 Conclusion

Forensic psychiatry and prison mental healthcare face numerous systemic challenges, which include an insufficiently trained workforce, overcrowding in the jails, limited infrastructure, and, at times, outdated legislation. Other factors such as cultural barriers, stigmatization of MSUD conditions, criminalization of substance use, traditional and alternative healing practices, faith healing, and poor coordination between legal and healthcare arms of the government systems further complicate the service delivery. There is a need for a multipronged approach to expand forensic psychiatry services in the South Asian region. This includes (1) increasing government spending on healthcare, specifically mental healthcare; (2) developing dedicated programs for forensic psychiatry training and dedicated forensic psychiatry units; (3) updating the legislation as per modern requirements and getting rid of the outdated, stigmatizing terminologies; (4) proper implementation of mental healthcare acts of the respective countries, with a focus on the human rights aspects of MSUD care; and (5) more research focused on the various aspects related to forensic psychiatry in the region. These steps could significantly improve the status of forensic psychiatry and overall MSUD care in the South Asian region.

References

Adhikari, A., Aryal, B., & Khatiwada, K. (2024). Addressing disability inclusion in Nepal: Barriers and actions. *Quest Journal of Management and Social Sciences, 6*(3), 540–549. https://doi.org/10.3126/QJMSS.V6I3.72486

Ahmed, A., Bose, P. K., & Arafat, S. M. Y. (2024). Forensic psychiatry in Bangladesh. *Mental Health in Bangladesh*, 167–183. https://doi.org/10.1007/978-981-97-0610-5_10.

Ahmed, T., Wassan, R., & Lashari, A. B. (2022). Impacts of vocational training and recreational activities on prison inmates: A case study of youthful offender's correctional facility, Hyderabad Pakistan. *Pakistan Languages and Humanities Review, 6*(4), 238–246. https://doi.org/10.47205/PLHR.2022(6-IV)24

Alam, Md. J., & Bari, K. M. A. (2014). The prevention of oppression against women and children act and special tribunal: Revisiting the law and its implementation. *Dhaka University Studies Part F, 25*. https://heinonline.org/HOL/Page?handle=hein.journals/dkauvylw25&id=112&div=&collection=

Arafat, S. M. Y., & Kar, S. K. (2024). Epidemiology of psychiatric disorders and overview of access to mental health Care in South Asia. In S. M. Y. Arafat & S. K. Kar (Eds.), *Access to mental health Care in South Asia*. Springer. https://doi.org/10.1007/978-981-99-9153-2_1

Arafat, S. M. Y., Kar, S. K., Abhayanayake, C., Sharma, P., & Marthoenis, M. (2024). Prison mental health in South-East Asia: A narrative review. *Brain and Behavior, 14*(8), e70004. https://doi.org/10.1002/BRB3.70004

Asokan, T. (2016). The insanity defense: Related issues. *Indian Journal of Psychiatry, 58*(6), 191–198. https://doi.org/10.4103/0019-5545.196832

Bakhadyo, L. (2021). Children victims of the justice system in Nepal with reference to the applicability of forensic psychology. *Kathmandu School of Law Review*, 9–10. https://heinonline.org/HOL/Page?handle=hein.journals/kslr10&id=32&div=&collection=

Balhara, Y. P. S., Parmar, A., Modak, T., & Vikram, V. (2022). From "Bhang Shops" to "Cannabis in Coffee Shops": Time to debate the option? *Indian Journal of Psychological Medicine, 44*(3), 285–289. https://doi.org/10.1177/0253717620957501/ASSET/IMAGES/LARGE/10.1177_0253717620957501-FIG1.JPEG

Balhara, Y. S., Parmar, A., Sarkar, S., & Verma, R. (2016). Stigma in dual diagnosis: A narrative review. *Indian Journal of Social Psychiatry, 32*(2), 128. https://doi.org/10.4103/0971-9962.181093

Bhatta, D. N., Bialous, S., Crosbie, E., & Glantz, S. (2020). Exceeding WHO framework convention on tobacco control (FCTC) obligations: Nepal overcoming tobacco industry interference to enact a comprehensive tobacco control policy. *Nicotine & Tobacco Research, 22*(12), 2213–2223. https://doi.org/10.1093/NTR/NTZ177

Bhugra, D., Pathare, S., Nardodkar, R., Gosavi, C., Ng, R., Torales, J., & Ventriglio, A. (2016). Legislative provisions related to marriage and divorce of persons with mental health problems: A global review. *International Review of Psychiatry, 28*(4), 386–392.

Chakma, J. K., Kumar, H., Bhargava, S., & Khanna, T. (2020). The e-cigarettes ban in India: An important public health decision. *The Lancet Public Health, 5*(8), e426. https://doi.org/10.1016/S2468-2667(20)30063-3

Choudhry, V., Dayal, R., Pillai, D., Kalokhe, A. S., Beier, K., & Patel, V. (2018). Child sexual abuse in India: A systematic review. *PLoS One, 13*(10), e0205086. https://doi.org/10.1371/JOURNAL.PONE.0205086

Ellis, A. (2020). Forensic psychiatry and mental health in Australia: An overview. *CNS Spectrums, 25*(2), 119–121. https://doi.org/10.1017/S1092852919001299

Garg, K., Kumar, C. N., & Chandra, P. S. (2019). Number of psychiatrists in India: Baby steps forward, but a long way to go. *Indian Journal of Psychiatry, 61*(1), 104. https://doi.org/10.4103/PSYCHIATRY.INDIANJPSYCHIATRY_7_18

Global Health Expenditure Database. (2025). Retrieved February 22, 2025, from https://apps.who.int/nha/database

Gold, L. H. ., & Frierson, R. L. . (2018). *The American Psychiatric Association publishing textbook of forensic psychiatry*.

Gupta, P., Panda, U., Parmar, A., & Bhad, R. (2019). Internalized stigma and its correlates among treatment seeking opium users in India: A cross-sectional observational study. *Asian Journal of Psychiatry, 39*, 86–90. https://doi.org/10.1016/J.AJP.2018.12.004

Gupta, R., Bhatt, G., Singh, R., Chahar, P., Goel, S., & Singh, R. J. (2025). Enforcement of COTPA in India- current status, challenges and solutions. *Indian Journal of Tuberculosis, 72*(1), 94–97. https://doi.org/10.1016/J.IJTB.2024.06.007

Harkavy-friedman, J., Aminoff, M. J., & Faulkner, L. R. (2012). The American Board of Psychiatry and Neurology: looking back and moving ahead. *169*(11), 1217–1218. https://doi.org/10.1176/APPI.AJP.2012.12070994

Hegde, P. R., Malik, Y., Kumar, C. N., & Math, S. B. (2024). The Bharatiya Nyaya Sanhita act (BNSA) 2023: Implications for forensic psychiatry in India. https://doi.org/10.1177/02537176241281465.

Hossain, M. M., Purohit, N., Sultana, A., Ma, P., McKyer, E. L. J., & Ahmed, H. U. (2020). Prevalence of mental disorders in South Asia: An umbrella review of systematic reviews and meta-analyses. *Asian Journal of Psychiatry, 51*, 102041. https://doi.org/10.1016/J.AJP.2020.102041

Jatchavala, C., Ransing, R., Sukavejworakit, N., Ramalho, R., & Devraj, N. (2024). Child sexual abuse, mental health, and legislation in India and Thailand: A cross-country comparison. *Journal of Forensic and Legal Medicine, 102*, 102655. https://doi.org/10.1016/J.JFLM.2024.102655

Javed, A., Khan, M. S., Nasar, A., & Rasheed, A. (2020). Mental healthcare in Pakistan. *Taiwanese Journal of Psychiatry, 34*(1), 6. https://doi.org/10.4103/TPSY.TPSY_8_20

Jejeebhoy, S. J., Santhya, K. G., & Acharya, R. (2014). Violence against women in South Asia: The need for the active engagement of the health sector. *Global Public Health, 9*(6), 678–690. https://doi.org/10.1080/17441692.2014.916736

Jiloha, R., Kukreti, P., & Kataria, D. (2019). *Forensic psychiatry: An Indian perspective* (1st ed.). Jaypee Brothers Medical Publishers.

Kathriarachchi, S., Seneviratne, V., & Amarakoon, L. (2019). Development of mental health care in Sri Lanka: Lessons learned. *Taiwanese Journal of Psychiatry, 33*(2), 55. https://doi.org/10.4103/TPSY.TPSY_15_19

Kaur, N., & Roy, S. (2022). Mental health status of incarcerated women in India: A perspective from a social worker. *Indian Journal of Gender Studies, 29*(1), 113–130. https://doi.org/10.1177/09715215211057930/ASSET/IMAGES/LARGE/10.1177_09715215211057930-FIG2.JPEG

Khan, M. M. (2024). Suicidal Behaviours in Pakistan. *Suicidal Behavior in Muslim Majority Countries*, 223–243. https://doi.org/10.1007/978-981-97-2519-9_15

Kline, S., & Sabri, T. (2023). The decriminalisation of suicide: A global imperative. *The Lancet Psychiatry, 10*(4), 240–242. https://doi.org/10.1016/S2215-0366(23)00057-3

Kuttala, D., Nandakumar, D., Joseph, R. G., 2025. Forensic psychiatric aspects of child sexual abuse in South Asia. *Forensic Psychiatry and Prison Mental Health in South Asia.*

Malathesh, B., & Das, S. (2017). Being a forensic psychiatrist in India: Responsibilities, difficulties, and criticalities. *Indian Journal of Psychological Medicine, 39*(6), 732–736. https://doi.org/10.4103/IJPSYM.IJPSYM_334_17/ASSET/IJPSYM.IJPSYM_334_17.FP.PNG_V03

Mental Health Act. (2018). *Laws of Bangladesh.* http://bdlaws.minlaw.gov.bd/act-1273.html. Accessed 23 February 2025

Mukherjee, A., & Bhandarkar, R. (2014). Need for decriminalisation of suicide in low- and middle-income countries. *International Psychiatry, 11*(2), 50–50. https://doi.org/10.1192/S1749367600004422

Murthy, R. S. (2017). National mental health survey of India 2015-2016. *Indian Journal of Psychiatry, 59*(1), 21–26. https://doi.org/10.4103/PSYCHIATRY.INDIANJPSYCHIATRY_102_17

Nambi, S. (2005). Marriage, mental health and the Indian legislation. *Indian Journal of Psychiatry, 47*(1), 3–14.

Nambi, S., & Sarkar, S. (2015). Mental illness and nullity of marriage: Indian perspective. *Indian Journal of Psychological Medicine, 37*(3), 366–369.

Namboodiri, V., George, S., & Singh, S. P. (2019). The mental healthcare act 2017 of India: A challenge and an opportunity. *Asian Journal of Psychiatry, 44*, 25–28. https://doi.org/10.1016/J.AJP.2019.07.016

Narayan, C. L., Narayan, M., Shikha, D., & Shekhar, S. (2015). Indian marriage laws and mental disorders: Is it necessary to amend the legal provisions? *Indian Journal of Psychiatry, 57*(4), 341–344.

Naveed, S., Waqas, A., Chaudhary, A. M. D., Kumar, S., Abbas, N., Amin, R., Jamil, N., & Saleem, S. (2020). Prevalence of common mental disorders in South Asia: A systematic review and meta-regression analysis. *Frontiers in Psychiatry, 11*, 573150. https://doi.org/10.3389/FPSYT.2020.573150/BIBTEX

Papalia, N., Mann, E., & Ogloff, J. R. P. (2020). Child sexual abuse and risk of Revictimization: Impact of child demographics, sexual abuse characteristics, and psychiatric disorders. *Child Maltreat, 26*(1), 74–86. https://doi.org/10.1177/1077559520932665

Parmar, A., Balhara, Y. P. S., & Singh, A. (2023a). Toward a national policy on alcohol: A complex public health issue in need of urgent action. *Indian Journal of Psychiatry, 65*(9), 974–978. https://doi.org/10.4103/INDIANJPSYCHIATRY.INDIANJPSYCHIATRY_440_23

Parmar, A., Bhatia, G., Sharma, P., & Pal, A. (2023b). Understanding the epidemiology of substance use in India: A review of nationwide surveys. *Indian Journal of Psychiatry, 65*(5), 498–505. https://doi.org/10.4103/INDIANJPSYCHIATRY.INDIANJPSYCHIATRY_791_22

Parmar, A., Gupta, P., & Bhad, R. (2022). An exploratory study of clinical profile, stigma and pathways to care among primary cannabis use disorder patients in India. *Journal of Substance Use, 27*(1), 74–79. https://doi.org/10.1080/14659891.2021.1897695

Parmar, A., Gupta, P., Panda, U., & Bhad, R. (2020). An observational study assessing the pathways to care among treatment seeking users of natural opiates. *Drugs: Education, Prevention and Policy, 27*(3), 199–204. https://doi.org/10.1080/09687637.2019.1649363

Parmar, A., Mohanty, D., Pal, A., & Singh, A. (2024). Substance use disorder in South Asia: Challenges and ways ahead. *Current Perspectives on Substance Use Disorders in South Asia, 149–164*. https://doi.org/10.1007/978-981-97-6619-2_9

Parmar, A., Narasimha, V. L., & Nath, S. (2024). National Drug Laws, policies, and programs in India: A narrative review. *Indian Journal of Psychological Medicine, 46*(1), 5–13. https://doi.org/10.1177/02537176231170534/ASSET/IMAGES/LARGE/10.1177_02537176231170534-FIG1.JPEG

Parmar, A., Nath, S., & Bhatia, G. (2022). Essential substance use disorder medications in Asia Pacific countries: An observational study. *Asian Journal of Psychiatry, 78*, 103276. https://doi.org/10.1016/j.ajp.2022.103276

Pathare, S., Nardodkar, R., Shields, L., Bunders, J. F., & Sagade, J. (2015). Gender, mental illness and the Hindu marriage act, 1955. *Indian Journal of Medical Ethics, 12*, 7–13.

Rajapaksa, S. W., Vidanapathirana, J., Nawaratne, S., & Suranga, M. A. (2021). Tobacco control strategies enrich the National Strategic Plan on prevention and control of cancer in Sri Lanka. *Asian Pacific Journal of Cancer Prevention, 22*(S2), 45–50. https://doi.org/10.31557/APJCP.2021.22.S2.45

Sabri, B., Renner, L. M., Stockman, J. K., Mittal, M., & Decker, M. R. (2014). Risk factors for severe intimate partner violence and violence-related injuries among women in India. *Women and Health, 54*(4), 281–300. https://doi.org/10.1080/03630242.2014.896445

Sarkar, S., Parmar, A., & Singh, A. (2020). An exploratory study of cannabis use pattern and treatment seeking in patients attending an addiction treatment facility. *Indian Journal of Psychiatry, 62*(2), 145–151. https://doi.org/10.4103/PSYCHIATRY.INDIANJPSYCHIATRY_132_19

Sebastian, L. (2012). Specialist training in forensic psychiatry: The UK experience. *Criminal Behaviour and Mental Health, 22*(4), 252–256. https://doi.org/10.1002/CBM.1839

Selengia, V., Thuy, H. N. T., Mushi, D., Selengia, V., Thuy, H. N. T., & Mushi, D. (2020). Prevalence and patterns of child sexual abuse in selected countries of Asia and Africa: A review of literature. *Open Journal of Social Sciences, 8*(9), 146–160. https://doi.org/10.4236/JSS.2020.89010

Sharma, I., Tripathi, C. B., & Pathak, A. (2015). Social and legal aspects of marriage in women with mental illness in India. *Indian Journal of Psychiatry, 57*(Suppl 2), S324–S332.

Singh, A., Joshi, M., & Parmar, A. (2024). Substance use disorder among women and children in South Asia. *Current Perspectives on Substance Use Disorders in South Asia*, 279–303. https://doi.org/10.1007/978-981-97-6619-2_14

UN Convention on Rights of a Child (UNCRC) - UNICEF UK. (2025). Retrieved February 23, 2025, from https://www.unicef.org.uk/what-we-do/un-convention-child-rights/

Vaishnav, M., Javed, A., Gupta, S., Kumar, V., Vaishnav, P., Kumar, A., Salih, H., Levounis, P., Bernardo, N., Alkhoori, S., Luguercho, C., Soghoyan, A., Moore, E., Lakra, V., Aigner, M., Wancata, J., Ismayilova, J., Islam, M., Da Silva, A., et al. (2023). Stigma towards mental illness in Asian nations and low-and-middle-income countries, and comparison with high-income countries: A literature review and practice implications. *Indian Journal of Psychiatry, 65*(10), 995–1011. https://doi.org/10.4103/INDIANJPSYCHIATRY.INDIANJPSYCHIATRY_667_23

Vashney, M., Parmar, A., & Mishra, A. K. (2020). The past, present and future of literature pertaining to betel (areca) nut: A citation analysis. *Substance Use and Misuse, 55*(9), 1403–1412. https://doi.org/10.1080/10826084.2019.1660677

Violence Against Women Prevalence Estimates. (2025). Retrieved February 23, 2025, from https://www.who.int/publications/i/item/9789240022256

World Bank Open Data | Data. (n.d.). Retrieved February 22, 2025, from https://data.worldbank.org/

World Drug Report 2024. (n.d.). Retrieved February 23, 2025, from https://www.unodc.org/unodc/en/data-and-analysis/world-drug-report-2024.html

World Health Organization. (2021). *WHO MH atlas 2020* (pp. 1–136).

Chapter 2
Forensic Psychiatry and Prison Mental Health in Bangladesh

S. M. Yasir Arafat

Abstract Forensic psychiatry is a neglected entity in Bangladesh. There is no certified forensic psychiatrist or available specialized training in the domain, even though a high prevalence of psychiatric disorders among prisoners has been revealed. There are only 15 inpatient beds for forensic psychiatry in the country. The prisons are overcrowded, and there is no prison mental health system. No psychiatrist or psychologist visits the prison to provide mental health services. We do not have regular data on prison suicide in Bangladesh. In this chapter, we discussed historical aspects of mental health legislation, epidemiology and burden of mental disorders among prisoners, the current status of prison mental health services, liaison between law enforcement and mental health service providers, available research and gaps, current challenges in prison mental health, and ways out.

Keywords Forensic psychiatry · Law · Mental health act · Bangladesh · Prison · Psychiatry · Mental health · Psychiatric services

1 Introduction

According to the last (2022) *Population & Housing Census* of Bangladesh (adjusted population), about 170 million people live in the country in an area of 147,570 square kilometers. Among them, more than 90% are Muslims, and about 70% live in rural areas (Bangladesh Bureau of Statistics, 2024). Bangladesh lies in the lower-middle income category with significant economic success in recent decades despite

S. M. Yasir Arafat (✉)
Department of Psychiatry, Bangladesh Specialized Hospital, Dhaka, Bangladesh

A. Parmar et al. (eds.), *Forensic Psychiatry and Prison Mental Health in South Asia*, South Asian Perspectives in Mental Health and Psychology,
https://doi.org/10.1007/978-981-96-7206-6_2

being affected by frequent natural disasters like cyclones and floods (World Bank, 2024). As per the constitution, it is a democratic country. However, there are struggles in ensuring a smooth transition of power in accordance with the democratic process. Along with the economic growth, there are critics of enforced disappearance, extra-judicial killing, limiting the freedom of expression, and politically motivated oppression and torture that has been accelerated during the recent decade (United Nations, 2025; Ahasan, 2023; Report, 2022; Amnesty International, 2024; Report, 2024). These conditions indicate the deterioration of human rights conditions in the country, which is affecting the general population.

Bangladesh gained its independence in 1971 from Pakistan after a war of nine months, which was part of the British Empire until 1947. Therefore, the structure of the legal system evolved from British law in almost every aspect, where forensic psychiatry is not an exception in the country. The justice system is a replica of the British judicial system (Ashraf et al., 2022). A fresh mental health act, the "Mental Health Act 2018," has been passed in Bangladesh and replaced the previously implemented colonial law, the "Lunacy Act 1912" (Karim & Shaikh, 2021; Mental Health Act, 2018). It mentions conditions for mental health services like the establishment and maintenance of mental hospitals, psychiatric assessment, conditions of hospitalizations, involuntary hospitalization, mental health capacity assessment, and legal guardianship of persons with mental illness (Karim & Shaikh, 2021; Mental Health Act, 2018). It is the basic guideline for dealing with persons with psychiatric disorders in Bangladesh. It attempts to protect the rights of persons with mental illness regarding their clinical assessment, medications, property, and legal proceedings in court (Karim & Shaikh, 2021; Mental Health Act, 2018). It is a great advancement in mental health care in Bangladesh, even though there are some complexities and areas of improvement (Barua, 2024). It also advocates the need for prison mental health services and mental health support for persons living under the custodial system. However, as an interface, forensic psychiatry needs collaborations with mental health professionals, lawyers, judges, law enforcement agencies, and policymakers. Therefore, some other laws are followed in forensic psychiatry practice in Bangladesh. They are the *Code of Criminal Procedure (1898)*, the *Bangladesh Jail Code, Revised Edition (2006)*, the *Penal Code (1860)*, and the *Police Ordinance (2008 Draft)* (Ashraf et al., 2022).

The development of psychiatric services has been linked to the prison system in Bangladesh. The earliest noted mental health asylum was founded in 1815 at Murlibazar, Dhaka, which was linked with the central jail (Arafat, 2019; Arafat, 2024). Then the first mental hospital, "Pabna Mental Hospital (PMH)," was established in Pabna in 1957 during the Pakistan period. After the liberation, psychiatric services expanded through medical college hospitals, medical university hospitals, and the *National Institute of Mental Health (NIMH)*, Dhaka. However, forensic psychiatry still remains an underdeveloped branch of psychiatry in Bangladesh.

2 Epidemiology and Burden of Mental Disorders Among Prisoners

2.1 Prison Population

In Bangladesh, there are 68 prisons (13 central prisons and 55 district jails). Among these 68 jails, there is one female-only jail (Khan et al., 2021), whilst the others have both male and female sections. Two child development centers for boys (Tongi and Jeshore [Pulerhat] each) and one child development center for girls (Konabari, Gazipur) are providing custodial services for juvenile delinquents in the country (Ahmed et al., 2024; Justice Audit Bangladesh, 2018). The official capacity of the prisons of Bangladesh is 42,887 (World Prison Brief, 2024). As of 15 October 2024, there were 53,831 prisoners with an incarceration rate of 44 per 100,000 population, and the occupancy rate was about 125.5% (World Prison Brief, 2024; Arafat et al., 2024). There was a release of more than 300,000 prisoners after the ousting of the authoritarian regime, followed by a mass uprising. The release reduced the burden on the prisons in the country. According to a previous estimate (2023), the occupancy rate was about 200%, which has reduced to 125.5%. The situation indicates the overall condition and mental health crisis in the prisons due to the political situation. Among the prison population of Bangladesh, about two-thirds of them are in the pre-trial stage, and about 4% were females (World Prison Brief, 2024; Arafat et al., 2024). The prisons are overcrowded with low amenities and are considered mostly punishment centers with negligible rehabilitation facilities (Sultana and Akter, 2023).

2.2 Psychiatric Disorders Among Prisoners

Psychiatric morbidities among prisoners have been poorly studied in Bangladesh. We did not find any national study assessing mental disorders among prisoners. The prevalence varies from 66.4% to 100% (Table 2.1). The majority of the studies were conducted in Dhaka, the capital city, and among prisoners referred to psychiatric care (Chowdhury et al., 1998; Mullick et al., 1998; Hamid et al., 2005; Yasmin et al., 2022), where at least 85.4% of the respondents had psychiatric disorders (Table 2.1). Only one study, we found, was conducted in prison settings among 250 female prisoners and revealed a lower rate (66.4%) and different patterns of disorders (neurotic disorders) (Hasan et al., 2004). Studies conducted among referred prisoners revealed psychoses as the major burden (Chowdhury et al., 1998; Mullick et al., 1998; Hamid et al., 2005; Yasmin et al., 2022).

Table 2.1 Prevalence of psychiatric disorders among prisoners in Bangladesh

Study	Sample size	Sample	Diagnostic tool	Prevalence (%)	Major disorder (%)
Chowdhury et al. (1998)	56	Outpatients who were sent to Pabna Mental Hospital from Pabna jail	Clinical diagnosis and record review	100	Schizophrenia (80.4)
Mullick et al. (1998)	67	Male prisoners referred from Dhaka Central Jail as outpatients	*International Classification of Diseases- 10 (ICD-10)*	91	Psychotic disorder (71)
Hasan et al. (2004)	250	Female prisoners staying at Dhaka Central Jail	*Structured Clinical Interview for DSM-III-R*	66.4	Depression (30.4)
Hamid et al. (2005)	48	Admitted patients at the National Institute of Mental Health (NIMH)	*Diagnostic and Statistical Manual of Mental Disorders-IV*	85.4	Schizophrenia (37.5)
Yasmin et al. (2022)	127	Indoor and outdoor patients at NIMH	ICD-10	94.4	Schizophrenia (34.6)
Kowser et al. (2022)	438	Dhaka Central Jail, Keraniganj	*Diagnostic and Statistical Manual of Mental Disorders-5*	63	Substance related disorder (60.1)

The initial study was conducted in Pabna at PMH among 56 prisoners referred from Pabna jail, and diagnoses were made by clinical assessment and document review (Chowdhury et al., 1998). The study reported a 100% prevalence rate of mental disorders, and 91% of disorders developed before committing the crime (Chowdhury et al., 1998). Another study was conducted among 67 referred prisoners from Dhaka Central Jail, assessed the disorders with *International Classification of Diseases-10 (ICD-10),* and found the prevalence of psychiatric disorders was 91%, with a major contribution to psychotic disorders (Mullick et al., 1998). Both of the studies were conducted among referred prisoners in an outpatient setting (Chowdhury et al., 1998; Mullick et al., 1998). One study was conducted among 250 female prisoners living in the Central Jail, assessed mental disorders using the *Structured Clinical Interview for DSM-III-R,* and found a prevalence of 66.4%, with a major contribution from neurotic disorders (Hasan et al., 2004). This is perhaps the only study conducted in a prison setting and only among female participants.

One study was conducted among 48 inpatient prisoners referred from prisons to NIMH, Dhaka, assigned diagnoses according to the *Diagnostic and Statistical Manual of Mental Disorders-IV* (DSM-IV), and found a prevalence of 85.4%, with a major contribution to psychotic disorder (Hamid et al., 2005). One recent study was conducted among prisoners referred from prisons in both inpatient and outpatient settings in 2017–18, assessed disorders by ICD-10, and found a prevalence of 94.4%, with a major contribution from psychotic disorder (Table 2.1) (Yasmin et al., 2022). As studies are discrete and mostly conducted among referred prisoners, a nationwide study is warranted to determine the burden of psychiatric disorders in Bangladesh (Khan et al., 2021). One recent study assessed psychiatric morbidity among 438 male prisoners living in the Dhaka Central Jail, Keraniganj, in 2018 through face-to-face interviews using DSM-5 criteria (Kowser et al., 2022). It found that the prevalence of psychiatric disorder was 63%; among them, 60% had substance-related disorder, 10.9% had depression, 10.5% had anxiety disorder, 7.6% had personality disorder, and 2.5% had psychosis.

2.3 Suicide in Prison

Little is known about suicidal behavior among prisoners in Bangladesh, as there is no public data covering the variables. There is also a lack of studies assessing suicidal behavior among prisoners in Bangladesh. Sometimes, some newspaper reports mention it; however, we do not know the extent of it (Arafat et al., 2024; Arafat, 2025; Rashid, 2023).

3 Current Status of Forensic Psychiatry Services in Bangladesh

3.1 Care Availing Pathway in Forensic Psychiatry in Bangladesh

Ideally, forensic psychiatric services are supposed to be available at tertiary care institutions like public medical college hospitals, medical university hospitals, and specialized institutions like NIMH, Dhaka. However, none of the public medical colleges has human resource support and hospitalization facilities to admit prisoners with mental illness. These services are available at only two institutions, i.e., NIMH, Dhaka, and the prison cell of *Bangabandhu Sheikh Mujib Medical University (BSMMU)*. Among these two institutes, only NIMH, Dhaka, has an independent forensic psychiatry department with both hospitalization facilities and outdoor services. On the other hand, BSMMU only liaises with other departments when prisoners are admitted at prison cell of the institute. Also, it arranges forensic psychiatry boards on an outdoor service basis when necessary.

Generally, deviated behaviors among prisoners are noticed by inmates, prison staff, and/or medical officers of the prison. Then, prisoners with suspected mental illness are sent to NIMH, Dhaka, with the direction of the jail authority. Sometimes, the court may send prisoners with directives to NIMH, Dhaka (Ashraf et al., 2022, Fig. 2.1). As per the Mental Health Act (Section 15), any prisoner with a criminal charge or punished for a criminal act should be accompanied by a "reception order" by a magistrate to be admitted to the mental hospital (Mental Health Act, 2018).

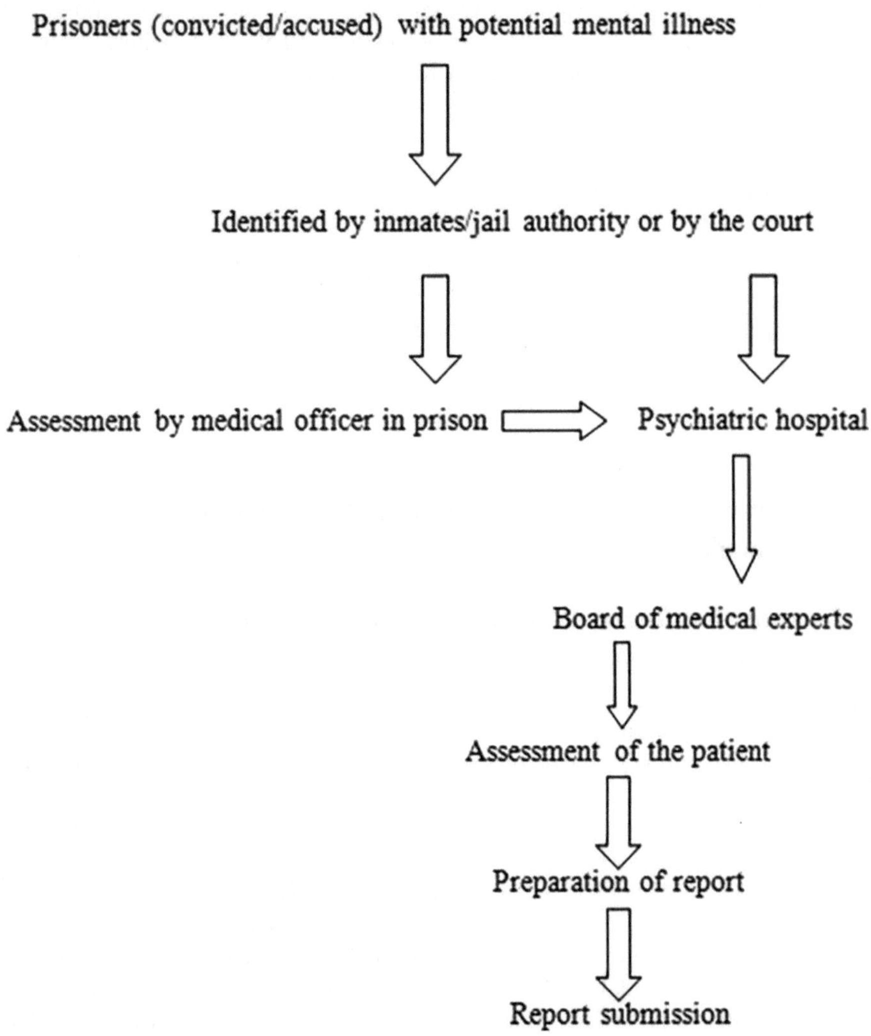

Fig. 2.1 Care availing pathway in forensic psychiatry in Bangladesh (adapted from Ahmed et al., 2024)

Then, as per the conditions and directives, the assigned persons of NIMH decide the next steps regarding hospitalization or treatment on an outdoor basis.

3.2 Forensic Psychiatric Services Spectrum

The NIMH, Dhaka, generally provides services covering four major areas of forensic psychiatry in Bangladesh. These are mentioned below.

3.2.1 Liaison with Legal System

It provides expert opinion and comments on mental health and illness for prisoners when directed by the Honorable Court or equivalent authority. It also helps to ensure legal support for mentally ill persons whenever necessary, as per the *Mental Health Act 2018*, i.e., issues with legal guardianship and property management of mentally disabled persons. Expert opinion has been provided through the *Mental Health Specialist Board (MHSB)* for prisoners in different phases, like convicts or detainees and mentally challenged persons, whenever directed by the Honorable Court or authorities equivalent to it. Some commonly handled issues are noticed, i.e., whether the accused prisoner has any mental illness, whether the accused had a mental disorder during the crime, fitness to stand trial, and diminished responsibility.

3.2.2 Disability Assessment

Ascertainment of disability is an important area of forensic psychiatry in Bangladesh. Generally, disability is certified through the Specialist Board under the "Rights and Protection of Disabled Persons Act 2013." This outdoor board assesses disabilities attributed to serious mental illness, neurodevelopmental disorders, and intellectual disability. It ensures that the government provides facilities, for example, disability allowance, for disabled persons due to mental illness.

3.2.3 Clinical Services to Prisoners with Psychiatric Disorder

The provision of clinical mental health services to prisoners with mental illness is another regular responsibility of forensic psychiatry. Psychiatric disorders may be developed before committing the crime, during detention, during the trial, or during punishment that may need psychiatric services in various spectrums, from hospitalization to usual counseling.

3.2.4 Reports on Mental Health

Reports on mental health have been sought from different Government, autonomous, or semi-autonomous organizations for their internal decisions. The forensic psychiatry department has provided these reports. Commonly, it has been sought to consider applications for job extensions after 65 years (Ahmed et al., 2024). It has also been noticed to consider job termination and carrying firearms for law-enforcing agencies.

3.3 Hospitalization Services

Studies conducted assessing the psychiatric morbidity among the prisoners revealed a 66.4–100% rate of suffering. However, hospitalization facilities are available at NIMH, Dhaka, for forensic psychiatric assessment, with 15 beds only (Ashraf et al., 2022). There are some facilities for admitting patients from prison at BSMMU, where occasional liaison is needed. No other hospitalization under forensic psychiatry is available in the country.

3.4 Involuntary Admission and Treatment

The recent Mental Health Act classifies hospital admissions into three categories: i.e., voluntary, non-protesting, and involuntary (Karim & Shaikh, 2021; Mental Health Act, 2018). Involuntary admissions can be attempted with the application or consent of the guardian or relative of the person suffering from mental illness, or the police officer working in the local jurisdiction, or the medical officer in charge. There is a prescribed form for this process. Emergency admission for up to 72 hours is based on the recommendation of the responsible medical officer; admission for treatment or assessment for up to 28 days, as recommended by a psychiatrist, has been allowed in the law. Further extensions are possible with the assessment and recommendations of the *Mental Health Review and Monitoring Committee* (Mental Health Act, 2018). The admission status could be changed over the course of time. Private hospitals use emergency medical services (EMS) for picking up patients from home settings for involuntary admission (Arafat et al., 2016). The government mental health services require an additional attendant to stay with the patients, and no public services are available to pick up violent, aggressive psychiatric patients and admit them to mental hospitals.

3.5 *Prison Mental Health in Bangladesh*

In the previous sections, we noticed that there is a high prevalence of psychiatric disorders among prisoners (>66–100%) and a double occupancy rate in the prisons. Officially, there are 141 posts for medical doctors in the 68 jails; however, among them, 137 posts were vacant, which indicates an extreme lack of the traditional healthcare system in the prisons of Bangladesh (Islam, 2022). A conventional mental health services system has not been available in the prisons in the country (Khan et al., 2024). The country also lacks any screening system for psychiatric disorders among prisoners (Khan et al., 2021). Initiatives from non-governmental organizations like *Dhaka Ahsania Mission (DAM)* did some important work on substance abuse, stress coping, anger management, and mindfulness practices among the prisoners. Mental health professionals like psychiatrists, psychologists, and psychiatric nurses do not attend prisons for clinical purposes. In case of any psychiatric necessity, prisoners are sent to nearby psychiatric service settings escorted by two police officers (Khan et al., 2021). Forensic psychiatric services for prisoners are provided free of cost. Some psychotropics, like conventional antipsychotics, mood stabilizers, sedatives and hypnotics, and amitriptyline, are provided without any charge.

3.6 *Education and Training in Forensic Psychiatry*

Forensic psychiatry and prison mental health have been included in postgraduate psychiatry courses as part of psychiatry in Bangladesh. However, there is no specialized degree, training, or courses on forensic psychiatry in the country. Forensic aspects of health, sexual health, and mental illness have been included in the forensic medicine and toxicology subject at the undergraduate level (Ahmed et al., 2024; BMDC, 2021).

4 Available Research and Gaps in Current Understanding

There is an extreme lack of research in forensic psychiatry in Bangladesh. A quick search in PubMed and Scopus with the search term "Forensic Psychiatry and Prison Mental Health in Bangladesh" revealed only two papers each. A search was done on 07 October 2024 at 2.30 pm, Dhaka Time. Yes, there are some concerns regarding the indexation of journals in well-reputed databases and the number of publications in well-indexed psychiatry journals from Bangladesh (Arafat et al., 2022). However, publications in local journals on forensic psychiatry and prison mental health are rare. Available studies are cross-sectional and descriptive in nature. The whole thing warrants attention to identify the research gaps and move forward.

5 Current Challenges and Ways Out of Forensic Psychiatry in Bangladesh

Forensic psychiatry is in the rudimentary stage, and there are no prison mental health services in Bangladesh. Lack of political will, high stigma, inadequate resources, lack of academic content, and specialized training programs are the major hurdles (Arafat, 2024; Ahmed et al., 2024; Arafat et al., 2024). Additionally, there are challenges in collaboration between the mental health professionals and the legal system, such as delays in delivering court orders to reach the mental health system, time shortages in psychiatric assessment, and misunderstanding of terms in communication forms. Additionally, a portion of forensic psychiatry services is dealt with by the forensic medicine department, which lacks collaboration among forensic psychiatry, forensic medicine, and law enforcement agencies. Prison is a restricted place. To conduct studies, the researcher needs to obtain permission from several agencies and offices. The process may raise concerns of paranoia from the prison management as well as the prisoners.

Improvements in academic courses, continued professional development (CPD), the enduring political will to improve the nascent stage of forensic psychiatry services, the establishment of a well-functioning prison mental health system, and sustainable collaboration with the legal system are warranted (Ahmed et al., 2024).

The collaboration between forensic mental health and the judiciary system will be an instrumental step in addressing service gaps and enabling a comprehensive understanding of the intersection between forensic psychiatry and the legal system in Bangladesh. The arrangement of joint CPD events could be an essential platform for interdisciplinary dialogue and shared learning. The establishment of a prison psychiatry services system could be an immediate step in the country. A study involving prisoners from all the prisons would reveal the actual service burden in the country.

6 Conclusion

Forensic psychiatry is in a rudimentary state in Bangladesh. There are no mental health services in prisons despite overcrowding and a high prevalence of psychiatric disorders. There are only 15 beds available for admission. The spectrum of services covers supporting the law enforcement authority with specific queries, disability assessments for social benefits, provision of clinical services for prisoners with mental illness, and mental health soundness reports necessary in different jobs for different purposes like service extensions. There is a lack of human resources, funding, training facilities, and collaboration between law enforcement authorities and mental health professionals. The country needs political attention to establish a mental health service system in prisons, ensuring training, and benefits, and sustained collaboration among law enforcement agencies, the judiciary, and mental health professionals.

References

Ahasan, N., 2023. Body count. Netranews. https://interactive.netra.news/extrajudicial-killings-bangladesh/. Accessed 07 October 2024

Ahmed, A., Bose, P. K., & Arafat, S. M. Y. (2024). Forensic psychiatry in Bangladesh. In S. M. Y. Arafat (Ed.), *Mental health in Bangladesh*. Springer. https://doi.org/10.1007/978-981-97-0610-5_10

Amnesty International. (2024). *Bangladesh 2023*. https://www.amnesty.org/en/location/asia-and-the-pacific/south-asia/bangladesh/report-bangladesh/. Accessed 07 October 2024

Arafat, S. M. Y. (2019). History of psychiatry in Bangladesh. *Asian Journal of Psychiatry, 46*, 11–12. https://doi.org/10.1016/j.ajp.2019.09.024

Arafat, S. M. Y. (2024). Mental health services in Bangladesh. In S. M. Y. Arafat (Ed.), *Mental health in Bangladesh*. Springer. https://doi.org/10.1007/978-981-97-0610-5_3

Arafat, S. M. Y., Kar, S. K., Abhayanayake, C., Sharma, P., & Marthoenis, M. (2024). Prison mental health in South-East Asia: A narrative review. *Brain and Behavior, 14*(8), e70004. https://doi.org/10.1002/brb3.70004

Arafat, S. M. Y., Uddin, M. S., Chowdhury, E. Z., Huq, N., Chouudhury, S. R., & Chowdhury, M. H. R. (2016). Demography and diagnosis of patients received emergency medical service from two private psychiatric hospital in Dhaka City. *International Journal of Neurorehabilitation, 3*(6), 240. https://doi.org/10.4172/2376-0281.1000240

Arafat, S. Y., Ali, S. A. E. Z., Saleem, T., Banerjee, D., Singh, R., Baminiwatta, A., & Shoib, S. (2022). Academic psychiatry journals in South Asian countries: Most from India, none from Afghanistan, Bhutan and the Maldives. *Global Psychiatry Archives, 5*(1), 1–9. https://doi.org/10.52095/gp.2021.4395.1036

Ashraf, S., Amin, Y. M., Sajib, M. S., & Al Azdi, Z. (2022). Situational analysis of forensic mental health in Bangladesh. *Forensic Science International: Mind and Law, 3*, 100074. https://doi.org/10.1016/j.fsiml.2022.100074

Arafat, S.M.Y., (2025). Prison Suicide in Bangladesh: A News Content Analysis. Health Secience Reports, 8, e70951. https://doi.org/10.1002/hsr2.70951

Bangladesh Bureau of Statistics. (2024). *Population & Housing Census 2022*. https://bbs.gov.bd/site/page/47856ad0-7e1c-4aab-bd78-892733bc06eb/Population-&-Housing. Accessed 28 September 2024

Barua, R. (2024). Bangladesh's mental health act 2018: A critical analysis. *Medical Law Review, 32*, 101–110. https://doi.org/10.1093/medlaw/fwad041

BMDC. (2021). *MBBS Curriculum Update – 2021*. https://www.bmdc.org.bd/curriculum-2020. Accessed 05 October 2024

Chowdhury, S. H., Rahman, S. M., & Begum, A. (1998). Mentally abnormal offenders A study of refereed patients from jail. *Bangladesh Journal of Psychiatry, 12*(1), 31–37.

Hamid, M. A., Hossain, M. D., Ahmed, H. U., Rahman, M. M., & Karim, M. E. (2005). Types of psychiatric disorder among patients attended in forensic psychiatry department of National Institute of Mental Health. *Dhaka. Bangladesh Journal of Psychiatry, 19*(2), 51–57.

Hasan, M. K., Jahan, N. A., Khanam, M., & Begum, A. A. (2004). Study on prison population: Psychiatric morbidity among female prisoners. *Bangladesh Journal of Psychiatry, 18*(2), 41–54.

Islam, R. (2022). Only four physicians for around 83,000 inmates. *Prothom Alo English*, https://en.prothomalo.com/bangladesh/2sw4r2cj3f . Accessed 06 October, 2024

Justice Audit Bangladesh. (2018). *Child Development Centers (CDC)*. https://bangladesh.justiceaudit.org/national-data/regional-services/child-development-centers/. Accessed 07 October 2024

Karim, M. E., & Shaikh, S. (2021). Newly enacted mental health law in Bangladesh. *BJPsych international, 18*(4), 85–87. https://doi.org/10.1192/bji.2021.1

Khan, A. A., Ryland, H., Hussain, M. A., & Forrester, A. (2024). Correctional and forensic mental health services in Bangladesh. In *Approaches to Offender Rehabilitation in Asian Jurisdictions* (pp. 193–205). Routledge.

Khan, A. A., Ryland, H., Pathan, T., Ahmed, H. U., Hussain, A., & Forrester, A. (2021). Mental health services in the prisons of Bangladesh. *BJPsych international, 18*(4), 88–91. https://doi.org/10.1192/bji.2021.34

Kowser, A. S. M., Parveen, M., & Reza, M. S. (2022). Psychiatric morbidity among prisoners. *Archives of NIMH, 5*(1), 31–37.

Mental Health Act. (2018). *Bangladesh.* [Online] [Accessed on 02.10.2024] Available from. http://bdlaws.minlaw.gov.bd/act-1273.html

Mullick, M. S. I., Khanam, M., & Nahar, J. S. (1998). Psychiatric Profile of the prisoners referred for psychiatric assessment. *Bangladesh Journal of Psychiatry, 12*(2), 69–75.

Rashid, M. (2023). One prison inmate dies daily. *NewAge Bangladesh.* https://www.newagebd.net/article/192965/one-prison-inmate-dies-daily. Accessed 07 October 2024

Report, N. (2022). Secret prisoners of Dhaka. *Netranews.* https://netra.news/2022/secret-prisoners-of-dhaka/. Accessed 07 October 2024

Report, W., 2024. Bangladesh: Events of 2023. *Human Right Watch.* https://www.hrw.org/world-report/2024/country-chapters/Bangladesh. Accessed 07 October 2024

Sultana, Z., & Akter, N. (2023). Life imprisonment in Bangladesh: Ensuring a constructive prison experience for life-sentenced prisoners. In D. van Zyl Smit, C. Appleton, & G. Vucong (Eds.), *Life imprisonment in Asia. Palgrave advances in criminology and criminal justice in Asia.* Palgrave Macmillan. https://doi.org/10.1007/978-981-19-4664-6_3

United Nations. (2025). *Human rights violations and abuses related to the protests of July and August 2024 in Bangladesh.* https://www.ohchr.org/sites/default/files/documents/countries/bangladesh/ohchr-fftb-hr-violations-bd.pdf. Accessed 21 February 2025

World Bank. (2024). *World Bank Country and Lending Groups.* https://datahelpdesk.worldbank.org/knowledgebase/articles/906519-world-bank-country-and-lending-groups. Accessed 07 October 2024

World Prison Brief. (2024). *Bangladesh.* https://www.prisonstudies.org/country/bangladesh. Accessed 26 November 2024

Yasmin, M., Mamun, A. A., Lopa, A. R., Khaleequzzaman, A. K. M., Sultana, S., & Karim, S. M. S. (2022). Patterns of psychiatric disorders in persons attending the Forensic Psychiatry Department of a tertiary care psychiatric hospital. *Archieves of NIMH, 5*(2), 24–28.

Chapter 3
Forensic Psychiatry and Prison Mental Health in India

Poulami Laha, Anirban Saha, and Guru S. Gowda

Abstract Forensic psychiatry and prison mental health in India intersect at the confluence of law, psychiatry, and human rights, presenting unique challenges in the country's evolving legal and healthcare landscape. The rights and treatment of persons with mental illnesses are governed by India's legal system, which has its roots in the country's colonial past and is impacted by changing viewpoints from a global perspective. The chapter examines how forensic psychiatry in India is influenced by social structure, the legal system, and Indian mental health laws. It delves into the epidemiology of mental disorders in prisons, emphasizing the high burden of psychiatric morbidity, substance use disorders, and suicidality among inmates. It also looks at policy frameworks and legislative measures for mental healthcare in prisons, including the function of the National Human Rights Commission. Special forensic psychiatry issues like competency to stand trial, insanity defense, admission, and involuntary medication are discussed too. The chapter also identifies research gaps and discusses the role of a multidisciplinary approach, combining psychiatry, law, criminology, and public health, which is necessary to ensure comprehensive and humane mental healthcare for incarcerated individuals in India.

Keywords Forensic psychiatry · Prison mental health · Human rights · Mental healthcare act · India · Treatment

P. Laha · G. S. Gowda (✉)
Department of Psychiatry, National Institute of Mental Health and Neuro Sciences (NIMHANS), Bengaluru, India

A. Saha
Department of Psychiatry, All India Institute of Medical Sciences (AIIMS), Raipur, India

A. Parmar et al. (eds.), *Forensic Psychiatry and Prison Mental Health in South Asia*, South Asian Perspectives in Mental Health and Psychology,
https://doi.org/10.1007/978-981-96-7206-6_3

1 Introduction

1.1 Social Structure in India

India is the largest democracy in the world, with over 1.4 billion people. It has a vast cultural diversity and a rich history and legacy (*World Population Prospects 2024*, 2024). India is a mix of vibrant modernity and deep-rooted traditions. Its cultural heritage is expressed through art, literature, festivals, and cuisine. Many ethnic, religious, and linguistic communities contribute to this diversity. The strong familial ties that underpin India's social and family structure offer decades of emotional and material support. In order to maintain stability in the face of adversity, the joint family structure promotes solidarity, shared obligations, and cultural continuity. A strong sense of belonging, group decision-making, and social cohesiveness are other benefits of close-knit societies (Srinivas, 1995). In India, caste and religion have a big impact on social structure. They affect social mobility, work opportunities, and educational opportunities. They can sometimes promote harmony but can also fuel prejudice and conflict. Wealth disparities among individuals and communities have an influence on healthcare, education, and general quality of life, which in turn affects a community (*Poverty and Shared Prosperity 2022*, n.d.). These problems are especially noticeable for underrepresented groups, like inmates, who are frequently left out of mainstream policy discussions (*India Justice Report: Ranking States on Police, Judiciary, Prisons & Legal Aid*, 2022). To understand prison mental health in India, one must consider the larger social context. Systematic injustices and cultural views on crime and rehabilitation affect the well-being of inmates (Mishra et al., 2021).

1.2 Legal and Justice Systems in India

India has a clear legal and judicial system that is based on the Constitution, which is the ultimate law of the land. The legal system is founded on a combination of religious law, common law, and customs that have been influenced by both indigenous and colonial traditions (Menski, 2006). In 1860, under British control, the Indian Penal Code (IPC) was created based on the suggestions made by the first Law Commission of India, which was chaired by Thomas Babington Macaulay. It was incorporated into the Republic of India's penal law by the Government of India upon independence. It lists offences and the associated punishments. With effect from 1st July, 2024, Bharatiya Nyaya Sanhita replaces it (*The Bharatiya Naya Sanhita*, 2023).

1.2.1 Hierarchy of Courts in India

A. **Supreme Court of India:** The Supreme Court of India is the apex court of India. It was established in Delhi on January 26, 1950, the day the Indian constitution went into effect. It acts as the last arbiter of constitutional interpretation and possesses the authority of judicial review.
B. **High Courts:** As the highest court in its jurisdiction, the High Court is present in every state.
C. **District and Session Courts:** Civil and criminal proceedings are handled by these. They operate at the district level. District Courts handle civil cases, whereas Sessions Courts deal with more serious criminal cases.
D. **Subordinate Courts:** These include Civil Judge Courts for minor civil matters and Magistrate Courts for minor criminal cases (*National Crime Investigation Bureau's*, n.d.).

1.2.2 Major Laws

A. **The Constitution of India, 1950:** The Constitution of India was effective from 26th January 1950 (*The Constitution of India*, 1950). It was the foundational document that established the rights, obligations, and governing framework of the people. The latest version was published on 1st May 2024 and is being followed currently (*The Constitution of India*, 2024).
B. **Bharatiya Nyaya Sanhita (BNS):** IPC has been substituted by it. It essentially keeps the IPC's provisions, adds a few new ones, and eliminates those that the courts have declared unlawful (*The Bharatiya Naya Sanhita*, 2023).
C. **Bharatiya Nagarik Suraksha Sanhita (BNSS):** It superseded the Code of Criminal Procedure (CrPC), 1973, on July 1st, 2024 (*The Code of Criminal Procedure*, 1973). It seeks to bring India's criminal justice system up to date (*The Bharatiya Nagarik Suraksha Sanhita*, 2023).
D. **Code of Civil Procedure (CPC), 1908:** Governs the handling of civil disputes (*The Code of Civil Procedure*, 1908).
E. **Evidence Act, 1872:** This law establishes guidelines for evidence admissible in court (*The Indian Evidence Act*, 1872).
F. **Juvenile Justice Act, 2015:** Addresses juvenile offences and their rehabilitation (*The Juvenile Justice (Care and Protection of Children) Act*, 2015).

1.3 Human Rights Condition in India

Article 21 of the Constitution is entitled to basic necessities such as clean air, clean water, wholesome food, healthcare, and sanitary living situations for citizens of India. It is an intrinsic part of the right to a dignified life, as encompassed in Article 21 of the Constitution. People with mental illnesses are frequently stigmatized and isolated, and institutional discrimination prevents them from integrating into society and enjoying their right to dignity. The state of human rights in India, especially with regard to mental health, brings to light important issues. A person's freedom is taken away by the legal process under involuntary admission under the previous Indian Mental Health Act of 1987. The Mental Healthcare Act, 2017 (MHCA), in India upholds this idea by ensuring the rights to informed consent, mental health care, and protection from inhumane treatment, which will be discussed in the following part (*The Mental Healthcare Act*, 2017). By acknowledging mental health as a human rights problem, the emphasis is shifted from treatment to overall well-being. It also encourages guaranteeing social inclusion, legal protection, and access to high-quality healthcare (Koccher & Sarkar, 2012).

1.3.1 National Human Rights Commission

The National Human Rights Commission of India (NHRC) is a statutory body constituted on 12th October, 1993, under the Protection of Human Rights Ordinance of 28th September, 1993. It was given a statutory basis by the Protection of Human Rights Act, 1993 (PHRA). Significant efforts have been made by the NHRC to enhance mental health services and defend the rights of those suffering from mental diseases. The Supreme Court entrusted the NHRC to oversee mental hospitals around the country while promoting improved treatment, rehabilitation, and living circumstances.

The Quality Assurance in Mental Health Care project with the National Institute of Mental Health and Neuro Sciences (NIMHANS) is one of the major initiatives. It examined 37 facilities and produced recommendations such as eliminating cell admissions, enhancing nutrition and hygiene, and switching to open wards. The NHRC also advocates for legal changes, sufficient staffing, and infrastructure improvements to bring mental health care into compliance with global human rights norms (Koccher & Sarkar, 2012).

1.4 History of Mental Health Legislation in India

The British monarch quickly passed a series of regulations to regulate the care and treatment of mentally ill people in British India after seizing control of the country's government in 1858 (Fig. 3.1). These laws were:

- The Lunacy (Supreme Courts) Act, 1858
- The Lunacy (District Courts) Act, 1858
- The Indian Lunatic Asylum Act, 1858 (with amendments passed in 1886 and 1889)
- The Military Lunatic Acts, 1877

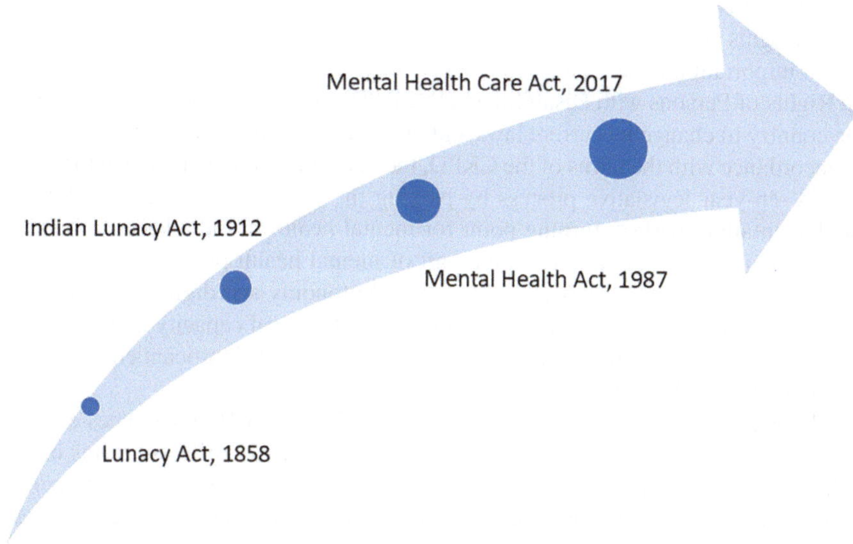

Fig. 3.1 Evolution of mental health legislations in India

The legal construction of lunacy in the eighteenth and nineteenth centuries, known as the "psychiatrization of criminal danger," which made "dangerousness" equivalent with "insanity" or mental disease, had an impact on the legislative aim of these. Because the "insane person" was viewed as dangerous by nature, the legal and psychiatric establishments had to work together to devise social control mechanisms that included both restorative and punitive measures. These regulations mainly dealt with the "segregation" or "detention" of two groups: indigenous people who were deemed a threat to others and Europeans with mental illnesses who were sent to England. In order to enforce this, institutional disciplinary measures like asylums and prisons were used (Foucault, 1978).

The Indian Lunacy Act (ILA), 1912, which was based on the English Lunacy Act, 1890, subsequently superseded these laws in order to control the confinement of mentally ill people in asylums and manage their private property. The ILA defined "lunatic" as "an idiot or a person of unsound mind" in order to describe people who have mental disease. In addition to being stigmatizing, these phrases mirrored the widespread belief that people with mental illnesses were illogical, not mentally capable, or incapable of handling their own affairs or making their own judgments (Ranade et al., 2022).

The United Nations General Assembly adopted the Universal Declaration of Human Rights following World War II. In 1950, the Indian Psychiatric Society proposed a Mental Health Bill to replace the outdated ILA-1912. After a lengthy and drawn-out process, the Indian Mental Health Act was ultimately enacted in 1987. MHA-87 defined mental illness in a progressive way and introduced a modern concept of treatment with an emphasis on care and treatment rather than on custody.

However, this act did not adequately address delivery of mental health care and human rights concerns (Narayan et al., 2011).

An important turning point was reached when India ratified the UN Convention on Rights of Persons with Disabilities (UNCRPD) in October 2007, which required the country to change its current laws and practices to comply with the Convention. In accordance with the terms of the CRPD, the Parliament finally repealed the MHA after a ten-year legislative process by passing the MHCA in 2017. The MHCA's implementation marks a turning point for mental health in India because it establishes a number of obligations on the part of mental health providers, the government, and other duty-bearers to safeguard the autonomy and dignity of those who have mental illness. The MHCA's recognition of the legal capacity and decisional autonomy of people with mental illness is one of the most significant changes from the ILA and MHA (Pathare & Kapoor, 2021).

The Rights of Persons with Disabilities (RPwD) Act, 2016, guarantees equality in accessing healthcare, work, education, and recognizes 21 different forms of disabilities, including mental illness, by protecting the rights and dignity of people with disabilities. The Act includes provisions for social security and legal protection, guardianship, as well as mandatory reservations in government employment and educational services. It also places a strong emphasis on removing obstacles from the workplace and makes discrimination against people with disabilities illegal. The law is implemented in accordance with UNCRPD in order to encourage empowerment and inclusion (*The Rights of Persons with Disabilities Act*, 2016).

The Narcotic Drugs and Psychotropic Substances (NDPS) Act, 1985 (*The Narcotic Drugs and Psychotropic Substances Act*, 1985), deals with the storage, consumption, transport, cultivation, possession, sale, purchase, and manufacturing of narcotics and psychotropic substances. The act defines these substances and imposes severe penalties for violation. It was amended four times in 1988, 2001, 2014, and 2021. The NDPS (Amendment) Act 2021 was passed on 29th December 2021. Depending on the amount of substance involved, the act stipulates harsh punishments, such as tough jail time and fines. Additionally, it permits the forfeiture of property resulting from drug-related offenses and contains provisions for the treatment and rehabilitation of drug addicts.

The Protection of Children from Sexual Offences (POCSO) Act, 2012 (*The Protection of Children from Sexual Offences Act*, 2012), deals with the protection of children under the age of 18 from sexual abuse, assault, and exploitation. The POCSO categories offences into penetrative and non-penetrative assault, sexual harassment, and pornography, as well as prescribes the severe penalties. The act guarantees child-friendly reporting, investigation, and trial processes, along with provisions for special courts to manage cases effectively and sensitively. The law requires mandatory reporting of offenses, and noncompliance is punishable (*The Protection of Children from Sexual Offences Act*, 2012).

2 Epidemiology and Burden of Mental Disorders Among Prisoners in India

The Institute for Criminal Policy Research and National Crime Records Bureau (NCRB), 2022, estimates the Indian prison population to be around 5,73,220. The prison population rate in India increased from 20 per 1,00,000 nationwide population in 2020 to 41 per 1,00,000 nationwide population in 2022, nearly doubling over 20 years. Worldwide, few countries have more than 100 per 1,00,000 prison population rates. The wide variation across countries is largely influenced by differences in legal policies, sentencing laws, and law enforcement practices. India's lower prison population rate reflects a legal system that relies more on bail provisions and underutilization of pretrial detention compared to countries with higher prison population rates. Among 5,73,220 inmates, 5,49,351 (95.8%) were male, 23,772 (4.1%) were female, and 97 (0.1%) were transgender (*Prison Statistics India*, 2022). In East Asian countries, the proportion of female prisoners ranges from 4.5% in Mongolia to 21% in Hong Kong (China) (*Asia | World Prison Brief*, n.d.). The NCRB Prison Statistics Report, 2022, revealed that 6283 (1.1%) inmates were foreigners (*Prison Statistics India*, 2022). According to the NCRB Prison Statistics Report, 2022, the stated numbers of convicts, undertrial inmates, and detenues were 1,33,415, 4,34,302, and 4324; they accounted for 23.3%, 75.8%, and 0.8% of the total, respectively. As of December 31, 2022, 1,179 inmates, or 0.2% of all inmates, were classified as other prisoners. Overcrowding occurs when the number of inmates remaining exceeds the authorized capacity. An occupancy rate of greater than 100 indicates overcrowding in the jail. The occupancy rate has increased from 130.2% in 2021 to 131.4% in 2022. Overcrowding has become one of the most significant issues faced by prisoners in recent years. It leads to sleep deprivation, poor hygiene, etc. It is crucial that inmates have adequate space and amenities in jails while also taking into account their human rights (*Prison Statistics India*, 2022).

Compared to the general population, prison inmates have a far greater rate of mental illness. Of all prisoners, 9084 were identified as having psychiatric illness, making up 1.6% of the total. 63.1% (5729) of the 9084 prisoners with mental illness were undertrials, and 35.7% (3246) were convicted (Table 3.1). According to the

Table 3.1 Types of prisoners across India (*Prison Statistics India*, 2022)

Category		Convicts	Undertrials	Détenues	Others	Total
State	Total	131029	411547	3753	1092	547421
	Suffering from mental illness	3155 (2.41%)	5110 (1.24%)	44 (1.17%)	55 (5.04%)	8364 (1.53%)
Union territory	Total	2386	22755	571	87	25799
	Suffering from mental illness	91 (3.81%)	619 (2.72%)	10 (1.75%)	0 (0%)	720 (2.79%)
Across India	Total	133415	434302	4324	1179	573220
	Suffering from mental illness	3246 (2.43%)	5729 (1.32%)	54 (1.25%)	55 (4.66%)	9084 (1.58%)

NCRB's Prison Statistics Report, 74.8% (119) of the 159 unnatural fatalities that occurred in Indian prisons in 2022 were primarily caused by suicide (*Prison Statistics India*, 2022).

According to several Indian research, the current prevalence of mental diseases among convicts, excluding substance-use disorders (SUDs), ranges from 21% to 33%. The inmates' SUD rates varied from 47.1% to 56.4% (Ayirolimeethal et al., 2014; Kumar & Daria, 2013). Overall, 83.5% of inmates had a psychiatric disorder, with depression (47.5%) being the most common, according to Tirumani *et al.* (Tirumani et al., 2020).

Rabiya and Raghavan's review of 12 studies in prisons in India found nicotine, alcohol, and cannabis as the prevalent substance use disorders (Rabiya & Raghavan, 2018). Suicide and self-harm are significant concerns in prisons. A ten-year study by Bardale and Dixit found that out of 179 autopsies, 14 were suicides, with 71.42% in lock-ups and 28.57% in prisons (Bardale & Dixit, 2015).

Crime and mental illnesses frequently have a reciprocal cause-and-effect relationship. In mental retardation, there are underlying characteristics that frequently make people more likely to commit crimes, including poor impulse control, disinhibition, suspicion and paranoia, distrust, delusions and hallucinations, and impaired judgment (Goyal et al., 2011). The NCRB Prison Statistics Report, 2022, revealed that the highest number of prisoners had education below class X (39.8%, 2,28,369), followed by prisoners with no education (25.6%, 1,46,879) (*Prison Statistics India*, 2022). Furthermore, overcrowding, a lack of privacy, uncertainty about the future, a lack of worthwhile activities, the depletion of prison facilities, and the widespread use of cruel practices that expose the inmates to a variety of physical (such as HIV infections and tuberculosis) and mental illnesses make the environment inside Indian prisons, at best, disgusting (Prasad et al., 2017). Anxiety, depression, chronic pain, and post-traumatic stress disorder are some of the long-lasting psychological effects of torture (de Williams & van der Merwe, 2013).

3 Current Status of Prison Mental Health Services and Liaison Between Law Enforcement and Mental Health Services Providers

3.1 Legal Provisions

In a positive step, Section 31(2) of the MHCA 2017 mandates basic and emergency mental health training for all prison medical officers. This ensures they are better prepared to handle mental health issues in prisons. Additionally, Section 103(6) of the Act requires every state government to set up mental health facilities in the medical wing of at least one prison. This helps improve access to mental healthcare for inmates. Most significantly, the MHCA 2017 guarantees inmates with mental illness the right to receive high-quality care. It also makes prison officials responsible for ensuring this right is protected. Section 31 of the Act mentions the need for mental health professionals. However, the Act does not explicitly specify the number of psychiatrists, nurses, or beds required in prisons (*The Mental Healthcare Act*, 2017). The Mental Healthcare (Rights of Persons with Mental Illness) Rules, 2018, recommends one doctor, two nurses, and four counselors for every 500 prisoners. In addition, one prison must have one psychiatrist. It advocates for at least 20-bed psychiatric facilities for every 500 prisoners. A list of essential allopathic psychiatric medications must be maintained, including risperidone, olanzapine, clozapine, haloperidol, chlorpromazine, trihexyphenidyl, imipramine, amitriptyline, fluoxetine, sertraline, paroxetine, valproate, carbamazepine, lithium, clonidine, atomoxetine, lorazepam, diazepam, oxazepam, disulfiram, naltrexone, acamprosate, nicotine gums, and varenicline. These medicines are made available free of cost to all persons with mental illness at all times at health establishments run or funded by the appropriate government, starting from community health centers and upward. It is important public mental health movement by government ensuring treatment at community; however, list has some omission not including clozapine and long acting benzodiazepine for alcohol use disorder (Parmar et al., 2022).

3.2 Policy Documents

The 2014 National Mental Health Policy recognized that people in detention, including convicts, are highly vulnerable to mental illness. This was the first time such a recognition was made. The policy suggests increasing awareness of mental health among law enforcement and judicial personnel. It emphasizes the connection between mental health and legal issues. This is one of the strategies to prevent mental illness and suicide (*National Mental Health Policy of India*, 2014). Model Prison Manual (MPM) 2016 mandates a comprehensive health screening at the time of admission. However, the screening primarily focuses on physical health, with mental health aspects often overlooked. MPM, 2016, emphasizes that rehabilitation does not end with prison release; sustained aftercare is essential to prevent relapse into criminal activity or mental health deterioration. Non-governmental organizations (NGOs) and rehabilitation centers play a role in providing continued care post-release (KGS, 2024). Substance abuse among prisoners is a significant concern in India. Several initiatives have been implemented to address this issue, including de-addiction centres, opioid substitution therapy (OST), and rehabilitation programs. The National Action Plan for Drug Demand Reduction (NAPDDR), run by the Ministry of Social Justice and Empowerment, supports the establishment of counseling and de-addiction centers (DACs) in prisons (KGS, 2024). The Government of India introduced the National Suicide Prevention Strategy in 2022 with the goal of lowering suicide rates by 10% by 2030. It emphasizes early detection, prevention, and better access to mental health care, particularly via digital platforms and community-based interventions. The plan places a strong emphasis on lowering stigma, limiting access to suicide tools, and bolstering suicide prevention research and surveillance. It is in line with the MHCA, 2017, which encourages compassionate care and decriminalizes suicide attempts (*National Suicide Prevention Strategy*, 2022).

3.3 Ground Reality in Prisons

India has a total of 1330 prisons (*Prison Statistics India*, 2022). The types of prison institutions include Central, District, Sub, Women's, Borstal, Open, and Special prisons, each serving different functions. Central and District prisons house long-term inmates. Sub-prisons operate at the sub-divisional level. Women's prisons cater to female inmates. Borstal schools focus on young offenders' rehabilitation. Open prisons offer a less restrictive environment with vocational training. Special prisons handle high-security cases like terrorism (Bhandari & Kaur, 2023). According to the Prison Statistics India (2022), 44.7% of inmates fall in the age group of 18–30 years, and 42.5% fall in the 30–50 age group. Of the total prisoners, 95.8% are male, 4.1% are female, and the rest are transgender. Additionally, 25.6% of prisoners are illiterate, and 39.8% are educated below the 10th standard (*Prison Statistics India*, 2022).

The state is in charge of making sure that inmates' fundamental right to mental health is upheld. This obligation starts as soon as a prisoner walks through the doors (KGS, 2024). Some states like Odisha, West Bengal, Delhi, Karnataka, Telangana, and Sikkim have implemented mental health screenings at intake, following NHRC or NIMHANS guidelines. However, only Odisha, Telangana, Karnataka, Manipur, and a few jails in Nagaland provide training of medical officers in prisons as recommended by MHCA 2017, leaving the majority of prison medical staff untrained in handling psychiatric conditions. Some prisons, such as in Chandigarh, have psychiatrists, clinical psychologists, and social workers on a contractual basis, but there is inconsistency in their deployment across states. Many states don't have DACs and instead refer prisoners to government hospitals. In some states, prisoners receive vocational training to facilitate economic independence upon release. Several states don't have formal aftercare program (KGS, 2024). There are only 68 approved positions for psychologists or psychiatrists to treat the mental health concerns of prisoners. But there are only 33 psychologists or psychiatrists in total, meaning that there is one mental health specialist for every 16,789 prisoners. Access to essential psychiatric medications in Indian prisons is often inadequate and inconsistent (*India Justice Report: Ranking States on Police, Judiciary, Prisons & Legal Aid*, 2022).

Inmates with mental health issues struggle to seek and receive proper care. Even though they have the same fundamental rights as others under the Indian Constitution, accessing mental health services is difficult for inmates. The COVID-19 pandemic made this problem worse. Repeated lockdowns, suspension of family visits, and delays in court hearings for undertrial prisoners increased the treatment gap more (Dhillon & Sasidharan, 2024).

4 Special Issues in Forensic Psychiatry such as Insanity Defense, Competency to Stand Trial, Admission, and Involuntary Medications

4.1 Insanity Defense

Section 84 of the Indian Penal Code (IPC) (1860) discusses the insanity defense and states, "Nothing is an offence which is done by a person who, at the time of doing it, by reason of unsoundness of mind, is incapable of knowing the nature of the act, or that he is doing what is either wrong or contrary to law"(*The Indian Penal Code*, 1860). Analysis of this statement gives two main criteria in the insanity defense. The first criterion is the presence of mental illness at the time of the act. The second criterion focuses on the loss of reasoning at the time of the act to understand it's nature- its wrongfulness, or its illegality. It is worth mentioning here that the term "unsoundness of mind" has not been defined in the IPC and has primarily been interpreted as being synonymous with insanity (Bada Math, 2015). However, criminal responsibility requires proof beyond a reasonable doubt of both the act committed (actus reus) and the intent or motive behind it (mens rea) (Jeremy Horder, 2022).

It is based on the McNaughten rule. In 1843, Daniel McNaughten, a delusional wood-turner from Glasgow, mistakenly killed Edward Drummond, believing he was Sir Robert Peel and that the Tories were persecuting him. After medical experts testified to his insanity, the judge halted the trial, leading to his committal to Bethlem Hospital and the establishment of the McNaughten Rules on criminal insanity (Asokan, 2007).

Not all mentally ill individuals are exempt from criminal responsibility, as legal insanity differs from medical insanity. "Medical insanity" is the term used to describe any individual experiencing any form of mental illness. "Legal insanity" is the term used to describe an individual with mental illness with a lack of reasoning ability. For example, partial delusion and impulsive or compulsive behaviors of a psychopath do not give protection under the insanity defense. A person could be deemed legally insane by doing the tests—"test of capacity to distinguish between right and wrong," "wild beast test," and "insane delusion test" (Bada Math, 2015).

Every person is legally presumed to be sane, aware of the consequences of their actions, and knowledgeable of the law unless proven otherwise (Admin, 2023). Hence, Section 105 of the Evidence Act (1872) places the burden of proving the insanity defense on the accused (*The Indian Evidence Act*, 1872). The accused must provide evidence, including expert testimony, documents, or prosecution evidence, to prove they were incapable of understanding the nature, wrongfulness, or illegality of their act. The plea of insanity has to be taken by the accused, his/her lawyer, or family members at the time of investigation or trial in lower courts, not while appealing for higher court (*The Indian Evidence Act*, 1872).

Psychiatrists play a crucial role in the insanity defense by conducting comprehensive mental health evaluations, assessing the defendant's mental state at the time of the offense, and determining fitness to stand trial. They provide objective, evidence-based opinions to the court through detailed assessments, serial mental status examinations, and forensic psychiatry proformas while reviewing all relevant legal and medical records. Despite considering opinions from psychiatrists, the court decides regarding accepting or rejecting the insanity defense (D. Kumar et al., 2014). Data from 13 out of 23 Indian High Courts revealed 102 cases where an insanity plea was raised, with murder being the most common crime (76.5%). The insanity plea was accepted in 17.65% of cases, and factors such as prior psychiatric documentation, the lower court's verdict, and expert psychiatric testimony significantly influenced the High Court's decision (Ramamurthy et al., 2019).

4.2 Competence to Stand Trial

A key idea in criminal law is competence to stand trial, which ensures that an accused individual has the mental capacity to comprehend and take part in court proceedings (Bonnie, 1992). A competent defendant is essential in the criminal justice system, as it upholds the integrity of legal proceedings, ensures fair and accurate judgments, and respects the defendant's right to make independent decisions (Hoge, 2016). Sections 328 and 329 of the Code of Criminal Procedure, 1973, govern the legal procedures for handling accused persons suspected to be of unsound mind, requiring a medical evaluation to determine their ability to enter a defense and directing either discharge or postponement of proceedings based on psychiatric assessment (*The Code of Criminal Procedure*, 1973).

Evaluation of competence to stand trial involved the assessment of the accused's ability to

- understand the purpose and nature of the trial proceedings,
- comprehend the charges against him and possible consequences,
- communicate meaningfully with their defense counsel, and
- participate in legal strategy and make informed decisions (Hoge, 2016).

It is worth mentioning here that a previously competent defendant may deteriorate during trial due to stress, and this possibility is generally acknowledged in competence assessment protocols (Bonnie, 1992). Psychiatric evaluation of the accused is sought for expert opinion on competence to stand trial (Hoge, 2016).

4.3 Admission

Admission to a psychiatric inpatient facility follows the MHCA 2017. Section 86 of the Act deals with the independent admissions. Section 89 and Section 90 of the Act deals with admissions of the major where the patient lacks the capacity to consent to admission and treatment (*The Mental Healthcare Act*, 2017). Consent from the nominated representative (NR) is needed for involuntary admissions. NR for persons with mental illness can be any person appointed by him in advance directive, a relative, a caregiver, or a suitable person appointed by a concerned board. If no suitable person is available to be appointed as an NR, the Mental Health Review Board (MHRB) shall appoint the Director of the Department of Social Welfare or their designated representative as the NR for him (*The Mental Healthcare Act*, 2017). The admission is for 30 days under Section 89. If the patient requires continued admission to a mental health establishment beyond 30 days and continues to lack capacity, Section 90 allows for 90 days of further stay with consent from the NR. Future admissions under Section 90 can be extended up to 120 days, then up to 180 days. Capacity assessment needs to be done every week under Section 89 and once in 14 days under Section 90. Admission of a minor (less than 18 years of age) happens under Section 87 of the Act on application from NR. The admissions need to be communicated to the Mental Health Review Board (MHRB) within 7 days for men and within 3 days for women and minors (*The Mental Healthcare Act*, 2017).

Compared to the Mental Health Act, 1987, the Mental Health Care Act, 2017, gives importance to human rights and privileges for the persons with mental illness. Section 103 of the MHCA deals with the prisoners with mental illness (Gautam et al., 2022). Subsection (1) of Section 103 of MHCA, 2017, states regarding admission:

> An order under section 30 of the Prisoners Act, 1900 or under section 144 of the Air Force Act, 1950, or under section 145 of the Army Act, 1950, or under section 143 or section 144 of the Navy Act, 1957, or under section 330 or section 335 of the Code of Criminal Procedure, 1973, directing the admission of a prisoner with mental illness into any suitable mental health establishment, shall be sufficient authority for the admission of such person in such establishment to which such person may be lawfully transferred for care and treatment therein:
>
> Provided that transfer of a prisoner with mental illness to the psychiatric ward in the medical wing of the prison shall be sufficient to meet the requirements under this section:
>
> Provided further that where there is no provision for a psychiatric ward in the medical wing, the prisoner may be transferred to a mental health establishment with prior permission of the Board.

The transfer procedure of any prisoner with psychiatric illness to the psychiatry ward in the medical wing of the prison or to a mental health establishment within or outside the state follows Subsection (6) of Section 103 of the MHCA, 2017. It is done in accordance with the orders from the State or the Central Government as applicable. Quality benchmarks should be followed in mental health services as per Subsection (7) of Section 103 of the MHCA, 2017. Every six months, the medical officer in charge of the mental health facility where any of the individuals listed in Subsection (1) are being held is required to provide a special report to the authority that ordered the detention about the mental and physical health of the detainee. On the other hand, the prison medical officer must submit a quarterly report to the Board confirming the absence of prisoners with mental illness. The Board may inspect the prison and question why any such prisoner has not been transferred to a mental health facility. This is mentioned in Subsections (3) and (4) of Section 103 of MHCA (*The Mental Healthcare Act*, 2017). The government has to establish a mental health unit in the medical wing of at least one of the prisons of each state and union territory for the care of the mentally ill. The requirement of a 20-bed inpatient facility for 500 prisoners has been proposed in the Act (*MHCA 2017—IV: PRISONERS WITH MENTAL ILLNESS*, n.d.; *The Mental Healthcare Act*, 2017). When the prisoner is fit for discharge from the mental health establishment, the prison authorities and the concerned court must be informed. The court decides the subsequent plan of action for under-trial prisoners. The prison authorities arrange transfer back to prison for convicted prisoners unless instructed otherwise. The Department of Psychiatric Social Work can work with the prisoner after discharge for rehabilitation if needed, and NR has to ensure the continuity of care (*The Mental Healthcare Act*, 2017).

4.4 Involuntary Medication

Involuntary medication refers to the administration of medication against the patient's wish. It is used when patients with mental illness refuse treatment due to a lack of understanding regarding the illness or a lack of the capacity to decide about treatment. The nominated representative (NR) or family facilitates treatment for a person with mental illness under beneficence either by forceful administration or concealing the treatment. The common involuntary medication practice can be oral or parenteral, and both are described below.

(A) Covert medication: Oral medicines are given in disguise mixed with food or drink in the absence of knowledge of the same in patients. It is not very relevant in prisoners with mental illness. A study from NIMHANS done on 300 patients found that covert administration of medication (CoAdM) was practiced by caregivers in 32% of persons with severe mental illness, particularly among males, those with poor insight, and those with medication non-adherence. While caregivers perceived significant improvements in self-care, interpersonal relationships, work, family functioning, and problem behaviors following CoAdM, the study highlights ethical concerns and suggests the need for legal frameworks, such as community treatment orders, to support caregivers while ensuring patient rights (Hegde et al., 2023).

(B) Parental medication:

(i) Rapid tranquilization: Rapid tranquilization is practiced legally when persons of mental illness imposing significant risk of harm to self or others are impending and other least restrictive options have failed, like verbal de-escalation. It can be symptom-triggered or fixed-dosage-basis in the form of chemical restraint, either intravenous or intramuscular. Fixed-dose regime should be reviewed every day to decide regarding the need to continue, frequency, and dosage for administration. Continuous monitoring of vitals is recommended after usage of sedation. It is considered a restrictive practice and should be administered when benefits outweigh risks with permission from NR.

(ii) Parental depot: If the patient does not take it voluntarily where needed, it can be administered with consent from the NR in the absence of capacity in persons with mental illness. For those refusing, each parenteral depot dose requires a capacity assessment within the preceding 7 days, and if capacity is lacking, it may continue with NR's consent, but once capacity is regained, the patient must provide consent (Hegde et al., 2025).

There is no specific law or clinical practice guidelines for involuntary medication in prisoners with mental illness in India (Baldaçara et al., 2024).

5 Research and Gaps in Current Understanding in Prison Mental Health

Regular prison statistics report is prepared by the National Crimes Record Bureau in India. The capacity of prisons increased by 2.5% from 2021 to 2022, but the number of prisoners increased by 3.5% during that period. Hence, the problem of overcrowding is increasing day by day (*Prison Statistics India*, 2022). Poor living conditions in prisons, along with the absence of meaningful recreational activities, social isolation, separation from family and friends, lack of privacy, shame and guilt, and worries regarding the future, make prisoners susceptible to developing mental illness (Suresh Bada Math, 2014). Even the prison architecture significantly impacts inmates' mental health by contributing to depressive symptoms (Gopinathan et al., 2024). Substance use disorder, depression and other neurotic disorders, psychosis, and personality disorders are found more commonly among them (Goyal et al., 2011; Prasad & Nagarajamurthy, 2011; SACJ, 2021). Mental illness and risk of suicide were more commonly found in young males compared to females (Ayirolimeethal et al., 2014; Rabiya & Raghavan, 2018). Available research shows that more than half of the prison population is under trial in India. Most of them are from underprivileged backgrounds without formal education and lack appropriate legal and financial assistance ('Indian Prisons Are Overcrowded & 2/3rd of the Inmates Are Under Trials', 2015). A study using the Mangal Emotional Intelligence Inventory (MEII) found that convicts scored significantly lower across all domains. It included intrapersonal and interpersonal awareness of emotions and intrapersonal and interpersonal management of emotions, and overall emotional quotient leading to challenges during hardship inside prison (Sharma et al., 2015). Another study found that prisoners exhibited poor social and emotional adjustment, which was significantly associated with mental health problems (Sinha, 2010). Kumar et al. found that prisoners are referred to mental health establishments by medical officers or the superintendent of the prison (62.2%) rather than by the court (37.8%) (Kumar et al., 2014).

A few interventional studies are done on prisoners for improving mental health. Prison courses for Vipassana started in India in 1975. The studies on the impact of Vipassana, one ancient meditation technique, in Tihar Jail indicate significant reductions in anxiety, depression, hostility, and feelings of helplessness among prisoners. It also enhanced well-being, hope, and reintegration into society, suggesting its potential as a cost-effective, large-scale intervention for psychiatric issues and prison reform (*Psychological Effects of Vipassana on Tihar Jail Inmates*, 1995). Similarly, Sudarshan Kriya, consisting of yoga movement, breathing, and meditation, done on non-psychotic male prisoners for 6 weeks, revealed significant improvement in anxiety, depression, general health, and psychological well-being. Hence, it improved overall functioning (Sureka et al., 2014). The feasibility and effectiveness of delivering opioid substitution therapy (OST) in opioid dependence has been demonstrated in a study done in 120-bed de-addiction center in Tihar Jail (Jhanjee et al., 2015). Thekkumkara et al. study developed and validated a peer support program for prisoners with common mental and substance use disorders. It incorporated key components like mental health education, early case identification, basic counseling, psychoeducation, substance use management, and suicide prevention (Thekkumkara et al., 2022).

Despite growing research on prison mental health, several gaps continue to prevail in understanding the complex interplay between incarceration and psychiatric morbidity. One significant gap is the lack of longitudinal studies exploring how incarceration affects mental health over time, particularly after release. Most of the studies rely on cross-sectional data, failing to capture the long-term consequences of imprisonment on psychological well-being. Additionally, the unique experiences of incarcerated women, who are often survivors of trauma and abuse, remain unexplored. Another critical gap is the effectiveness of existing mental health interventions in prison settings. While cognitive-behavioral therapy (CBT) and pharmacological treatments have been implemented in some facilities, there is little research evaluating their outcomes within the unique constraints of the prison environment. Furthermore, there is inadequate attention given to culturally sensitive interventions.

6 Current Challenges in Prison Mental Health and Way Forwards

Prison management in India falls under state government jurisdiction. It leads to inconsistent implementation of the Model Prisons and Correctional Services Act 2023 across different states (*Model Prisons and Correctional Services Act, 2023*, 2023). Overcrowding, inadequate prison staff, and a lack of dedicated medical and psychiatric facilities create barriers to effective rehabilitation. Additionally, the accessibility of substances despite restrictions increases the vulnerability of inmates to psychiatric disorders, self-harm, and suicide. Several countries other than India follow the Risk-Need-Responsivity (RNR) model. It assesses the reoffending risk of the prisoners, identifies their criminogenic needs, and tailors interventions based on their responsiveness to treatment. It balances security with rehabilitation (Allen-Flores et al., 2024). The lack of systemic mental health provisions in many prisons, along with judicial discretion in deciding the fate of mentally ill individuals, exacerbates the problem. Absence of mandated psychiatric evaluations during medical screenings results in non-diagnosis of mental illness in prisoners (SACJ, 2021). The incorporation of RNR model focusing on individualized treatment can aid in designing interventions that target the specific mental health and criminogenic factors of inmates. Separating offenders based on their crime type and psychological profile, integrating tele-mental health services (TMHS), and multidisciplinary collaborations among psychiatry, criminology, and public health can ensure evidence-based policies to improve prison mental health care (Khanna et al., 2018).

Prison officials should introduce program emphasizing inmate well-being, skill-building, and psychological support to strengthen reform and rehabilitation (Vajawat et al., 2024). Buddy systems, psychological first aid, stress management courses, and awareness campaigns can help prevent suicides and promote resilience among prisoners (Gowda et al., 2021). Several non-governmental organizations can take part in the implementation of culturally sensitive reformation programs. Investing in human resources, adequate funding, improved prison architecture, and recreational activities can significantly enhance mental health, which is a legal right of the prisoner. Further research is needed to develop policies and guidelines and strict application of the same for regular monitoring of mental health, long-term follow-ups, and strategies to eliminate illegal substances within prisons. Multi-sectional involvement of psychiatry, law, criminology, and public health can ensure prisoners' rights to timely and effective mental health care.

7 Conclusion

In India, forensic psychiatry and prison mental health continue to be intricate yet vital facets of mental health treatment that touch on human rights, ethics, and the law. Compared to the normal community, prisoners have a greater frequency of mental illness. Even while laws like the Mental Healthcare Act of 2017 and other Supreme Court orders are designed to protect the rights of mentally ill prisoners, structural issues including stigma and restricted access to qualified mental health specialists still exist. A multidisciplinary strategy is needed to close these gaps, combining psychiatry with the legal and penitentiary systems to guarantee prompt diagnosis, suitable treatment, and rehabilitation. Effectively treating these issues requires community-based reintegration techniques, controlled diversion programs, and specialized forensic psychiatric treatments. Additionally, emphasis on the rights of prisoners and the involvement of non-governmental organizations in the rehabilitation and reformation of prisoners could be of help. Multi-sectional collaboration of psychiatry, law, criminology, and public health could aim at developing evidence-based policies to improve mental health care in prisons. Lastly, improving human resources and providing adequate funding could offer a fair mental health care within the criminal justice system.

References

Admin. (2023, October 5). *STATE OF M.P VS AHAMADULLAH AIR 1961, SC 998—Legal Vidhiya*. https://legalvidhiya.com/state-of-m-p-vs-ahamadullah-air-1961-sc-998/

Allen-Flores, B., Hamilton, Z., Ursino, J., & Kigerl, A. (2024). Risk-contamination and Dilution: Advancing the RNR model in prison settings. *Crime & Delinquency, 00111287241287139*. https://doi.org/10.1177/00111287241287139

Asia | World Prison Brief. (n.d.). Retrieved 24 February 2025, from https://www.prisonstudies.org/map/asia

Asokan, T. V. (2007). Daniel McNaughton (1813–1865). *Indian Journal of Psychiatry, 49*(3), 223–224. https://doi.org/10.4103/0019-5545.37328

Ayirolimeethal, A., Ragesh, G., Ramanujam, J. M., & George, B. (2014). Psychiatric morbidity among prisoners. *Indian Journal of Psychiatry, 56*(2), 150–153. https://doi.org/10.4103/0019-5545.130495

Bada Math, S. (2015). Insanity defense: Past, present, and future. *Indian Journal of Psychological Medicine*, *37*(4), 381–387.

Baldaçara, L., Pinto, A. L. d. C. B., Díaz, A. P., Sanches, M., & da Silva, A. G. (2024). Rapid tranquilization in a psychiatric emergency room: A naturalistic cohort study in 12 h. *Psychiatry Research Communications, 4*(2), 100168. https://doi.org/10.1016/j.psycom.2024.100168

Bardale, R. V., & Dixit, P. G. (2015). Suicide behind bars: A 10-year retrospective study. *Indian Journal of Psychiatry, 57*(1), 81–84. https://doi.org/10.4103/0019-5545.148531

Bhandari, B., & Kaur, S. (2023). *Prison System in India*. https://www.lawjournals.org/assets/archives/2023/vol9issue2/9062-857.pdf

Bonnie, R. J. (1992). The competence of criminal defendants: A theoretical reformulation. *Behavioral Sciences & the Law, 10*(3), 291–316. https://doi.org/10.1002/bsl.2370100303

de Williams, A. C., & van der Merwe, J. (2013). The psychological impact of torture. *British Journal of Pain, 7*(2), 101–106. https://doi.org/10.1177/2049463713483596

Dhillon, H. S., & Sasidharan, S. (2024). Prison mental health – An Indian perspective. *Annals of Indian Psychiatry, 8*(1), 80. https://doi.org/10.4103/aip.aip_105_21

Foucault, M. (1978). About the concept of the 'dangerous individual' in 19th-century legal psychiatry. *International Journal of Law and Psychiatry, 1*(1), 1–18. https://doi.org/10.1016/0160-2527(78)90020-1

Gautam, S., Jain, A., Gupta, I. D., Gautam, M., Gaur, N., & Shekhawat, B. S. (2022). Clinical practice guidelines for human rights and privileges of mentally ill persons. *Indian Journal of Psychiatry, 64*(Suppl 1), S35. https://doi.org/10.4103/indianjpsychiatry.indianjpsychiatry_697_21

Gopinathan, B., Vijayshankar, V., & Roy, S. (2024). Exploring the relationship between the built environment of prisons and the mental health of inmates. *International Journal of Prison Health, 20*(3), 360–374. https://doi.org/10.1108/IJOPH-11-2022-0071

Gowda, G. S., Shadakshari, D., Vajawat, B., Reddi, V. S. K., Math, S. B., & Murthy, P. (2021). Suicide in Indian prisons. *The Lancet Psychiatry, 8*(8), e19. https://doi.org/10.1016/S2215-0366(21)00233-9

Goyal, S. K., Singh, P., Gargi, P. D., Goyal, S., & Garg, A. (2011). Psychiatric morbidity in prisoners. *Indian Journal of Psychiatry, 53*(3), 253. https://doi.org/10.4103/0019-5545.86819

Hegde, P., Gowda, G. S., Vajawat, B., Basavaraju, V., Moirangthem, S., Kumar, N., & Bada Math, S. (2023). Study on covert administration of medications practices among persons with severe mental illness: A cross-sectional study. *International Journal of Social Psychiatry, 69*, 28–37. https://doi.org/10.1177/00207640211065675

Hegde, P. R., Gautham, M., Kumar, C. N., Manjunatha, N., & Math, S. B. (2025). Clinical practice guidelines for long-stay psychiatric services: Focus on admission procedures, covert medications, and proxy consultations. *Indian Journal of Psychiatry, 67*(1), 168. https://doi.org/10.4103/indianjpsychiatry.indianjpsychiatry_688_24

Hoge, S. K. (2016). Competence to stand trial: An overview. *Indian Journal of Psychiatry, 58*(Suppl 2), S187–S190. https://doi.org/10.4103/0019-5545.196830

India Justice Report: Ranking States on Police, Judiciary, Prisons & Legal Aid. (2022). https://indiajusticereport.org/files/IJR%202022_Full_Report.pdf

Indian Prisons are Overcrowded & 2/3rd of the Inmates are Under Trials. (2015, April 25). *FACTLY*. https://factly.in/indian-prisons-are-overcrowded-23rd-of-the-inmates-are-under-trials/

Jeremy, H. (2022). *Ashworth's principles of criminal law* (10th ed.). Oxford University Press. https://doi.org/10.1093/he/9780192897381.001.0001

Jhanjee, S., Pant, S., Girdhar, N. K., Sethi, H., Gunasekaran Rengaswamy, R., Jain, R., & Sarangi, J. (2015). Opioid substitution treatment in Tihar prisons, India: Process of implementation. *The International Journal on Drug Policy, 26*(9), 890–891. https://doi.org/10.1016/j.drugpo.2015.05.016

KGS. (2024, November 20). Prisons in India: Mapping Prison Manuals and Measures for Reformation and Decongestion. *UPSC Current Affairs 2025*. https://currentaffairs.khanglobalstudies.com/prisons-in-india-mapping-prison-manuals-and-measures-for-reformation-and-decongestion/

Khanna, M., Gowda, G. S., Bagevadi, V. I., Gupta, A., Kulkarni, K., Shyam, R. P., Basavaraju, V., Ramesh, M. B., Sashidhara, H. N., Manjunatha, N., Channaveerachari, N. K., & Math, S. B. (2018). Feasibility and utility of tele-neurorehabilitation service in india: Experience from a quaternary center. *Journal of Neurosciences in Rural Practice, 9*(4), 541–544. https://doi.org/10.4103/jnrp.jnrp_104_18

Koccher, J. S., & Sarkar, U. N. (2012). *Care and treatment in mental health institutions: Some glimpses in the recent period*. National Human Rights Commission.

Kumar, D., Viswanath, B., Sebestian, A., Holla, B., Konduru, R., Chandrashekar, C. R., & Math, S. B. (2014). Profile of male forensic psychiatric inpatients in South India. *The International Journal of Social Psychiatry, 60*(1), 55–62. https://doi.org/10.1177/0020764012461334

Kumar, V., & Daria, U. (2013). Psychiatric morbidity in prisoners. *Indian Journal of Psychiatry, 55*(4), 366–370. https://doi.org/10.4103/0019-5545.120562

Menski, W. F. (2006). *Comparative law in a global context: The legal systems of Asia and Africa* (2nd ed.). Cambridge University Press. https://doi.org/10.1017/CBO9780511606687

MHCA 2017—IV: PRISONERS WITH MENTAL ILLNESS. (n.d.). Retrieved 8 February 2025, from https://mhca2017.com/index.php/rules/iv-prisoners-with-mental-illness

Mishra, A., Shreya, A., & Shukla, A. (2021). Promotion of mental health and well-being in Indian prisons. *International Journal of Community Medicine And Public Health, 8*(1), 482–488. https://doi.org/10.18203/2394-6040.ijcmph20205740

Model Prisons and Correctional Services Act, 2023. (2023). https://www.mha.gov.in/sites/default/files/2024-12/ModelPrisonsCorrectionalServicesAct_20122024.pdf

Narayan, C. L., Narayan, M., & Shikha, D. (2011). The ongoing process of amendments in MHA-87 and PWD Act-95 and their implications on mental health care. *Indian Journal of Psychiatry, 53*(4), 343–350. https://doi.org/10.4103/0019-5545.91910

National Crime Investigation Bureau's. (n.d.). Retrieved 8 February 2025, from https://www.ncib.in/

National Mental Health Policy of India. (2014, October). Ministry of Health and Family Welfare, Government of India. https://nhm.gov.in/images/pdf/National_Health_Mental_Policy.pdf

National Suicide Prevention Strategy. (2022). Ministry of Health and Family Welfare, Government of India. https://mohfw.gov.in/sites/default/files/National%20Suicide%20Prevention%20Strategy.pdf

Parmar, A., Nath, S., & Padhy, S. K. (2022). List of essential psychotherapeutic medicines 2019 of India: When science was left behind. *Indian Journal of Psychiatry, 64*(2), 209–212. https://doi.org/10.4103/indianjpsychiatry.indianjpsychiatry_286_21

Pathare, S., & Kapoor, A. (2021). Decisional Autonomy and India's Mental Healthcare Act, 2017: A comment on emerging Jurisprudence. In C. Sunkel, F. Mahomed, M. A. Stein, & V. Patel (Eds.), *Mental health, legal capacity, and human rights* (pp. 155–170). Cambridge University Press. https://doi.org/10.1017/9781108979016.013

Poverty and Shared Prosperity 2022. (n.d.). World Bank. Retrieved 8 February 2025, from https://www.worldbank.org/en/publication/poverty-and-shared-prosperity

Prasad, B. M., Thapa, B., Chadha, S. S., Das, A., Babu, E. R., Mohanty, S., Pandurangan, S., & Tonsing, J. (2017). Status of Tuberculosis services in Indian Prisons. *International Journal of Infectious Diseases, 56*, 117–121. https://doi.org/10.1016/j.ijid.2017.01.035

Prasad, P., & Nagarajamurthy, B. (2011). A study of anxiety and depression among undertrial prisoners in Central Jails in Karnataka. *Asian Journal of Developmental Matters, 5*, 143–147.

Prison Statistics India. (2022). National Crime Records Bureau (Ministry of Home Affairs), Government of India. https://www.ncrb.gov.in/uploads/nationalcrimerecordsbureau/custom/psiyearwise2022/1701613297PSI2022ason01122023.pdf

Psychological Effects of Vipassana on Tihar Jail Inmates. (1995). Vipassana Research Institute. https://www.vridhamma.org/research/Psychological-Effects-of-Vipassana-on-Tihar-Jail-Inmates

Rabiya, S., & Raghavan, V. (2018). Prison Mental Health in India: Review. *Indian Journal of Social Psychiatry, 34*(3), 193. https://doi.org/10.4103/ijsp.ijsp_9_18

Ramamurthy, P., Chathoth, V., & Thilakan, P. (2019). How does India decide insanity pleas? A review of high court judgments in the past decade. *Indian Journal of Psychological Medicine, 41*(2), 150–154. https://doi.org/10.4103/IJPSYM.IJPSYM_373_18

Ranade, K., Kapoor, A., & Fernandes, T. N. (2022). Mental health law, policy & program in India – A fragmented narrative of change, contradictions and possibilities. *SSM - Mental Health, 2*, 100174. https://doi.org/10.1016/j.ssmmh.2022.100174

SACJ, T. (2021, January 30). *Mental Health of Prisoners in India: An Analysis*. The NUJS SACJ. https://www.nujssacj.com/post/mental-health-of-prisoners-in-india-an-analysis

Sharma, N., Prakash, O., Sengar, K. S., Chaudhury, S., & Singh, A. R. (2015). The relation between emotional intelligence and criminal behavior: A study among convicted criminals. *Industrial Psychiatry Journal, 24*(1), 54–58. https://doi.org/10.4103/0972-6748.160934

Sinha, S. (2010). Adjustment and mental health problem in prisoners. *Industrial Psychiatry Journal, 19*(2), 101–104. https://doi.org/10.4103/0972-6748.90339

Srinivas, M. N. (1995). *Social change in modern India*. Orient Blackswan.

Sureka, P., Govil, S., Dash, D., Dash, C., Kumar, M., & Singhal, V. (2014). Effect of Sudarshan Kriya on male prisoners with non psychotic psychiatric disorders: A randomized control trial. *Asian Journal of Psychiatry, 12*, 43–49. https://doi.org/10.1016/j.ajp.2014.06.010

Suresh Bada Math. (2014). *Minds Imprisoned: Mental Health Care in Prisons*.

The Bharatiya Nagarik Suraksha Sanhita. (2023, December 25). Ministry of Law and Justice (Legislative Department), New Delhi. https://www.mha.gov.in/sites/default/files/2024-04/250884_2_english_01042024.pdf

The Bharatiya Naya Sanhita. (2023). Ministry of Law and Justice (Legislative Department), New Delhi. https://www.mha.gov.in/sites/default/files/2024-04/250883_english_01042024.pdf

The Code of Civil Procedure. (1908). https://cdnbbsr.s3waas.gov.in/s380537a945c7aaa788ccfcdf1b99b5d8f/uploads/2022/12/2022122853.pdf

The Code of Criminal Procedure. (1973). Ministry of Law and Justice (Legislative Department), New Delhi. https://cdnbbsr.s3waas.gov.in/s380537a945c7aaa788ccfcdf1b99b5d8f/uploads/2022/12/2022122878.pdf

TheConstitutionofIndia.(1950).https://archive.org/details/the-constitution-of-india-original-1950/page/n15/mode/2up

The Constitution of India. (2024, January 5). Ministry of Law and Justice (Legislative Department), New Delhi. https://lddashboard.legislative.gov.in/sites/default/files/coi/COI_2024.pdf

The Indian Evidence Act. (1872, March 15). Ministry of Law and Justice (Legislative Department), New Delhi. https://cdnbbsr.s3waas.gov.in/s380537a945c7aaa788ccfcdf1b99b5d8f/uploads/2022/12/2022122817.pdf

The Indian Penal Code. (1860, June 10). Law Commision of India. https://ia600805.us.archive.org/35/items/THEINDIANPENALCODE1860/THE%20INDIAN%20PENAL%20CODE,%201860.pdf

The Juvenile Justice (Care and Protection of Children) Act. (2015, December 31). Ministry of Law and Justice (Legislative Department), New Delhi. https://www.indiacode.nic.in/bitstream/123456789/19022/1/juvenile_justice_%28care_and_protection_of_children%29_act%2C_2015_%282_of_2016%29.pdf

The Mental Healthcare Act. (2017, July 4). Ministry of Law and Justice (Legislative Department), New Delhi. https://acrobat.adobe.com/id/urn:aaid:sc:AP:368ceefb-6e71-4412-8847-69c66d1a7418

The Narcotic Drugs and Psychotropic Substances Act. (1985, September 16). Ministry of Law and Justice (Legislative Department), New Delhi. https://narcoticsindia.nic.in/legislation/ndpsact.pdf

The Protection of Children from Sexual Offences Act. (2012). Ministry of Law and Justice (Legislative Department), New Delhi. https://www.indiacode.nic.in/bitstream/123456789/2079/1/AA2012-32.pdf

The Rights of Persons with Disabilities Act. (2016, December 28). Ministry of Law and Justice (Legislative Department), New Delhi. https://cdnbbsr.s3waas.gov.in/s3e58ae-a67b01fa747687f038dfde066f6/uploads/2023/10/2023101061053958942.pdf

Thekkumkara, S. N., Jagannathan, A., Muliyala, K. P., & Murthy, P. (2022). Development and validation of a peer support programme for the prisoners with mental and substance use disorders in India. *Indian Journal of Psychiatry, 64*(3), 316–321. https://doi.org/10.4103/indianjpsychiatry.indianjpsychiatry_416_21

Tirumani, S. R., Vennam, B. S. V., & Seepana, R. (2020). A study on prevalence of psychiatric morbidity and substance abuse among prisoners. *Open Journal of Psychiatry and Allied Sciences, 11*(2), 96–99. https://doi.org/10.5958/2394-2061.2020.00020.8

Vajawat, B., Gowda, G. S., Sarkar, J., & Murthy, P. (2024). Care, Management and Rehabilitation of Offenders in India. In *Approaches to Offender Rehabilitation in Asian Jurisdictions.* Routledge.

World Population Prospects 2024: Summary of Results | DESA Publications. (2024, July 11). https://desapublications.un.org/publications/world-population-prospects-2024-summary-results

Chapter 4
Forensic Psychiatry and Prison Mental Health in Nepal

Pawan Sharma, Devavrat Joshi, and Srijana Kunwar

Abstract Nepal is governed as a federal democratic republic after the adoption of the 2015 Constitution, ending a decade-long civil war and the abolition of the monarchy. The mental health sector has been under slow and steady development for decades. The vulnerable prison population of Nepal faces mental health challenges, from high prevalence to limited access to services. Though legal provisions are there for people with mental disorders, lack of implementation has affected a large group of patients. Forensic psychiatry as a subspecialty has not been recognized, and there is a challenge in this sector in terms of workforce, services, and research. In this chapter, we aim to discuss the historical aspects, epidemiology, current scenario, and challenges with way-outs in the field of forensic psychiatry and prison mental health.

Keywords Forensic psychiatry · Prison mental health · Correctional psychiatry · Nepal

1 Introduction

Nepal, a South Asian nation characterized by its landlocked geography, is bordered by China to the north and India on the remaining three sides. Renowned for its rich cultural heritage and breathtaking geographical diversity, the country spans the mighty Himalayas and the lush plains of the Terai region, which support agricultural

---

P. Sharma (✉)
Department of Psychiatry, Patan Academy of Health Sciences, Lalitpur, Nepal
e-mail: pawansharma@pahs.edu.np

D. Joshi
Mental Hospital Lagankhel, National Academy of Medical Sciences, Lalitpur, Nepal

S. Kunwar
Department of Forensic Medicine, Patan Academy of Health Sciences, Lalitpur, Nepal

A. Parmar et al. (eds.), *Forensic Psychiatry and Prison Mental Health in South Asia*, South Asian Perspectives in Mental Health and Psychology,
https://doi.org/10.1007/978-981-96-7206-6_4

productivity. As of the most recent census, Nepal has a population exceeding 30 million, composed of diverse ethnic and cultural groups (Census Nepal, 2021). It has been governed as a federal democratic republic since the adoption of the 2015 Constitution. Nepal underwent decades of political turmoil, including a decade-long civil war (1996–2006), the abolition of monarchy in 2008, and subsequent transitions to establish democratic systems. The Constitution ensures governance through a three-tier federal structure, including central, provincial, and local levels.

Nepal is home to a mosaic of ethnic, linguistic, and cultural groups, with over 125 ethnic communities and 123 distinct languages documented (Gurung, 2001). The social fabric is deeply influenced by historical and cultural traditions, including the caste system rooted in Hinduism. Despite the legal abolition of caste-based discrimination and untouchability in 1963, these practices continue to impact marginalized communities, such as *Dalits, Janajatis* (indigenous people), and women, limiting their access to education, healthcare, and employment (Bennett, 2008). The legal framework of Nepal is enshrined in the 2015 Constitution, which guarantees fundamental rights such as equality, freedom, and justice for all citizens (Secretariat & Durbar, 2015). The judiciary operates independently, comprising the Supreme Court, seven High Courts, and numerous District Courts. Additionally, specialized constitutional bodies, like the National Human Rights Commission (NHRC), were established to monitor human rights violations and advocate for justice and accountability (Vyas et al., 2024).

2 Prison System in Nepal

The history of prison in Nepal starts in 1914. "Sadar Jail" (present-day Jagannath Dewal jail office in Kathmandu) as Nepal's first prison. The jail administration was under "*Mukhtiyar,*" and the chief was Rana General. After the people's revolution of 1950, the prison administration came under the Ministry of Home Affairs. After the repeal of the Prisons Act, 1963 AD, the Prisons Act, 2022, came into effect, along with the implementation of the 15th Amendment to the Prisons Rules, 2020 (Department of Prison Management, 2022). The Ministry of Home Affairs established the Prison Management Department at the central level in 1993 AD to streamline and improve the effectiveness of work pertaining to prison administration and management. The Department of Prison Management is responsible for overseeing the management of prisons in Nepal (Department of Prison Management, 2022).

There are 75 prison offices spread over 72 of Nepal's 77 districts. The appropriate Chief District Officer is in charge of overseeing Prison management and administration on a local level. The Prison Management department has been assisting in the fields of policy, administration, and prisoner management. Besides this, the Code of Conduct for Prison Office Staffs, Security personnel, Prisoners, and Visitors, 2022 imposes restrictions and safety for the prisoners living in the prisons of Nepal covering all 77 districts (Department of Prison Management, 2022).

Inadequate space is one of the main causes of the overcrowding of convicts in several prisons, especially those located within the Kathmandu Valley. There is a discrepancy between the number of prisoners housed in these institutions and their capacity. For instance, there were 3488 prisoners in the central jail, while the stated capacity is for only 1500 people in the year 2023. Many of the prisons are accommodating more prisoners than their actual capacity, and hence, the overall occupancy level was 153.7% (World Prison Brief, 2024).

3 Epidemiology and Burden of Mental Disorders Among Prisoners

A study done in Jhumka Regional Prison, which is the largest prison in eastern Nepal, among 434 randomly selected inmates using the Center for Epidemiologic Studies Depression Scale, showed that the prevalence of depression was 35.3%, and around 2.3% of inmates reported suicidal ideation during imprisonment, and 0.9% attempted suicide inside the prison. Depression was associated with previous incarceration and frequent appointments when encountering health problems (Shrestha et al., 2017). Another study in western Nepal examined 223 inmates selected through systematic random sampling from eight district-level prisons. Using the Beck Depression Inventory-II, it was found that 18.8% of the inmates exhibited symptoms of depression. Factors such as health issues, suicidal ideation during imprisonment, and attempted suicide before incarceration had a significant relationship with depression (Bhusal et al., 2024). Similarly, data from male prisoners at a prison in Kathmandu, using the Major Depression Inventory (MDI) tool of the WHO, indicated that the prevalence of depressive symptoms was 45.6%. Among them, 28.2% met the criteria for severe depression, 6.7% met the criteria for moderate depression, and 10.8% met the criteria for mild depression. Additionally, a history of past illness, drug abuse, and previous episodes of depression were significantly associated with current depressive symptoms (Baral et al., 2020). Among female inmates, it was seen that out of 92 recruited participants, 37 (40.1%) respondents had symptoms of depression (Regmi et al., 2019). Among male-only prisons, it was seen that among 490 prisoners, psychiatric morbidity was seen in 10.41% of prisoners using the Modified Mini Screen. Suicidality and post-traumatic stress disorder were present among 3.47% and 3.06%, respectively. There was a significant association of psychiatric morbidity with length of stay in prison, satisfaction with living facilities, regular health check-ups, and doctor appointments during health problems (Parajuli, 2023). Among the prisoners attending OPD of the central jail hospital during a period of six months, 40.33% had psychiatric morbidity, with male preponderance. The most common diagnosis was neurotic, stress-related and somatoform disorder (57%), followed by mood disorder (32.2%) (Bhattarai et al., 2018). A WHO-AIMS report of 2007 showed that the percentage of persons with mental retardation in prison is about 3%. Up to 20% of prisons had at least one prisoner per month in treatment contact with a mental health professional (WHO, 2008). As per a report published in 2008 by the Office of the High Commissioner for Human Rights in Nepal, it was reported that 84% of the mentally disabled detainees in Dhulikhel prison were detained in relation to homicide. They reside in the poorest living section of the prison, which is a separate section for the severely mentally disabled (Office of United Nations High Commissioner for Human Rights in Nepal, 2008).

4 Current Status of Prison Mental Health Services

In the past, due to the inability to treat people with severe mental illnesses and the discriminatory attitude of society towards such individuals, words such as *baulaa-haa/paagal/magaz bigreko* (mad/insane) were commonly used to indicate persons with mental health conditions, and the same concept was formally recognized in major policies such as the first *Muluki Ain* (Civil Code) of 1854 AD, the previous *Muluki Ain*, 1963, and the Prison's Act, 1963, with discriminatory provisions such as chaining and imprisonment of people with mental health conditions until they became 'normal' after treatment. The agreed rule was: "chain those who are insane and send them to the jail." As a result, most of those with severe mental illnesses were sent to prisons (Gurung et al., 2023).

As per historical data, Maryknoll Nepal, a non-governmental organization, reached an agreement with the Directorate of Jail Administration and the then His Majesty's Government of Nepal in 1994 to stop the system of keeping mentally ill patients without any criminal offences in jails of the Kathmandu Valley. It also agreed upon the release of all the mentally ill women from the Central Female Jail, Kathmandu, and all the mentally ill male patients without criminal offences from Dhulikhel Jail, Kavre district. Treatment and then rehabilitation of the 48 mentally ill women released as per this agreement within their own families was started, and, similarly, the male patients from Dhulikhel Jail were also treated in a residential facility named Ashadeep at Nayapati, Kathmandu. Since 1994, no patients with mental disorders without any criminal offences have been wrongfully imprisoned.

The Central Prison Hospital in the Kathmandu district and the Hospital for Prisoners with Psychosocial Problems in Nakkhu, Lalitpur district, are the allocated authorities to treat prisoners in Nepal. In other prisons, health workers and assistant health workers oversee the medical section, and inmates mostly get medical treatment in other hospitals situated near the prison. Presently, psychosocial counseling is being provided in 40 prisons in Nepal, which is set to be extended to all existing prisons. But still, the appropriate interventions being provided to the mentally ill prisoners are grossly inadequate. The Central Jail Hospital has a dedicated post for a psychiatrist. However, there are no permanently appointed psychiatrists and mental health professionals in this center. There is a hospital run in the prison at Nakkhu, Lalitpur, which is supposed to function as a prison mental hospital. A psychiatric clinic was run thrice a month in this hospital, which till now was being overseen by a general medical practitioner. There has been a recent appointment of a psychiatrist in a permanent post, which has created a hope that this hospital may become fully functional within a year or two and may serve as the focal point for all the mentally ill prisoners. In other prisons, there have been periodic mental health assessments and treatment of inmates by some psychiatrists, psychologists, and nongovernment organizations. In addition to this, mental health assessment and support for children detained for criminal offenses have been initiated (WHO, 2021).

Regarding the mental health treatment of prisoners, the existing Civil Code (2017) has also undergone extensive amendments, and regarding mental health, the recent version states, "(1) Treatment of the physically or mentally sick detainees or prisoners shall be done by the government doctor. Provided that, if any detainee or prisoner wishes to have his/her treatment done by any other doctor at his/her own cost, permission shall be granted to have such treatment as prescribed" (Nepal Law Commission, 2018).

5 Legal Provisions for Mental Health in Nepal

Nepal became the 86th country to ratify the UNCRPD and the 53rd country to ratify the Optional Protocol on May 7, 2010 (UN CRPD, 2010). The constitution of Nepal, Article 35, mentions that every citizen has the right to receive basic health services free of charge from the state and to have equal access to health services under the right to health (Secretariat & Durbar, 2015). The Mental Health Policy of 1996 had one of the objectives of protecting the human rights of mentally ill people (Singh & Khadka, 2022). The overarching health policy of 2019 also aims at protecting the fundamental human rights of people with psychosocial disabilities and mental illnesses, which has been emphasized in the National Mental Health Strategy and Action Plan 2020 (Sharma et al., 2024). Different acts in Nepal have addressed mental health issues, which are mentioned in Table 4.1.

One of the important achievements in Nepal has been the introduction of the One Stop Crisis Management Centre (OCMC) in 2010, which is available in 94 different hospitals throughout the nation. This center aims to provide integrated services like health services, medicolegal services, mental health and psychosocial counseling services, along with security through district police, established safe homes and rehabilitation centers, district bar/bar association/para-legal services, and rehabilitation through a one-door system as a part of comprehensive support to the people who are facing the gender-based violence, i.e., the victim and the perpetrator (Joshi et al., 2023; Atreya et al., 2020).

Table 4.1 Acts of Nepal related to mental illness (Nepal Law Commission, 2018)

SN	Act	Description
1	Act Relating to Rights of Persons with Disabilities, 2017	This Act identifies mental disability and intellectual disability and ensures their rights. The Act also states that for the person with mental or psychosocial disabilities, the government of Nepal shall • make provisions for the treatment in community hospitals or health centers as chosen by them or any member of their families or their guardians • provide free medicines and consultancy service • make arrangements for the treatment and rehabilitation or family reunion of the persons who have been disregarded by their families • not be held in prison in the name of treatment or protection However, nothing shall bar the keeping in prison of any person with a disability who is undergoing action or has been sentenced for any criminal offence, in accordance with the prevailing law. There is provision for punishment on contravention of • Prohibition on hatred, disregard, or neglect • Prohibition on engagement in begging
2	The Public Health Service Act, 2018	This Act states that every citizen shall have the right to obtain free basic health services, including service relating to mental disease. If any person treats the persons having mental health problems by committing acts such as keeping them tied up or detaining them in a cell, the person shall be deemed to have committed an offence under this Act and shall be subject to punishment.
3	The National Penal (Code) Act, 2017	Act of a person of unsound mind not to be offence: No act done by a person who, at the time of doing it, because of unsoundness of mind, is incapable of knowing the nature, characteristic, fault, or consequence of such act shall be considered to be an offence. The Act done for benefit by consent of guardian not to be offence. No act done in good faith and with due care for the benefit of a person below 18 years of age, or of unsoundness of mind due to mental illness, by his or her guardian or another person by consent of the guardian, which causes harm to that person, shall be considered to be an offence. Provided that, except where done to prevent death or grievous hurt, no person who does an act with the knowledge that it is likely to cause death or grievous hurt shall be dispensed with criminal liability. Regarding consent, the Act states, "Provided that consent given by a person who, being of unsound mind due to mental illness, is unable to understand characteristic, fault and consequence of the consent given by him or her when he or she was in a state of unsoundness of mind shall not be considered to be consent." The offence committed against an elderly person above 75 years of age, or a person being of unsound mind by reason of physical or mental illness, or a person incapable of defending himself or herself because of disability, or a child, has been put under the factors aggravating the gravity of the offence.

(continued)

Table 4.1 (continued)

SN	Act	Description
4	The National Civil (Code) Act, 2017	In this act, a person who has not attained ten years of age or, even if he or she has attained that age, is unable to protect his or her rights and interests for the reason of unsoundness of mind, shall be considered to be legally incompetent. In the family law of this act, no one shall conclude, or cause to be concluded, a marriage with a man or a woman who is of unsound mind by way of misrepresentation. The exception to joint parental authority: either of the mother and father is of unsound mind, the mother or father of sound mind, during the period of existence of such state of mind. A person of unsound mind is prohibited from adopting a child and forming a contract.

6 Available Research and Gaps in Current Understanding

Most of the research done on the epidemiology of mental disorders among prison inmates has been cross-sectional research using tools. They have estimated the prevalence of common mental disorders only. There have been some reports of the use of interventions like *Vipassanā* meditation, which have resulted in changes in attitude, anger reduction, and improvement of physical and mental health (Pandey, 2022). There are some qualitative studies conducted, like a study with 100 quantitative surveys and 14 key informant interviews, which showed that the major problems faced by elderly prison inmates were physical, psychological, economic, and legal challenges. It was difficult for inmates to maintain relationships with their families outside. The major coping factors were religion and maintaining relationships with other prisoners (Chettri et al., 2024). However, despite these small efforts, there is a gross lack of systematic information on national prevalence data on the prison population. Also, there are no longitudinal studies or cohort studies on any of the domains of mental health of the prison population. Also, in terms of forensic psychiatry, there is gross unavailability of research.

7 Current Challenges and Ways Out

Despite the recent development in the field of psychiatry in terms of workforce and services as compared to the past, there are many challenges that Nepal faces. Following are the challenges and ways out in this neglected field of psychiatry:

7.1 Prison Mental Health

7.1.1 Lack of Data

There is no national data on the prevalence and types of mental disorders among prisoners in Nepal (Arafat et al., 2024). Though the available data suggest psychiatric disorders are relatively common in this population, there is a need to do a national survey on recognizing the actual burden of mental disorders. The Epidemiology and Disease Control Division under the Department of Health Services, Nepal, has recently announced its plans to conduct a national-level mental health survey among all prisoners/detainees throughout the country, commencing from the Bagmati Province. If this is continued in all seven provinces, it could be an important achievement (The Kathmandu Post, 2024).

7.1.2 Lack of Manpower and Mental Health Services

The mental health services in the prison are grossly inadequate. There are no dedicated psychiatric units to treat the huge morbidity of mental disorders in prison. There are no rehabilitation programs to address issues like trauma and substance use. There is a need to uplift this poor service regarding mental health in this population.

7.1.3 Overcrowding and Poor Living Conditions

Nepalese prisons are overcrowded, with inmates often living in cramped, unsanitary environments, which can lead to undue stress and anxiety. There is a need to modify or improve the existing prison infrastructure.

7.1.4 Limited Access to Mental Health Services

Mental health services are rarely prioritized within the prison system. Inmates often go undiagnosed or untreated for serious mental health conditions. Also, those who are already diagnosed with mental disorders are not provided regular treatment. As a lot of patients in jails of Nepal have a history of severe mental disorder. These people need rehabilitation programs so that they can be integrated into society later. One of the ways forward would be to integrate comprehensive mental health services into the prison system, including regular psychiatric evaluations.

7.2 *Forensic Psychiatry*

7.2.1 Lack of Trained Manpower and Services

The country still lacks trained forensic psychiatrists. Hence, the burden of assessing and handling prisoners with mental illness lies on the general psychiatrists working mostly in government hospital setups. Similarly, there is inadequate training for lawyers in handling cases of mentally ill prisoners (Singh & Khadka, 2022). In addition, though brief training and orientation programs related to the mental health of prisoners for the police and law enforcement agencies are held occasionally by the experts, their exposure to this matter is grossly inadequate. Hence, specialized training for mental health professionals, legal practitioners, and law enforcement officers is required in this field. There is also a need to establish dedicated forensic psychiatry units in hospitals to address the needs of individuals in the legal system. This can be done in collaboration with countries with advanced forensic psychiatry systems to adopt best practices.

7.2.2 Lack of Standardized Forensic Psychiatric Evaluation Protocols

There are no standardized forensic psychiatric evaluation protocols. Also, there is an act on the rights of people with disabilities, but there are no clear-cut guidelines on grading disability due to mental illnesses. Hence, bodies like the Psychiatrists' Association of Nepal need to develop the assessment protocol and guidelines in collaboration with forensic medicine experts and law experts to be endorsed by the government of Nepal.

7.2.3 Limited Implementation of Law

Though the laws are passed, there are always problems with proper implementation (Prajapati et al., 2024). Hence, there is a need to implement the legal provisions that are in place.

7.2.4 Lack of Mental Health Act

There is no Mental Health Act in Nepal. Though the process of drafting the Act has been ongoing for the last decade, there hasn't been much development in this regard until recently (Stephens et al., 2024). There is a need to expedite the process and pass the act.

8 Conclusion

There has been a slow and steady improvement in forensic psychiatry and prison mental health in Nepal over a period of time. However, the existent prison infrastructure, number of medicolegal experts/law enforcers specializing in mental health, baseline epidemiological data, and the efforts in this area to date are not enough to cater to the mental health needs of the prison population. Also, there is a need to improve the forensic mental health workforce and services in Nepal.

Acknowledgment We would like to thank Dr. Divyanshu Jha, Madhesh Institute of Health Sciences, Provincial Hospital, Janakpurdham, Nepal, for providing his help in compiling the acts in Nepal related to people with mental disabilities.

References

Arafat, S. M. Y., Kar, S. K., Abhayanayake, C., Sharma, P., & Marthoenis, M. (2024). Prison mental health in South-East Asia: A narrative review. *Brain and Behavior, 14*(8), e70004. https://doi.org/10.1002/brb3.70004

Atreya, A., Shrestha, R., Nepal, B., Nepal, S., Shrestha, D., & Mahato, S. (2020). When sexual offence is an unexpected diagnosis – exploration of medical, legal and social aspects in Nepalese scenario. *Medico-Legal Journal, 88*(4), 192–195. https://doi.org/10.1177/0025817220935878

Baral, K., Dahal, M., Khadka, G., & Adhikari, A. (2020). Prevalence of depressive symptoms and its associated factors among male prisoners at Dillibazar prison, Kathmandu, Nepal. *Europasian Journal of Medical Sciences, 2*(1). https://doi.org/10.46405/ejms.v2i1.21

Bennett, L. (2008). *Caste, ethnic, and regional identity in Nepal: Further analysis of the 2006 Nepal Demographic and Health Survey*. Population Division, Ministry of Health and Population, Government of Nepal.

Bhattarai, P., Sharma, V. D., Chapagai, M., & Tulachan, P. (2018). Prevalence of psychiatric morbidity among prisoners attending OPD of Central Jail Hospital, Kathmandu. *Journal of Psychiatrists' Association of Nepal, 7*(1). https://doi.org/10.3126/jpan.v7i1.22934

Bhusal, R., AP, C., Bhattarai, N., Mishra, D. K., Sapkota, S. K., Sharma, S., & Sapkota, K. P. (2024). Depression among inmates of Gandaki Province, Nepal: A cross-sectional study. *BMC Psychiatry, 24*(1), 446. https://doi.org/10.1186/s12888-024-05896-9

Census Nepal 2021. (2021). Retrieved January 19, 2025, from https://censusnepal.cbs.gov.np/Home/Index/EN

Chettri, R., Subedi, L., & Chimariya, S. (2024). Problems and coping strategies of elderly inmates in prisons of Nepal. In A. B. Soletti (Ed.), *Contemporary issues in late adulthood: Perspectives from India* (pp. 49–61). Springer Nature. https://doi.org/10.1007/978-981-97-4449-7_5

Department of Prison Management. (2022). Retrieved January 20, 2025, from https://www.dopm.gov.np/en/#

Gurung, D., Neupane, M., Bhattarai, K., Acharya, B., Gautam, N. C., Gautam, K., Koirala, S., Marahatta, K., Gurung, P., Khadka, K. B., Kohrt, B. A., Thornicroft, G., & Gronholm, P. C. (2023). Mental health–related structural stigma and discrimination in health and social policies in Nepal: A scoping review and synthesis. *Epidemiology and Psychiatric Sciences, 32*, e70. https://doi.org/10.1017/S2045796023000823

Gurung, H. B. (2001). *Nepal, social demography and expressions* (2nd ed.). New ERA. https://cir.nii.ac.jp/crid/1130000794959985920

Joshi, S., Baniya, S., Bhandari, A. R., & Shakya, R. (2023). Hospital based one-stop crisis management centre at patan academy of health sciences: New avenues for the mental health professionals. *Journal of Psychiatrists' Association of Nepal, 12*(2). https://doi.org/10.3126/jpan.v12i2.63409

Nepal Law Commission | Nepal Law Commission. (2018). Retrieved January 21, 2025, from https://lawcommission.gov.np/

Office of United Nations High Commissioner for Human Rights in Nepal. (2008). Retrieved January 17, 2025, from https://nepal.ohchr.org/en/index.html

Pandey, M. P. (2022). Applying Vipassanā meditation as a jail reform technique: A case of Nakkhu Prison, Lalitpur, Nepal. *International Journal of Law and Society, 13*(4). https://doi.org/10.11648/j.ijls.20220503.11

Parajuli, S. (2023). Screening of psychiatric morbidity in a male only prison. *Journal of Patan Academy of Health Sciences, 10*(1). https://doi.org/10.3126/jpahs.v10i1.54529

Prajapati, R., Lamichhane, A., Shrestha, B., Shah, L. K., Siddique, M., Singh, P. K., Bhattarai, S., Manandhar, S., & Giri, S. (2024). Addressing mental health challenges in Nepal: A review of policies, status, and strategies for improvement. *Journal of Multidisciplinary Research Advancements, 2*(1). https://doi.org/10.3126/jomra.v2i1.66645

Regmi, S., Shrestha, P., Gaihre, S., & Thagunna, N. S. (2019). Depression among female inmates in central prison of Kathmandu. *Nepal. Global Journal of Medicine & Public Health, 8*(1) https://nicpd.ac.in/ojs-/index.php/gjmedph/article/view/3917

Secretariat, C. A., & Durbar, S. (2015). Constitution of nepal 2015. *Kathmandu: Constituent Assembly Secretariat, 19*, 505.

Sharma, P., Gautam, K., & Marahatta, K. (2024). Access to Mental Health Care in Nepal: Current status, potential challenges, and ways out. In S. M. Y. Arafat & S. K. Kar (Eds.), *Access to mental health care in South Asia: current status, potential challenges, and ways out* (pp. 91–111). Springer Nature. https://doi.org/10.1007/978-981-99-9153-2_6

Shrestha, G., Yadav, D. K., Sapkota, N., Baral, D., Yadav, B. K., Chakravartty, A., & Pokharel, P. K. (2017). Depression among inmates in a regional prison of eastern Nepal: A cross-sectional study. *BMC Psychiatry, 17*(1), 348. https://doi.org/10.1186/s12888-017-1514-9

Singh, R., & Khadka, S. (2022). Mental health law in Nepal. *BJPsych International, 19*(1), 24–26. https://doi.org/10.1192/bji.2021.52

Stephens, J., Simkhada, P., van Teijlingen, E., Porter, J., & Eaton, J. (2024). An analysis of Nepal's Draft Mental Health Acts 2006–2017: Competing values and power. *Health Policy and Planning, 39*(5), 499–508. https://doi.org/10.1093/heapol/czae023

The Kathmandu Post. (2024). *Health authorities to screen prisoners for mental health conditions.* Retrieved February 7, 2025 from https://kathmandupost.com/health/2024/12/15/health-authorities-to-screen-prisoners-for-mental-health-conditions

UN CRPD - Convention on the Rights of Persons with Disabilities. (2010). UNDP. Retrieved January 24, 2025, from https://www.undp.org/nepal/publications/un-crpd-convention-rights-persons-disabilities

Vyas, R. P., Kanel, P., & Kharel, A. (2024). *Chapter 13 The Impact of the United Nations Human Rights Treaties on the Domestic Level in Nepal.* Brill. https://doi.org/10.1163/9789004377653_015

WHO. (2008). *WHO-AIMS Report on Mental Health System, Nepal.* Retrieved January 17, 2025, from https://scholar.googleusercontent.com/scholar?q=cache:vRNH8RVbwGIJ:scholar.google.com/&hl=en&as_sdt=0,5

WHO(2021) *WHOSpecialInitiativeforMentalHealth*,Nepal.RetrievedJanuary28,2025,fromhttps://www.who.int/publications/m/item/nepal%2D%2D-who-special-initiative-for-mental-health

World Prison Brief. Nepal (2024). Retrieved January 20, 2025, from https://www.prisonstudies.org/country/nepal

Chapter 5
Forensic Psychiatry and Prison Mental Health in Pakistan

Mudassar Abdullah, Muhammad Tahir Khalily, and Brian Hallahan

Abstract This chapter explores the current challenges and trends in forensic psychiatry and prison mental health in Pakistan. It emphasizes the challenges impacting this field in systematic, social, and cultural domains. A lack of awareness about mental health has prevented many prisoners from attaining appropriate input, resulting in a deleterious impact on their well-being. Consequently, increased governmental funding is required to provide mental health practitioners, forensic psychiatry, and prison mental health services for implementing evidence-based interventions where required. Additionally, training of prison staff to increase awareness of mental illness, as well as training of newly appointed mental health practitioners, is needed, which will likely require international collaboration. Particular focus is required for protecting women and juveniles with mental health difficulties. Supporting such changes with empirical evidence will be optimal, with culturally adapted, evidence-based randomized controlled trials targeting mental health disorders and other factors potentially impacting engagement in therapeutic interventions, including stigma pertaining to mental illness.

Keywords Forensic psychiatry · Prison mental health · Social and cultural domains · Interventions · Legislative · Randomized control trials

---

M. Abdullah
Department of Business Administration (Psychology Program), Faculty of Management and Social Sciences, IQRA National University, Peshawar, Pakistan

M. T. Khalily (✉)
Khushal Khan Khattak University Karak Khyber Pakhtunkhwa Pakistan and Academic Fellow Department of Neuroscience, School of Medical Sciences, Universiti Sains Malaysia, Kotabaru, Malaysia

B. Hallahan
Department of Psychiatry, University of Galway, Galway, Ireland

A. Parmar et al. (eds.), *Forensic Psychiatry and Prison Mental Health in South Asia*, South Asian Perspectives in Mental Health and Psychology,
https://doi.org/10.1007/978-981-96-7206-6_5

1 Introduction

The Islamic Republic of Pakistan, a Muslim-majority country, has a population of more than 220 million people and incorporates a complex social structure representing a mixture of urban and rural populations and a strong patriarchal society (Chauhan, 2014). The social hierarchical system in Pakistan is usually characterized by family, tribe, and social class, with conventional belief systems about mental illness often misattributing symptoms to cultural viewpoints and with traditional healing pathways sometimes followed rather than evidence-based medical interventions for major mental health disorders, including psychotic illnesses (Shah et al., 2019; Tabassum, 2024). Pakistan has been divided into four provinces (Punjab, Sindh, Khyber Pakhtunkhwa, and Balochistan) as well as the semi-autonomous territories of Azad (Free) Jammu and Kashmir and Gilgit Baltistan, each with distinct cultural and socioeconomic characteristics. The chapter explores the current state of forensic psychiatry and prison mental health services in Pakistan and examines associated social, cultural, legal, and systemic dimensions impacting the same.

1.1 Social Structure

Pakistan has a traditional patriarchal society where males are usually the dominant figures providing all care for children, and women seldom work outside of the home. This societal system has been criticized as unfair to both men and women in modern times. Patriarchal society has a significant impact on mental health outcomes. Mental health-related stigma and the contrast between rural and urban lifestyles have affected access to and perceptions of care within the traditional family system (Abbas et al., 2024; Uddin, 2017). Individuals with low socioeconomic backgrounds with less educational attainments and employment opportunities are disproportionately vulnerable to mental health problems (Raza, & Khan, 2025). Furthermore, prioritizing mental health interventions in the context of cultural and religious beliefs can play a significant role in mitigating or exacerbating these challenges (Yusuf, 2021).

Inequalities in mental health care have been suggested to relate to socioeconomic conditions, with economically deprived communities facing greater barriers to accessing mental health services due to limited financial support, less awareness of mental illness, and difficulty in accessing services due to geographic isolation. For example, most of the country's population lives in rural regions that lack access to specialized psychological services, which are more available in urban centers (Rasul & Karki Nepal, 2024). These local challenges and disparities need to be addressed by targeting efforts to critically understand economic, cultural, and geographic barriers to health care. Even in urban areas, mental health facilities are concentrated in more affluent neighborhoods, leaving more disadvantaged communities reliant on comparatively limited healthcare support (GBD 2019 Pakistan Collaborators,

2023). Therefore, integrated policies, including outreach programs, are required to provide more equitable access to mental health services.

1.2 *Discrimination and Stigmatization*

Many individuals in Pakistan misattribute symptoms of a range of mental illnesses to other factors such as supernatural powers (i.e., engagement in previous evil deeds, an "evil eye," or "black magic"). This misattribution of symptoms results in poor management of both mild and major mental health disorders and engagement in traditional healing practices (i.e., for treatment of "jinn" or "Ta'wiz") that may have an adverse impact both on symptoms and prognosis rather than engagement with mental health services. This is despite evidence that engagement with mental health services is associated with an amelioration in symptomatology, a reduction in the intensity of conventional beliefs, and subsequent increased preference for engagement with mental health services. The presence of a mental illness in an individual or a family in Pakistan is viewed by many as a significant social stigma (Waqas et al., 2014), further impacting engagement in evidence-based mental health interventions. These beliefs and attitudes are particularly prevalent in (but not solely limited to) marginalized communities and those of lower socioeconomic class, resulting in less discourse about mental health-related problems (including suicide and related stigma) (Husain et al., 2020; Mirza, 2023; Abdullah et al., 2018). Within prisons, the stigma and/or misattribution of beliefs can result in prisoners experiencing neglect or increasing their risk of suffering abuse. Thus, even where mental health supports are available in prison services, prisoners with mental health difficulties are unlikely to request support, and staffs working within prison services are unlikely to identify symptoms and attribute them to mental health difficulties.

Integrating policies to reform educational disparities and engaging religious leaders, educators, and community influencers to make mental health a shared responsibility rather than an individual burden have been suggested as strategies to improve understanding and decrease stigmatization (Noorullah et al., 2024; Waqas et al., 2020; Mubeen et al., 2024; Siddiqui, & Khan, 2021).

1.3 *Legal and Justice System*

Pakistan's legal basis for mental health care stems from colonial-era laws (Pakistan Penal Code, 1860). Initial reforms include the Mental Health Ordinance 2001 and its amendment, the Mental Health Act of 2018. However, their implementation has been limited due to resource constraints and systemic failures (Government of Pakistan, 2001; Khan & Khan, 2021). These laws have emphasized the protection of individuals with mental health problems from human rights violations but provide limited guidance regarding the detailed implementation of these rights in closed environments like prisons (Tareen & Tareen, 2016). The 2018 amendments to the Mental Health Ordinance 2001 promote collaboration between various agencies for mental health care provision; however, the delivery of these resources is still incomplete (Khan & Khan, 2021). The field of forensic psychiatry has yet to receive the required structural support and effective implementation of available resources.

According to the Pakistan Prison Rules (1978), the explicit directives concerning mental health are based on medical care provisions for prisoners. There is consequently a lack of clarity about requirements for mandatory mental health screenings, regular evaluations, and strengthening and defining the protocols for handling psychiatric emergencies, which is imperative for improving care and outcomes in the prison population (Shah & Iqbal, 2018).

1.4 Human Rights Conditions

According to the Human Rights Commission of Pakistan (HRCP) (2020), persecution and maltreatment are a pervasive trend in jails, encompassing physical and psychological violence in various forms experienced by prisoners. Trauma, anxiety, and depressive disorders are common risks associated with increased levels of maltreatment for prisoners (Lakhdir et al., 2021). Previous studies have unsurprisingly indicated limited access to healthcare services, including mental healthcare, in prisons (Noorullah et al., 2024; Husain et al., 2020), with a delay in diagnosis, treatment, and resultant worse prognosis (Husain et al., 2020). Women, juveniles, and minority groups are at increased risk of abuse in prisons in Pakistan (UNICEF, 2020; Liaquat et al., 2016), with the International Commission of Jurists (ICJ, 2019) suggesting that women prisoners are vulnerable to sexual harassment, abuse, and exploitation (Gaja, 2019).

1.5 Mental Health Legislation

Initial reforms include the Mental Health Ordinance 2001, subsequent regional Acts (the Punjab Mental Health Act of 2014, the Khyber Pakhtunkhwa Mental Health Act of 2017, and the Baluchistan Mental Health Act of 2019), and its amendment, the Mental Health Act of 2018. However, their implementation has been limited due to resource constraints and systemic failures (Government of Pakistan, 2001; Khan & Khan, 2021). These laws have emphasized the protection of individuals with mental health problems from human rights violations but provide limited guidance regarding the detailed implementation of these rights in closed environments like prisons (Tareen & Tareen, 2016). The 2018 amendments to the Mental Health Ordinance 2001 promote and foster collaboration between agencies for mental health care provision; however, the delivery of these resources is still incomplete (Khan & Khan, 2021). The field of forensic psychiatry has yet to receive the structural support and effective implementation of these resources (Malik et al., 2021). The integrity of an individual's mental health is highlighted in the implementation of safety guidelines to enforce the rights of prisoners in prison (HRCP, 2020).

Other lawful schemes, including the Pakistan Prison Rules (1978), have laid the foundation for providing appropriate medical care, but clear guidelines for mental health difficulties are lacking. The non-inclusion of mental health facilities has limited the importance of the provision of mental health care and accountability within prison jurisdictions. Proposed actions, including guidelines with standardized measurements for screening and diagnosis and the provision of psychiatric patients in emergency units, are yet to be universally implemented (Dayani et al., 2024).

1.6 Conditions in Prison

Pakistan's prisons are overpopulated and lack adequate water, food, and sanitation facilities. Data obtained from the Justice Project Pakistan (2024) has estimated that 108,643 prisoners were held in 127 prisons (overpopulation rate of 152%), with, on occasion, 15 individuals residing in three-person cells (World Prison Brief, 2025) (see Table 5.1). This highlights the near impossibility of meeting mental health needs, with minimal mental health input available despite an estimate of 14.5% of prisoners facing significant mental health difficulties (HRCP, 2025; Ahmad, 2007; Gilani et al., 2005). These shortcomings violate established national and international standards for human rights and require further improvements (HRCP, 2020).

There is a lack of funding and proper implementation in the provision of rehabilitation strategies in prison. Reducing prisoner numbers or creating more prisons to reduce overcrowding, establishing appropriate mental health sections in each prison service, and appropriately training disciplinary professionals in the delivery of awareness of mental health symptoms are required (Gilani et al., 2005).

Table 5.1 Prison population in Pakistan

Classifications	n	%	Year
Population in prison Prison capacity	108,643 66,625	152	2024
Prison population rate	45/100,000	–	2024
Pre-trial detainees/remand prisoners	–	70	2021
Deaths in prison	521	0.63	2022
Female prisoners		1.6	2021
Juveniles (<18 years of age)	1543	1.6	2021
Number of prisons	116	–	2022

2 Epidemiology and Burden of Mental Disorders Among Prisoners

According to Shahid and colleagues (2014), individuals in prison settings have higher rates of mental health disorders compared to the general population, with depressive, anxiety, and substance use disorders particularly prevalent in prison settings. Approximately 30% of all prisoners experience one of these disorders, with other conditions less common but still present at greater frequency than in the general population (i.e., schizophrenia) (HRCP, 2020). Many factors exacerbate or increase the risk of mental health disorders in prisoners. These include overcrowding and exposure to violence (both physical and psychological), which can, for example, cause or exacerbate symptoms of post-traumatic stress disorder (PTSD) (Rehan et al., 2023). Limited access to mental health services, as stated, results in many prisoners not being diagnosed or treated for their difficulties in a timely fashion. Additional stressors unique to the prison environment, such as uncertainty regarding legal proceedings and prolonged detentions without charges, further exacerbate symptoms for many prisoners.

3 Current Status of Prison Mental Health Services

3.1 Available Services

Pakistan's prison mental health services, as stated, are currently underdeveloped (Human Rights Watch, 2025), with only 400 psychiatrists serving a population exceeding 220 million. This scarcity is particularly acute in prisons, where mental health services are often lacking.

1. The inadequacy of mental health care extends beyond mere numbers. Facilities are often unequipped to handle mental health emergencies, and prison staff rarely receive training on identifying and managing mental health issues. The overreliance on general physicians for psychiatric care, combined with the stigma attached to mental illness, exacerbates the condition (Human Rights Watch, 2025). This environment leads to prisoners with mental health disorders being ignored or subjected to punitive measures, worsening their conditions.
2. The situation is particularly concerning for vulnerable populations, such as women, juveniles, and minority groups. Women prisoners often face unique mental health challenges due to trauma, abuse, and lack of gender-sensitive care. Similarly, juveniles are exposed to adult offenders and may experience psychological harm due to separation from family and lack of rehabilitation opportunities. Addressing these systemic shortcomings is essential to ensuring equitable and effective mental health care in prisons.

3. Globally, models of integrated mental health services in prisons emphasize comprehensive care, including mental health screenings upon entry, ongoing assessments, and structured rehabilitation programs. Countries like Norway and Canada have demonstrated the efficacy of such models. Replicating similar systems within Pakistan's socioeconomic context could significantly improve outcomes for prisoners (Alvi et al., 2023). The Canadian "Psychiatric In-reach Programme" provides timely care for inmates suffering from severe mental illnesses. Incorporating such structured programs in Pakistan, with culturally adapted practices, could help fill the significant care gaps currently observed. Additionally, technological solutions such as mobile apps for mental health monitoring, which have been trailed in Europe, could offer scalable solutions for Pakistan's underfunded system (Human Rights Watch, 2025).
4. Advanced strategies could also include establishing mobile mental health units to serve rural prisons. These units could deliver essential psychiatric care, conduct mental health screenings, and train prison staff to recognize early signs of mental health crises (Alvi et al., 2023). With proper funding and collaboration, these units could bridge the urban-rural divide in mental health services.

3.2 *Model Programs*

Despite these challenges, some success stories and model programs exist in Pakistan. For example, the Pakistan Prison Reform Programme aims to improve prison conditions and provide mental health services. This program has been successful in providing mental health services to prisoners and improving prison conditions. Another example is the mental health program established by the non-governmental organization, the Pakistan Mental Health Association (PMHA). This program provides mental health services, including counseling and medication, to prisoners in Pakistani jails.

Countries with well-developed forensic mental health services, such as Norway and Australia, provide regular evaluations and interventions within correctional facilities, offering models for potential reforms in Pakistan.

1. **Vocational Training and Rehabilitation**: In Sindh's correctional facilities, a rehabilitation program offering workshops in carpentry, tailoring, and electronics led to significant reductions in anxiety and depressive symptoms among participants over six months (Ahmed et al., 2022). One participant, a 30-year-old male convicted of theft, reported that acquiring new skills gave him hope for reintegration into society (Tariq, 2020). Follow-ups indicated a 40% decrease in recidivism among program graduates, highlighting the role of skill development in psychological and social rehabilitation (Basit, 2015).
2. **Mental Health Interventions for Juveniles**: In 2019, a collaboration between an NGO and the Khyber Pakhtunkhwa government introduced a mental health intervention program in juvenile detention centers (Dayani et al., 2024). The

program provided cognitive-behavioral therapy (CBT) sessions to 100 juvenile detainees (12 to 18 years of age). Assessments revealed a 60% improvement in emotional regulation and a 45% decrease in aggressive behaviors. A 15-year-old participant previously involved in violent altercations learned techniques to manage anger through therapy sessions (Najmussaqib & Mushtaq, 2023). This program demonstrates the potential benefits of targeted mental health interventions for juveniles.

3. **Trauma-Informed Care for Women Prisoners**: A 2020 study in Karachi's women's prison examined the prevalence of PTSD among inmates (Human Rights Watch, 2025). Out of 200 surveyed prisoners, 75% reported experiencing domestic abuse prior to incarceration, and 60% exhibited symptoms of PTSD. The introduction of trauma-informed care, including counseling, group therapy, and support groups, led to significant reductions in PTSD symptoms within a year. One inmate stated that group therapy sessions helped her process her traumatic past and regain confidence, emphasizing the importance of gender-sensitive approaches to mental health care in prisons.
4. **Implementation of Technological Mental Health Support:** In recent years, a pilot project in Lahore's central prison introduced telepsychiatry services, connecting inmates with psychiatrists through secure video conferencing (Zahid et al., 2017). This initiative addressed the shortage of on-site mental health professionals and enabled timely interventions. Initial results showed improved diagnosis rates and better adherence to treatment plans. One inmate, who had suffered from undiagnosed bipolar disorder for years, reported a significant improvement in his condition following interventions provided to him following these virtual consultations.

3.3 Liaison Between Law Enforcement and Mental Health Service Providers

Joint Training Programs Collaborative training programs for law enforcement officers and mental health practitioners can ameliorate responses to mental health crises and improve communication and understanding of each other's roles (Casas & Kegel, 2024; Tareen & Tareen, 2016). Such programs can learn from the success of similar programs worldwide, including the Crisis Intervention Team (CIT) model in the USA (Nick et al., 2022). Additional benefits of such programs can be increasing empathy and reducing stigma for law enforcement officers not used to recognizing mental health difficulties. Police training curricula can also be a transformative step by including modules on Psychological First Aid. Structuring "train-the-trainer" programs can create a cascading effect to ensure that the knowledge is consistently disseminated among law enforcement ranks. If policymakers create standardized curricula for these programs and explore international collaborations (including with the World Health Organization), transformative management of mental health crises or distress can quickly evolve in prisons in Pakistan. Indeed, collaborative assessments of individuals referred for mental health difficulties between mental health practitioners and prison officers have been associated with improved mental health outcomes in other jurisdictions (Lowder et al., 2024).

3.4 Barriers to Collaboration

There is a critical need for collaboration between law enforcement and mental health practitioners, as alluded to. However, currently, a gap in communication between these groups allows for divergent perceptions of each other's roles, differences in terminology, priorities, and methodologies (Lavoie et al., 2022), and limited resources for training and infrastructure to implement joint training programs exist (Watson & Fulambarker, 2012).

A broader public health framework is needed for integrating mental health services with the development of robust referral and review systems in Pakistan, with a streamlining of referrals and timely interventions for mental health disorders. The implementation of technology-driven solutions, including centralized databases accessible to law enforcement and healthcare practitioners, may support timely review and further collaborative management.

4 Specific Issues in Forensic Psychiatry in Pakistan

Forensic psychiatry in Pakistan faces many challenges in delivering an effective mental health service within the criminal justice system. Detailed below are some specific pertinent issues:

1. **Insanity Defense** is an infrequent utilization of limited understanding and resources. The misconception about insanity and an inadequate legal framework can lead individuals with mental ill health to be held criminally responsible instead of receiving necessary treatment.
2. **The Competency to Stand Trial Assessments** can determine an individual's capacity to understand legal proceedings, which have many inaccuracies. The inaccurate evaluations potentially cause miscarriages of justice, further propelling the need to fill these gaps with trained professionals and adequate resources.
3. Current laws governing **Involuntary Medication and Admission Procedures** are often insufficient and can lead to potential human rights violations. The necessary guidelines and safeguards regarding the mental ill health of individuals need to be ensured for dignified and respectful treatment.

5 Forensic Psychiatry and Its Scope

5.1 Training Expertise

In Pakistan, the field of forensic psychiatry is at an embryonic stage due to the limited infrastructure, trained personnel, and professionals, with around 12% of psychiatrists specializing in this field (Hassan et al., 2017). Due to the dearth of resources, there are frequent delays in attaining competency assessments, including for insanity defenses and care for mentally ill prisoners (Husain et al., 2020).

Building expertise is critical to integrating forensic psychiatry into legal and disciplinary frameworks. Training programs must include international best practices tailored to Pakistan's specific sociocultural and legal contexts. Standardized curricula for postgraduate medical education and certification systems for forensic psychiatrists, including ongoing continuous professional learning, can collectively enhance capacity (Malik et al., 2021). By engaging with law enforcement agencies, courts, and correctional facilities, forensic psychiatrists can confer policy-making processes that emphasize mental health in the justice system.

5.2 Capacity Building and Recommendations

1. Specialized Training: Forensic psychiatry is a specialized field that needs targeted education and expertise. Introducing modules on forensic psychiatry as a postgraduate requirement will provide a foundational understanding and interest in this area among future psychiatrists (Arboleda-Flórez, 2006). Postgraduate training should include placements in forensic psychiatry for all trainee psychiatrists, with future forensic psychiatrists spending at least three years in approved forensic psychiatry placements. Given Pakistan's limited forensic psychiatry services, governmental sponsorship of psychiatrists in international placements in centers of excellence for forensic psychiatry is strongly advised. Ongoing training for all health practitioners working in forensic psychiatry, encompassing workshops and courses affiliated with universities resulting in diplomas or degrees, is suggested, with universities partnering with international institutions to organize comprehensive programs, including at Master's and PhD levels, are suggested.
2. Resource Provision: Adequate financial support is essential for establishing forensic psychiatry centers in Pakistan (Hassan et al., 2017). These centers can serve as hubs for assessment, research, and training of health professionals of all disciplines in forensic psychiatry. Sustainable funding models must be evolved to establish consistent service delivery.
3. Public-Private Organizations: Collaboration between governmental and non-governmental organizations (NGOs) can add to governmental efforts by providing expertise, training, and funding (Ejaz et al., 2011). These partnerships could

potentially include innovative approaches, such as ambulant forensic units, to expand services to remote areas.

4. International Partnerships: Psychiatry staff working in all disciplines (not just psychiatrists in training) should be able to engage in placements in centers of excellence of forensic psychiatry internationally. Global best practices of cultural exchange programs can help practitioners stay updated in forensic psychiatry and enable the adaptation of successful models of forensic care within the cultural and legal contexts of Pakistan (Hassan et al., 2017). Such initiatives will also enable joint research initiatives and subsequent participation in international conferences and dissemination of research in peer-reviewed international journals.
5. Engaging Stakeholders: A better awareness on behalf of judicial and law enforcement officers pertaining to the principles of forensic psychiatry can enable informed decision-making in legal cases involving individuals with mental health disorders or difficulties. Trained staff working in forensic psychiatry services delivering workshops and seminars to such staff will support the same (Khalily et al., 2021). The importance of accurate psychiatric evaluations in determining competency, culpability, and rehabilitation needs to be highlighted in such sessions.
6. Research: In addition to engagement in collaborative research initiatives with other international centers, the development of a robust database on mental health cases within prison services will be imperative for future evidence-based policymaking (Khan & Khan, 2021). Mental health needs among prisoners have been minimally examined. Research initiatives that focus on the prevalence of mental health disorders and the effectiveness of potential interventions will benefit prisoners and educate staff working in forensic psychiatry. Future forensic psychiatry centers should include research hubs that facilitate data collection and analysis in addition to collaboration with other national forensic centers, universities, and international centers of excellence.

6 Available Research and Gaps in Current Understanding

Some important gaps in the current understanding of research on mental health in Pakistan are as follows:

1. **Limited Epidemiological Studies:** Lack of reliable data on the prevalence of mental illnesses, which hinders effective policy development. Therefore, this gap can be filled by conducting longitudinal studies.
2. **Inadequate Training Programs:** Training programs organized by law enforcement and mental health professionals require an adequate framework for developing and evaluating comprehensive training programs.

3. **Lack of Standardized Assessment Tools:** Developing and validating tools may be considered a priority. Also, a lack of culturally sensitive, standardized assessment tools leads to inaccurate diagnoses and treatment plans.

Future research should focus on:

1. Determining the prevalence and distribution of mental illnesses in Pakistan.
2. Assessing the impact of training programs on professionals' knowledge and attitudes.
3. Validating standardized assessment tools for local use.
4. Developing and implementing policy reforms to enhance mental health services.
5. Exploring the role of technology in bridging gaps in service delivery, especially in remote areas.

7 Current Challenges in Prison Mental Health and Ways Out

Pakistan faces several challenges in the prison system and needs adequate reforms in mental health services, as follows:

a. Inadequate **Funding** for mental health services and professionals can be entertained by allocating them an appropriate budget to overcome shortages at all levels. Therefore, the evidence-based approaches require funding grants in the public-private and international partnerships.
b. Adequate mental health services can be an important step in overcoming **Infrastructure Limitations** in the prison system. It should also be listed as a proposed recommendation for a phased approach to upgrade facilities and construct dedicated mental health units.
c. **Policy Gaps**: Ensuring the presence of clear guidelines and standards leads to consistent care in mental health services. This gap can also be filled to reform policies by including specific provisions for prison mental health.

Recommendations for Reforms
Stepwise recommendations for these challenges are as follows:

i. **Enhance Training and Resources**: Can improve understanding of mental health issues and the insanity defense by providing comprehensive training for legal, mental health, and law enforcement professionals and cultivating better interdisciplinary awareness in collaborative workshops (Lorey & Fegert, 2021).
ii. **Develop Clear Guidelines and Protocols**: For competency assessments, involuntary medication, and admission procedures, align with international best practices while considering cultural context in view (Khalily et al., 2021).
iii. **Reform Legal Frameworks**: To govern the insanity defense and involuntary treatment and align it with international human rights standards, including the

provisions of periodic review for mental health legislation (Tareen & Tareen, 2016).

iv. **Stakeholder Engagement**: Should engage government officials, NGOs, and professionals in developing and implementing effective policies and programs in the prison system.

v. **Community-Based Programs**: The criminal justice system needs to work on establishing evidence-based approaches to serve as preventive measures at the community level in targeting the influx of individuals with untreated mental illnesses.

8 Conclusion

In Pakistan, the field of forensic psychiatry is at an embryonic stage due to the limited infrastructure, trained personnel, and professionals. Despite a high prevalence of mental health disorders within prisons, there is currently limited support available for prisoners with limited detection of mental health difficulties and treatments available to prisoners even if diagnosed. In addition, prison environments with overcrowding, exposure to violence, and uncertainty regarding time duration in prison given delays in report writing and prolonged detention without charges exacerbate symptoms, particularly in certain groups (women, juveniles, minorities, and individuals with pre-existing major mental health disorders such as schizophrenia). Resource allocation, either governmental alone or in combination with NGOs, is urgently required. The provision and subsequent training for all staff, including psychiatrists working in forensic psychiatry, is essential, with the provision of opportunities to engage in some training in international centers of excellence optimal, with future ongoing continuous professional development required. The development of advanced forensic psychiatry services with research hubs allowing data collection and analysis, engagement in trials for culturally adapted interventions, and international collaborations is suggested. The introduction of model programs (i.e., the Prisoners' Rehabilitation Program) should enable the introduction of appropriate evidence-based interventions and emphasize the importance of research, policy updates, and inter-sectoral partnerships in addressing gaps and fostering a humane, equitable criminal justice system that prioritizes systematic reforms in mental health care in prison settings.

References

Abbas, R., Delaruelle, K., & Bracke, P. (2024). Prevalence and correlates of mental health stigma among Pakistani adolescents and young adults. *FWU Journal of Social Sciences*, 114–126. https://doi.org/10.51709/19951272/winter2024/8

Abdullah, M., Khalily, M. T., Ahmad, I., & Hallahan, B. (2018). Psychological autopsy review on mental health crises and suicide among youth in Pakistan. *Asia-Pacific Psychiatry, 10*(4), e12338. https://doi.org/10.1111/appy.12338

Ahmad, K. (2007). Shortage of psychiatrists a problem in Pakistan. *Lancet (London, England), 370*(9590), 817–818. https://doi.org/10.1016/S0140-6736(07)61397-X

Ahmed, T., Wassan, R., & Bakhsh Lashari, A. (2022). Impacts of vocational training and recreational activities on prison inmates: A case study of youthful offender's correctional facility, Hyderabad Pakistan. *Pakistan Languages and Humanities Review, 6*(4), 238–246. https://doi.org/10.47205/plhr.2022(6-IV)24

Alvi, M. H., Ashraf, T., Kiran, T., Iqbal, N., Gumber, A., Patel, A., & Husain, N. (2023). Economic burden of mental illness in Pakistan: an estimation for the year 2020 from existing evidence. *BJPsych international, 20*(3), 54–56. https://doi.org/10.1192/bji.2023.4.

Arboleda-Flórez, J. (2006). Forensic psychiatry: Contemporary scope, challenges and controversies. *World Psychiatry, 5*(2), 87–91.

Basit, A. (2015). Pakistan's militant rehabilitation programme: An overview. *Counter Terrorist Trends and Analyses, 7*(9), 10–17. http://www.jstor.org/stable/26351388

Casas, J. B., & Kegel, A. (2024). Law enforcement mental health: A systematic review of qualitative research. *Psychological Services, 21*(4), 938–946. https://doi.org/10.1037/ser0000803

Chauhan, K. (2014). Patriarchal Pakistan: Women's representation, access to resources, and institutional practices. In *Gender inequality in the public sector in Pakistan*. Palgrave Macmillan. https://doi.org/10.1057/9781137426475_4

Dayani, K., Zia, M., Qureshi, O., Baig, M., & Sabri, T. (2024). Evaluating Pakistan's mental healthcare system using World Health Organization's assessment instrument for mental health system (WHO-AIMS). *International Journal of Mental Health Systems, 18*(1), 32. https://doi.org/10.1186/s13033-024-00646-6

Ejaz, I., Shaikh, B. T., & Rizvi, N. (2011). NGOs and government partnership for health systems strengthening: A qualitative study presenting viewpoints of government, NGOs and donors in Pakistan. *BMC Health Services Research, 11*, 122. https://doi.org/10.1186/1472-6963-11-122

Gaja, G. (2019). Chapter 2 general principles in the Jurisprudence of the ICJ. In *General principles and the coherence of international law*. Brill | Nijhoff. https://doi.org/10.1163/9789004390935_004

GBD 2019 Pakistan Collaborators. (2023). The state of health in Pakistan and its provinces and territories, 1990–2019: A systematic analysis for the Global Burden of Disease Study 2019. *The Lancet. Global Health, 11*(2), e229–e243. https://doi.org/10.1016/S2214-109X(22)00497-1

Gilani, A. I., Gilani, U. I., Kasi, P. M., & Khan, M. M. (2005). Psychiatric health laws in Pakistan: From lunacy to mental health. *PLoS Medicine, 2*(11), e317. https://doi.org/10.1371/journal.pmed.0020317

Government of Pakistan. (2001). *Mental Health Ordinance*. Government of Pakistan Printing Press. Available at http://punjablaws.punjab.gov.pk/public/dr/MENTAL%20HEALTH%20ORDINANCE%20FOR%20PAKISTAN%202001.doc.pdf

Hassan, T., Nizami, A. T., & Asmer, M. S. (2017). Forensic psychiatric service provision in Pakistan and its challenges. *BJPsych International, 14*(2), 40–44. https://doi.org/10.1192/s205647400000177x

HRCP. (2020). *State of Human Rights in Pakistan*. Retrieved from: https://www.google.com/search?q=HRCP+(2020).+State+of+Human+Rights+in+Pakistan.&rlz=1C1GCEA_enPK1088PK1088&oq=HRCP+(2020).+State+of+Human+Rights+in+Pakistan.&gs_lcrp=EgZjaHJvbWUqBggAEEUYOzIGCAAQRRg7MgcIARAhGKABMgcIAhAhGKAB0gEHNzk3ajBqNKgCALACAQ&sourceid=chrome&ie=UTF-8

Human Rights Watch. (2025). *"A Nightmare for Everyone": The Health Crisis in Pakistan's Prisons*. Retrieved from: https://www.hrw.org/report/2023/03/29/nightmare-everyone/health-crisis-pakistans-prisons

Husain, M. O., Zehra, S. S., Umer, M., Kiran, T., Husain, M., Soomro, M., Dunne, R., Sultan, S., Chaudhry, I. B., Naeem, F., Chaudhry, N., & Husain, N. (2020). Stigma toward mental and physical illness: Attitudes of healthcare professionals, healthcare students and the general public in Pakistan. *BJPsych Open, 6*(5), e81. https://doi.org/10.1192/bjo.2020.66

Khalily, M. T., Rehman, A. U., Bhatti, M. M., Hallahan, B., Ahmad, I., Mehmood, M. I., Khan, S. H., & Khan, B. A. (2021). Stakeholders' perspective on mental health laws in Pakistan: A mixed method study. *International Journal of Law and Psychiatry, 74*, 101647. https://doi.org/10.1016/j.ijlp.2020.101647

Khan, R. Q., & Khan, A. M. (2021). Crime and punishment: Pakistan's legal failure to account for mental illness. *BJPsych International, 18*(4), 94–96. https://doi.org/10.1192/bji.2020.30

Lakhdir, M. P. A., Akber Ali, N., Peerwani, G., Farooq, S., Khaliq, A., Nathwani, A. A., & Azam, S. I. (2021). The role of parent-to-child maltreatment in the pathway of self-reported depressive symptoms in Pakistani adolescents. *Health Psychology Open, 8*(2), 20551029211065614. https://doi.org/10.1177/20551029211065614

Lavoie, J. A. A., Alvarez, N., & Kandil, Y. (2022). Developing Community co-designed scenario-based training for police mental health crisis response: A relational policing approach to de-escalation. *Journal of Police and Criminal Psychology, 37*(3), 587–601. https://doi.org/10.1007/s11896-022-09500-2

Liaquat, S., Qaisrani, A., & Khokhar, E. N. (2016). Introduction. In *Freedom of Expression in Pakistan: A myth or a reality* (pp. 3–3). Sustainable Development Policy Institute. http://www.jstor.org/stable/resrep02846.3

Lorey, K., & Fegert, J. M. (2021). Increasing mental health literacy in law enforcement to improve best practices in policing-introduction of an empirically derived, modular, differentiated, and end-user driven training design. *Frontiers in Psychiatry, 12*, 706587. https://doi.org/10.3389/fpsyt.2021.706587

Lowder, E. M., Grommon, E., Bailey, K., & Ray, B. (2024). Police-mental health co-response versus police-as-usual response to behavioral health emergencies: A pragmatic randomized effectiveness trial. *Social Science and Medicine*, (*1982*), *345*., 116723. https://doi.org/10.1016/j.socscimed.2024.116723

Malik, W. A., Arnold, C., Vithiananthan, A., & Hassan, T. (2021). Forensic psychiatry in Pakistan: An update. *International Journal of Risk and Recovery, 4*(2), 42–50. https://doi.org/10.15173/ijrr.v4i2.4622

Mirza, S. (2023). The recent decriminalization of suicidal behavior in Pakistan as a critical opportunity for research and clinical progress. *Asian Journal of Psychiatry, 82*, 1–2. https://doi.org/10.1016/j.ajp.2023.103481

Mubeen, Z., Fatmi, Z., Hameed, W., & Asim, M. (2024). Barriers and facilitators to accessing adolescents' mental health services in Karachi: Users and providers perspectives. *BMC Health Services Research, 24*(1), 157. https://doi.org/10.1186/s12913-024-10593-0

Najmussaqib, A., & Mushtaq, A. (2023). Estimation and linkage between behavioral problems and social emotional competence among Pakistani young school children. *PloS One, 18*(5), e0278719. https://doi.org/10.1371/journal.pone.0278719

Nick, G. A., Williams, S., Lekas, H. M., Pahl, K., Blau, C., Kamin, D., & Fuller-Lewis, C. (2022). Crisis intervention team (CIT) training and impact on mental illness and substance use-related stigma among law enforcement. *Drug and Alcohol Dependence Reports, 5*, 100099. https://doi.org/10.1016/j.dadr.2022.100099

Noorullah, A., Asad, N., Pirani, S., Iqbal, S., & Khan, M. M. (2024). Mental health care in Pakistan. In S. M. Y. Arafat & S. K. Kar (Eds.), *Access to mental health care in South Asia*. Springer. https://doi.org/10.1007/978-981-99-9153-2_7

Pakistan: Penal Code, Act No. XLV, 6 October 1860, (accessed 08 February 2025). https://www.refworld.org/legal/legislation/natlegbod/1860/en/41422

Rasul, G., & Karki Nepal, A. (2024). Addressing poverty and inequality in the mountains of Pakistan. *Discover Global Society, 2*(1), 60. https://doi.org/10.1007/s44282-024-00086-0

Raza, S. H., & Khan, L. (2025). Beyond numbers: Mapping poverty disparities in Pakistan through a spatial lens. *Applied Spatial Analysis and Policy, 18*(1), 28. https://doi.org/10.1007/s12061-024-09626-2

Rehan, S. T., Shan, M., Shuja, S. H., Khan, Z., Hussain, H. U., Ochani, R. K., Shaikh, A., Ratnani, I., Nashwan, A. J., & Surani, S. (2023). Workplace violence against healthcare workers in Pakistan; Call for action, if not now, then when? A systematic review. *Global health action, 16*(1), 2273623. https://doi.org/10.1080/16549716.2023.2273623

Shah, I., Khalily, M. T., Ahmad, I., & Hallahan, B. (2019). Impact of conventional beliefs and social stigma on attitude towards access to mental health services in Pakistan. *Community Mental Health Journal, 55*(3), 527–533. https://doi.org/10.1007/s10597-018-0310-4

Shah, M. Q., & Iqbal, A. (2018). Pakistan prison rules Vis-a-Vis international standards for the treatment of prisoners; A critical analysis. *Journal of Law and Society, 49*, 89.

Siddiqui, F., & Khan, Q. u. a. (2021). Barriers and challenges to mental health care in Pakistan. *Pakistan Journal of Neurological Sciences (PJNS), 16*(3), Article 1. Available at: https://ecommons.aku.edu/pjns/vol16/iss3/1

Tabassum, M. (2024). Family traditions, social expectations, state influence and the fabric of patriarchy. In B. S. Nayak & N. Tabassum (Eds.), *Impact of patriarchy and gender stereotypes on working women. Diversity and inclusion research.* Springer. https://doi.org/10.1007/978-3-031-74406-8_10

Tareen, A., & Tareen, K. I. (2016). Mental health law in Pakistan. *BJPsych International, 13*(3), 67–69. https://doi.org/10.1192/s2056474000001276

Tariq, A. (2020). Reintegration prospects for the Ex-convicts in Pakistan: A legal perspective. *Policy Perspectives, 17*(1), 35–52. https://doi.org/10.13169/polipers.17.1.0035

Uddin, S. (2017). Exploring Perceptual Changes and Stigma Relating to Mental Health and Wellbeing within the South Asian Community.

Unicef. (2020). *Global status report on preventing violence against children 2020.* https://www.unicef.org/reports/global-status-report-preventing-violence-against-children-2020

Waqas, A., Zubair, M., Ghulam, H., Wajih Ullah, M., & Zubair Tariq, M. (2014). Public stigma associated with mental illnesses in Pakistani university students: a cross sectional survey. *PeerJ, 2*, e698. https://doi.org/10.7717/peerj.698

Waqas, A., Malik, S., Fida, A., Abbas, N., Mian, N., Miryala, S., Amray, A. N., Shah, Z., & Naveed, S. (2020). Interventions to reduce stigma related to mental illnesses in educational institutes: A systematic review. *The Psychiatric Quarterly, 91*(3), 887–903. https://doi.org/10.1007/s11126-020-09751-4

Watson, A. C., & Fulambarker, A. J. (2012). The Crisis intervention team model of police response to mental health crises: A primer for mental health practitioners. *Best Practices in Mental Health, 8*(2), 71.

World Prison Brief. (2025). Retrieved from: https://www.prisonstudies.org/country/pakistan

Yusuf, H. (2021). Culture and mental health in Pakistan. In R. Moodley & E. Lee (Eds.), *The Routledge international handbook of race, culture and mental health* (pp. 434–444). Routledge/Taylor & Francis Group.

Zahid, Z., Atique, S., Saghir, M. H., Ali, I., Shahid, A., & Malik, R. A. (2017). A commentary on telerehabilitation services in Pakistan: Current trends and future possibilities. *International Journal of Telerehabilitation, 9*(1), 71–76. https://doi.org/10.5195/ijt.2017.6224

Chapter 6
Forensic Psychiatry and Prison Mental Health in Sri Lanka

Chittahari Abhayanayaka, Lucien Angelo Prashantha de Alwis, and Thommadura Susitha Sampath Mendis

Abstract Sri Lanka has underdeveloped specialist forensic mental health services. The country does not have a purpose-built forensic hospital or widespread community forensic services. Assessment of mentally ill offenders, prison mental health services, and providing reports to courts make up a significant portion of the work of generalist psychiatrists in the country. Specialist forensic psychiatric services are concentrated in several large cities. At present, there are only two forensic psychiatrists in the country. In Colombo, two wards located within the National Institute of Mental Health act as the forensic unit, and in Kandy and Galle, some beds within the regional psychiatry units are allocated for forensic patients. Prison mental health services are staffed and funded by the Ministry of Health and are in-reach services. The legislative framework for forensic patients is outdated and needs urgent reform. Workload, overcrowding within forensic units and prisons, and lack of trained staff are challenges that forensic services must overcome.

Keywords Sri Lanka · Forensic services · Prison mental health

1 Introduction

Sri Lanka is an island nation located at the southern tip of the Indian subcontinent. It is a 65,610 Km^2 island with a rapidly aging population of 22 million (De Silva & De Silva, 2023; Department of Census and Statistics, Sri Lanka, 2024). It is a lower-middle-income country with a GDP of around 84.4 billion USD and a per capita

C. Abhayanayaka
Department of Forensic Psychiatry, Kandy Teaching Hospital, Kandy, Sri Lanka

L. A. P. de Alwis (✉)
Gold Coast Mental Health Service, Griffith University, Gold Coast, Australia

T. S. S. Mendis
Victorian Institute of Forensic Mental Health, Fairfield, VIC, Australia

A. Parmar et al. (eds.), *Forensic Psychiatry and Prison Mental Health in South Asia*, South Asian Perspectives in Mental Health and Psychology,
https://doi.org/10.1007/978-981-96-7206-6_6

income of 3823 USD in 2023 (Central Bank of Sri Lanka, 2024). The country has faced significant challenges in recent decades, including a 26-year civil war (1983–2009), resulting in an estimated 100,000 deaths and the devastating 2004 Indian Ocean tsunami that claimed over 35,000 lives. A financial crisis in 2022 led to severe food and fuel shortages, with inflation reaching 70% in 2023. Although the economy has shown signs of stabilization in 2023 and 2024, the country continues to face significant economic challenges. Sri Lanka was a British colony from 1796 to 1948. The legacy of British colonial rule in Sri Lanka is evident in its judicial and healthcare systems, with courts, prisons, and hospitals still reflecting the structure and practices of the English system.

1.1 Legal and Justice System

Laws in Sri Lanka are a complex amalgamation of statutory law, common law, religious law, and personal (customary) law. This intricate mix reflects Sri Lanka's rich legal heritage owing to the different ethnicities that inhabit the country, as well as due to invasions from different European powers since the sixteenth century (Nadaraja, 1972). Sri Lanka's criminal law is based on English law and is largely codified. The Penal Code of Sri Lanka serves as the primary source of criminal law. The current Penal Code and Criminal Procedure Code (CPC) were originally enacted in the late nineteenth century and were derived from similar statutes in India.

The courts in Sri Lanka are independent institutions, separate from the executive and legislative branches of the government. The country has a three-tiered court system. The two highest courts are the Supreme Court and the Court of Appeal. The Supreme Court is the country's highest court and the court of final appeal. The second tier consists of provincial High Courts. High Courts are courts of first instance for serious crimes and a court of appeal for both civil and criminal matters. The lowest tier consists of first-instance courts, such as district courts and magistrates' courts. The courts, mirroring the British model, employ an adversarial approach rather than an inquisitorial one. There were a total of 416 judges serving in different courts and tribunals by the end of 2023 (Ministry of Justice, 2024). The number of judges per 100,000 population was 1.9, which is a low figure compared to European countries but comparable to other South Asian nations (Deseau et al., 2019; Ministry of Justice, 2024; World Bank Group, 2013).

Political interference over the past several decades has diminished the public perception of judicial independence. This is further aggravated by resource limitations that have led to delays in the administration of justice. By the end of 2023, there were more than 1.1 million cases that were pending unsolved. More than 95% of this backlog is at the courts of first instance, with each judge or magistrate having more than 4,000 cases to process. While this backlog is primarily driven by non-criminal matters, there were more than 26,000 serious criminal matters to be resolved even at the High Court level (Ministry of Justice, 2024).

1.2 Human Rights Conditions

Chapter III of Sri Lanka's constitution secures certain fundamental rights and freedoms for all its citizens. It contains provisions to enshrine equality and equal protection under the law. Additionally, it guarantees freedom of belief and religion, freedom of speech and expression, freedom of assembly and association, and freedom from torture and cruel, inhuman, or degrading treatment. All citizens are entitled to directly apply to the Supreme Court, bypassing lower courts, to seek redress for actual or potential infringement of their rights by government action.

In addition to constitutional guarantees, Sri Lanka has ratified numerous key international human rights treaties (Office of the United Nations High Commissioner for Human Rights (OHCHR), 2025). These include the International Covenant on Civil and Political Rights (ICCPR), the Convention on the Elimination of All Forms of Discrimination Against Women (CEDAW), and the Convention on the Rights of Persons with Disabilities (CRPD), among others. However, the implementation and enforcement of these treaties have faced significant challenges. Sri Lanka has endured two armed insurrections and a 30-year-long civil war. All parties involved in these insurgencies, including the government, have been accused of serious human rights violations. This has led the UN Human Rights Council to pass several resolutions expressing concern over the human rights situation in Sri Lanka (OHCHR, 2021).

It is widely considered that Sri Lanka has inadequate rights and protections for LGBTQI+ individuals, women (and girls), and people with disabilities. The country has many laws, such as the Prevention of Terrorism Act (PTA), the Vagrancy Act, and the Online Safety Act, which have been criticized by human rights organizations for violating the principles of human rights (Human Rights Watch, 2024).

2 Health Care in Sri Lanka

Sri Lanka has a robust healthcare system despite allocating only 4% of its GDP to health expenditure. The health system comprises a state-funded curative and preventative healthcare network (free at the point of delivery) and a limited, privately funded hospital-based care network. Although the private sector has expanded in recent years, state-funded public health services still provide more than 95% of inpatient care and over 50% of outpatient care (Rajapaksa et al., 2021). In addition to an extensive government hospital network, the country has robust state-funded maternal and childcare services, as well as a community healthcare network focused on primary prevention. As of mid-2022, the state-run health sector comprised over 1500 institutions, including 588 hospitals and 517 primary care institutes (Ministry of Health (MoH), 2025).

The provision of health services in Sri Lanka is decentralized. The country is divided into 26 health administrative regions within nine provinces. Each health administrative region is divided into medical officer of health (MOH) divisions for community-based preventive health services. There is a total of 340 MOH divisions in the country. This hierarchical, multi-tiered structure has succeeded in providing accessible and affordable health care to the Sri Lankan populace (Rajapaksa et al., 2021). Over the last two decades, the country has been striving to achieve a community-based, decentralized service structure for mental health services (Fernando et al., 2017). The government allocates less than 2% of the annual health budget for mental health, amounting to about US $0.44 per capita (Raja et al., 2010), an amount higher than some of its neighboring countries.

Systematic epidemiological data on mental illness in the Sri Lankan population is not readily available. The WHO estimates that the burden of mental disorders in Sri Lanka is 1379.4 disability-adjusted life years (per 100,000 population), a figure that, while considerable, is lower than the average for the region and the world (WHO, 2021). The Sri Lanka Demographic and Health Survey (SLDHS) in 2016 revealed that up to 0.7% of the population acknowledged that they were receiving treatment for a mental illness. The most common illnesses were depression (37%) and psychosis (17%) (DCS and MoH, 2017). This is also reflected in admissions to public inpatient services, where the majority of admissions are due to depressive illness and schizophrenia (Directorate of Mental Health, 2023). The country's suicide rate of 15 per 100,000 is high compared to the global value of 9.2 (WHO, 2025). The burden of mental illness appears to be increasing over the last several years, with a nationally representative survey revealing high mental health difficulties in 6.1% of the population in the 2021–2022 period. A value more than double of what was found by the same survey in the 2018–2019 period (Deivanayagam et al., 2024).

Treatment for mental illness is provided by both the public and private sectors. In 2021, up to 73% of the hospitals had psychiatric outpatient services, while close to half (46%) had facilities to provide inpatient admissions for mental illness. Acute inpatient units are now present in every district, with many also offering intermediate-care rehabilitation facilities. In 2021, there were 21 inpatient units and three child and adolescent units (WHO, 2022). Psychiatrist-led multidisciplinary teams provide inpatient and outpatient services in most tertiary-care hospitals in the country. Where there are no psychiatrists, services are provided by medical officers who have a year of additional training in psychiatry and have obtained a Diploma in Psychiatry. In many districts, specially appointed medical officers, known as Medical Officers of Mental Health (MOMH), provide psychiatric services under the supervision of a psychiatrist or a diploma-trained medical officer. MOMH are fully qualified doctors with three months of additional training in common mental illnesses who provide community-based care in many districts around the country. They are expected to be the first level of specialist care for those with mental illness. They work closely with the country's primary care network, accepting referrals and passing on the more complex patients to specialist psychiatric care. The MOMH and the diploma-trained medical officers fill the gap in services due to the lack of an adequate number of psychiatrists in the country. Sri Lanka has only 0.6 psychiatrists per 100,000 population (WHO, 2021).

3 Correctional Services

Sri Lanka has four large prisons for convicted prisoners, 18 remand prisons, and 12 prison camps (two of which are open camps), with a capacity for approximately 10,000 prisoners (Arafat et al., 2024; Department of Prisons, 2024). However, in 2023, these institutions housed an average daily population of about 27,000 detainees, exceeding capacity by more than double. Sri Lanka has an incarceration rate of 127 per 100,000 population, a figure much higher than her neighbors India, Pakistan, and Bangladesh but comparable with other Asian countries (World Population Review, 2025). Sri Lankan prisons employ about 5200 prison guards. This number is about 1000 positions short of the available cadre positions for the authorized number of inmates (Department of Prisons, 2024). Furthermore, the number of staff involved in rehabilitation, vocational training, and welfare are limited in comparison with the total number of inmates and the high turnover rate. This results in most prisoners never getting access to individualized rehabilitative activities during their period of incarceration. Despite the availability of free healthcare within prisons, severe shortages of medications, equipment, and qualified staff hinder the effectiveness of prison health services (Human Rights Commission of Sri Lanka, 2020).

The prevalence of psychiatric illness is largely unknown in the prison population. A prison survey conducted in the southern part of the island revealed that 17.5% of new prisoners were documented as having a mental illness and were receiving treatment (Wickramatilake et al., 2023). Another study of suicidal behaviors in prisons revealed a prevalence of 22.7%, a value much higher than what is found in the general population (Rajapakse, 2017; Suranga & Vidanapathirana, 2022). Surveys conducted in Sri Lanka's prisons reveal a high prevalence of drug use (Darshana et al., 2023; Dissabandara et al., 2009; Dissanayake, 2017; Hapangama et al., 2021). The illicit drugs predominantly used by detainees appear to be cannabis and heroin. A large portion of prisoners who continue to use illicit substances in prison have been found to have a dependence on these drugs. Despite these findings, Sri Lankan prisons do not have dedicated drug services. There are no harm minimization services, such as opioid replacement therapy. There are state-run rehabilitation centers in the country where prisoners may be diverted for compulsory rehabilitation. Two of the largest rehabilitation centers, with a capacity of close to 1000 inmates, are run by the military and function under a nonmedical model. Even these centers do not have robust post-discharge support for detainees who complete the one-year-long rehabilitation program, leading to high rates of relapse and recidivism (Satkunanathan, 2021). The recidivism rate in Sri Lanka is about 20% (Department of Prisons, 2024). However, the recidivism among mentally ill offenders is not known.

4 Forensic Psychiatry Services (FPS) in Sri Lanka

In Sri Lanka, Forensic Psychiatric Services (FPS) are very much centralized, with most specialist services concentrated around the major cities of Colombo, Kandy, and Galle. At the time of writing, there are only two forensic psychiatrists in the country. Thus, FPS are routinely carried out by general adult psychiatrists as well as child and adolescent psychiatrists throughout the country. Services such as assessing mentally ill offenders and victims, providing opinions to courts and advice to Judicial Medical Officers[1] (JMOs) constitute a significant portion of the daily workload of a general psychiatrist. Many generalist psychiatrists offer in-reach services to their local prisons. Sri Lanka does not have a purpose-built forensic hospital. Instead, the care of mentally ill offenders is primarily provided by the Forensic Inpatient Service (FIS) at the NIMH and, to a lesser extent, by regional inpatient units. Sri Lanka only started specialist training in forensic psychiatry in 2011. Since then, six forensic psychiatrists have completed training. However, four of the six have migrated out of the country.

4.1 Services in Colombo

FPS in Colombo are organized around the Forensic Inpatient Service of the National Institute of Mental Health (NIMH)[2] in Angoda (an outer suburb of Colombo, around 8 km from Colombo City). In addition to the large inpatient service, the Colombo service conducts outreach clinics in the National Hospital of Sri Lanka and an in-reach clinic at the Welikada Prison Hospital.

4.1.1 Forensic Inpatient Service (FIS)

The NIMH in Angoda has the largest and busiest forensic inpatient service in the country. Located within the NIMH, it is the only unit recognized under the law to receive and detain forensic patients. Thus, it is the only facility in the country that can accept patients after a finding of not guilty by reason of insanity (NGRI) or unfit for trial for detainment as part of their disposal.

The Colombo FIS consists of two inpatient units: one male and the other female. The male unit has a bed capacity of 100 beds, and the female unit 22 beds. These

[1] Judicial medical officers are specialist doctors in forensic medicine and pathology. They are employed by the government of Sri Lanka to conduct autopsies, examine injuries, and give expert evidence to courts.

[2] The National Institute of Mental Health (NIMH) is the largest tertiary hospital for mental health care in Sri Lanka. It has a bed capacity of over 1000 beds. It opened in 1926 as the Angoda Mental Asylum and was later upgraded in 2008 as a NIMH.

units are not purpose-built; instead, existing wards of the Angoda Mental Hospital have been converted into forensic psychiatry wards. Thus, the Colombo FIS is ill-equipped to contain and rehabilitate high-risk offenders. Such offenders are almost always screened at the prison level to prevent admission. Consequently, the milieu within the Colombo FIS is not significantly different from that of a general inpatient unit, other than the fact that the detainees are undergoing a legal inquiry.

4.1.1.1 The FIS Male Unit—Ward 21

The FIS male ward is located on the third floor of a three-floor building, which was one of the original six three-story blocks present at the time the Angoda Mental Asylum opened in 1926. The ward occupies a single floor of this building, arranged as a dormitory, with 100 beds taking up most of its floor space. It is more common than not for the ward to be over capacity with more patients than beds. Due to the design of these wards (high ceilings, thick walls with ample ventilation through large barred windows), temperature, humidity, and ventilation are maintained despite the overcrowding and the tropical climate in the region.

The FIS male ward has a level of security comparable to that of a medium-secure unit. The ward is always locked, with a staff member or a security officer posted at the entry. The main entrance opens into an airlock before the entry door into the patient area. Patients and visitors are searched before entry into the ward. All searches are conducted manually without the aid of X-ray baggage screening systems or hand-held security wands. Conducting a body search on a patient or visitor would be unusual. There are no seclusion facilities within the FIS male ward. The male FIS ward, being on the third floor, can only be reached by climbing a stairwell of six flights of stairs arranged in a spiral. There is no lift access, which makes it difficult for anyone with disabilities to access the unit.

Detainees are not stratified according to risk or acuity of illness. Thus, it is common for acutely unwell patients to share the same space as those who are cured of illness or for someone with a minor offence to share the same space as someone with a very serious offence, such as murder.

4.1.1.2 Forensic Rehabilitation Unit (FRU)

One floor below the FIS male ward is the Forensic Rehabilitation Unit (FRU). The FRU has the same level of environmental security available in the male ward of the FIS. There are facilities for arts and crafts as well as exercise equipment. From the FRU, a staircase leads to an enclosed, secure garden area of approximately 500 m^2, which is divided into a horticulture project and a playground. The FRU has a full-time occupational therapist and several nurses who run activities on most days of the week. They can provide group activities for about 20 to 30 patients.

4.1.1.3 The FIS Female Unit—Ward 25

The FIS female ward is a 22-bed unit located in a single-story building within the NIMH. The ward has a simple design, typical of most other adult psychiatry units in the NIMH. The ward is a long structure, with 22 beds arranged in two rows in the form of a dormitory. At one end of the ward, there is the entrance and the nursing station, and at the other end, there are the toilets and a seclusion room. Just outside the female unit, there is a hall for rehabilitation activities. The security level in the female ward is similar to a low-secure unit, with little to no perimeter security. The entrance to the female ward has no airlock design and opens into the campus grounds of the NIMH. The hall built for rehabilitation is an open structure with no locking-up facilities. Thus, only patients with a very low risk of aggression and absconding can be taken for rehabilitation activities. Overcrowding is rarely a problem in the female ward.

4.1.1.4 Detainees in the Colombo Forensic Inpatient Service

The majority of the patients admitted to the FIS are remandees who have been committed for trial, where judicial authorities have inquired about the mental state of the defendant. In some, the issue of fitness for trial has been raised, while in others, their behavior in the courts has raised doubts about the presence of a mental illness. Some magistrates refer defendants who are acutely unwell for treatment through a direct referral to the FIS, despite a different pathway being in existence for prisoners to be referred for treatment under the Mental Diseases Ordinance (De Alwis et al., 2024). A few are sent by higher courts for assessment of their criminal responsibility when an issue of NGRI has been raised. In addition to the above patients, about one-fourth of the detainees in the unit have been detained under the CPC after a finding of NGRI or unfitness for trial. This group often ends up spending months to years in hospital, as opposed to the other patients who are often summoned back to courts within a few weeks. The male ward of the FIS receives close to 10 admissions every week, while in the female ward, this number is close to two or three. Most admissions are acutely unwell, suffering from acute psychosis, mania, or severe depression requiring assertive treatment. Once treatment is completed and where no detention orders exist, the patients are sent back to custody to face their court matters.

4.2 Services in Kandy and Galle

Kandy and Galle are UNESCO World Heritage cities located about 100 km from Colombo in the Central and Southern Provinces of Sri Lanka, respectively. Out of the two forensic psychiatrists in Sri Lanka, one works in Colombo and the other in Kandy. A forensic psychiatrist was working in Galle until 2023. Both the Kandy and

Galle services consist of an inpatient service, a prison in-reach program, and a community forensic service. In the absence of a dedicated physical unit for forensic patients, male and female beds have been allocated from the male and female general psychiatry inpatient units of the Kandy Hospital and Galle (Karapitiya) Hospital to be used for admissions of forensic patients. These beds are serviced by the nursing and the allied health staff of the hospitals' general inpatient psychiatry units. In Kandy, the forensic psychiatrist is assisted by several psychiatry registrars and one medical officer. In Galle, since the forensic psychiatrist there left his post for employment overseas, a general psychiatrist has been providing cover for the functions of the forensic unit. Prisoners from regional prisons, from the Central and Southern Provinces, are admitted to the Kandy and Galle Hospital inpatient psychiatry beds when in need of assessment or treatment under the Prison Ordinance. The typical duration of stay is a few days to weeks, much less than the average stay in the Colombo FIS.

Unlike the Colombo service, which refers all discharges back to local mental health services, Kandy and Galle's forensic services conduct limited outpatient follow-up clinics for forensic patients once released from custody. High-risk patients are identified and provided additional input, including closer follow-up and liaisons with local general psychiatric services. Similar to the Colombo service, the Kandy and Galle services have outpatient clinics for noncustodial mentally ill offenders, victims of crime, and other patients requiring capacity assessments referred by the local Magistrate and High courts. In addition, multiple referrals come from JMOs attached to regional hospitals and university forensic departments. Preparing forensic reports constitutes a major workload for both services.

5 Prison Mental Health Services (PMHS) in Sri Lanka

All PMHS services in Sri Lanka are in-reach services funded and run by the health staff of the Ministry of Health (MoH). Many regional generalist psychiatrists conduct clinics in their local prisons. In addition to in-reach prison services, there are non-specialist medical officers appointed by the MoH working within the different prisons who assess and follow up with patients with mental illness as part of their role in providing health care within prisons. There are often close liaisons between these medical officers and the prison in-reach service staff. There are no legal provisions allowing for the involuntary treatment of prisoners in custody.

The Prison Ordinance authorizes the Commissioner General of Prisons to transfer any prisoner to a government hospital for assessment or treatment of any medical illness. These provisions are used to transfer prisoners to the forensic inpatient services in Colombo, Kandy, and Galle. Only the FIS at the NIMH can accept and take over the custody of prisoners due to the secure nature of the unit. In other places, the prisoners are accompanied by correctional officers, and physical restraints are employed to prevent escape. Due to the high level of manpower necessary, the duration of stay for prisoners in general psychiatry inpatient units (even when admitted to specified forensic beds in Kandy and Galle) is short.

The Colombo group of prisons, housing more than 60% of the total prison population, which includes the Welikada Prison (the largest maximum-security prison in Sri Lanka), Colombo Remand Prison, Magazine Prison, and Welikada Female Prison, provides in-reach services through the FPS of the NIMH. The Kandy FPS provides services to New Bogambara Prison in Pallekele, which is the second-largest maximum-security prison in the country. The Galle FPS supports the Galle and Boossa prisons. Prisoners are referred to these in-reach clinics by courts, JMOs, and medical officers.

Both the Welikada prison and the New Bogambara prison have hospitals built within the prison compounds. Both hospitals have psychiatric wards where prisoners with serious mental illnesses deemed unmanageable in the general prison population are transferred. Despite the psychiatry unit inside the Welikada prison hospital having a bed capacity of about 50 beds, the ward houses between 100 and 120 mentally ill prisoners. The majority of the patients do not have access to a bed and sleep on the floor. This ward is very much overcrowded and understaffed at the time of writing. It is serviced by one medical officer (a medical officer of mental health) with the help of other prisoners who are part of a work party. There are no dedicated nursing staff, but general nurses from the main Welikada hospital would assist when needed. Like the Welikada prison hospital, the New Bogambara prison hospital has a 30-bed psychiatry ward. There are only three doctors for the whole of the New Bogambara prison hospital, and only one has had training in managing mental illness. The psychiatry ward in the New Bogambara prison is often overcrowded. From both prison psychiatry units, those prisoners requiring more intensive care or further observation and assessment are transferred to the FIS in Colombo or the Kandy Hospital psychiatry unit.

6 Treatment in Forensic Psychiatry

At present, FPS in Sri Lanka mostly concentrates on the treatment of acute exacerbations of serious mental illness among mentally ill offenders and on providing court reports. Forensic rehabilitation services are very much in their infancy. Overcrowding, high turnover, and limited availability of trained allied health staff make having a biopsychosocial approach challenging. Even in the Colombo FIS with a dedicated FRU, many of the activities that take place are not tailored to the individual but focused on groups. The activities are not addressed to fulfilling criminogenic or vocational needs; rather, they are to keep detainees entertained and occupied. The beds in the FIS in Colombo are the only beds that can be considered specialized forensic beds in the country. For a population of 22 million people, this number of forensic beds is grossly inadequate. Treatment disruptions are common at the point of transfer between the inpatient units and the prison, with a significant number relapsing while awaiting their judicial inquiry in custody. The level of overcrowding in prisons means that monitoring and supervising the treatment of a prisoner with mental illness becomes a challenging task.

7 Legislative Framework

7.1 Mental Health Act of Sri Lanka—Mental Diseases Ordinance No 27 of 1956

The Mental Diseases Ordinance (MDO) regulates involuntary detention and treatment of those with serious mental illness. This statute was originally enacted in 1873 as the Lunacy Ordinance by the British Colonial Government. After undergoing multiple amendments, with the last and most significant one taking place in 1956, the Lunacy Ordinance became the current act (De Alwis, 2017). The MDO allows for people with serious mental illness to be committed to a mental hospital through courts or to be temporarily detained for treatment by two doctors. It does not contain provisions for an independent, external review of these detentions but allows for "Visitors" appointed by the government to supervise the mental hospital and inquire into the welfare of those detained. At present, only the NIMH would be considered a "mental hospital." However, all large hospitals in the different provinces of the country have psychiatry inpatient units, where people with serious mental illnesses are treated involuntarily. The legal status of these admissions remains unclear. The act does not allow for involuntary treatment in the community. A new Mental Health Act has been under deliberation since 2005.

The provisions for the insanity defense or for those who are unfit for trial are not contained within the Mental Diseases Ordinance. Instead, they are found in the Penal Code and the CPC of Sri Lanka. The Prisons Ordinance allows for mentally ill prisoners to be transferred to a mental hospital for involuntary treatment (De Alwis et al., 2024).

7.2 Insanity Defense

Provisions for the insanity defense are found in Section 77 of the Penal Code of Sri Lanka. Section 77 states that "Nothing is an offence which is done by a person who, at the time of doing it, because of unsoundness of mind, is incapable of knowing the nature of the act, or that he is doing what is either wrong or contrary to the law." This allows for complete exoneration from any crime if a defendant is found to be unsound at the time of the offence. The defense is considered to have been derived from the McNaughten Rules but is considered to be broader in its application (De Alwis, 2019). The defense is based on an intellectual understanding of the offence. Thus, if a defendant was unaware of the nature of their actions or the wrongfulness due to mental illness, they would be considered to have been unsound at the time of the offence and would be exonerated from punishment.

Once found unsound, the subsequent management of this person is directed by provisions within the CPC of Sri Lanka. Section 381 of the CPC, reflecting an older Victorian tradition, states that a person who is of unsound mind would be detained in a safe place of custody until the (Justice) Minister's wishes are known. The safe place of custody may be a mental hospital, prison, or other "suitable place" of custody. The mental hospital referred to in this section is the NIMH. The person detained would be periodically reviewed by the Visitor's board to decide if they have sufficiently recovered to be handed over to a family member or friend or be released back into the community (De Alwis et al., 2024).

7.3 Unfitness for Trial

Sections 374 and 375 of the CPC specify that any person unable to make a defense (unfit to plead and stand trial) as a result of mental illness will have their trial or inquest postponed until recovery. However, nowhere in the CPC is the legal test for this determination defined. Instead, this is defined in case law. In *K v. Pindorissa* (1927), Lyall Grant J referred to the legal test used in the English case of *R v. Prichard* (1836) when defining the relevant capacities that are needed to be present in the defendant to be able to make their defense. When a defendant is found to be unfit for trial, they may be given bail until they have recovered sufficiently to resume the trial. If unsuitable for bail, they would be detained in custody and periodically reviewed until they have recovered from their mental illness adequately to be able to make their defense. Sri Lankan law does not contain specific legal provisions on how to dispose of those who are permanently unfit for trial. This has resulted in defendants who are permanently unfit for trial languishing in detention indefinitely if they are unable to secure bail. This has been identified as a contravention of human rights against this vulnerable population (De Alwis et al., 2024).

7.4 Burden and the Quantum of Proof

Unlike in other criminal matters, where the burden of proof lies with the prosecution to prove the case against a defendant beyond a reasonable doubt, the burden of proof for the insanity defense rests with the defense and needs to be proved on a balance of probabilities (De Alwis & Fernando, 2013). The issue of unfitness may be raised by the defense, the prosecution, or the presiding judicial official during any stage of a criminal inquiry. The burden lies upon the party that raises the issue and is decided on a balance of probabilities (De Alwis, 2014).

7.5 Disposal of Those Found NGRI and Unfit for Trial

Sri Lanka does not have any legal provisions specifically establishing forensic mental health orders or supervision orders for those found NGRI or unfit for trial. Instead, the limited disposal options include release from custody with friends or family or detention until the Justice Minister's wishes are known. The Minister's decision is influenced by recommendations made by the Visitor's Board, who review detainees every three months. The Visitor's Board consists of an independent psychiatrist, a representative from the Ministry of Justice, and a high-ranking prison official representing the Commissioner General of Prisons. They would review those detained under sections 376 and 381 of the CPC in prison as well as in the FIS in Colombo and make recommendations that would be sent to the Minister. It is a process with long bureaucratic delays and inefficiencies. When decisions are made, they are made at a judicial or administrative level without much clinical input. Once released, there are no legal mechanisms to monitor the ex-detainees (De Alwis et al., 2024). Sri Lankan law, including the Mental Health Act, lacks provisions for compulsory and supervised outpatient treatment. Patients may only be treated involuntarily in a hospital setting. Thus, forensic patients cannot be given graduated leave or a trial of community-based activities before release.

8 Conclusion

Forensic psychiatric services in Sri Lanka are very much underdeveloped and underfunded. The overcrowding in forensic units, the high volume of work (under time pressure from courts), and the prospects of having to potentially testify in courts make jobs in forensic psychiatry less desirable. This is further compounded by the brain drain of the psychiatry resource pool due to better prospects in other countries.

Moving forward, Sri Lanka would benefit from making forensic services less centralized. Developing services around the major cities in the country is a viable option as more trained staff become available. Having a purpose-built forensic inpatient service with multiple units to house acute, subacute, and long-term detainees, with a higher bed strength, will ease the pressure for beds in the existing units. However, this would do little to help with overcrowding in prisons. Changes to bail laws and sentencing options are necessary before overcrowding in prisons can be addressed.

Sri Lanka's legal framework is lagging behind that of its neighbors, many of whom have modernized their mental health acts to better address contemporary challenges. Reform in current laws that affect forensic patients is urgently needed, as existing laws have become a hindrance to developing forensic mental health services in the country.

Statutes

Children and Young Persons Ordinance, No. 48 of 1939 (1956 Revision)
Code of Criminal Procedure Act 1979
Mental Diseases Ordinance, No 27 of 1956 (1956 Revision)
Penal Code (Ordinance No. 2 of 1883)
Prisons Ordinance No. 16 of 1877

References

Arafat, S. Y., Kar, S. K., Abhayanayake, C., Sharma, P., & Marthoenis, M. (2024). Prison mental health in South-East Asia: A narrative review. *Brain and Behavior, 14*(8), e70004. https://doi.org/10.1002/brb3.70004

Central Bank of Sri Lanka. (2024). *Sri Lanka Socio-Economic Data 2024* (No. Volume 47). Central Bank of Sri Lanka. https://www.cbsl.gov.lk/sites/default/files/cbslweb_documents/publications/otherpub/publication_sri_lanka_socio_economic_data_folder_2024_e.pdf

Darshana, N., Ruben, R., & Wijesinghe, C. (2023). Previously used substances and predictors of illicit drug use among incarcerated male prisoners in Galle, Sri Lanka. *Heroin Addiction and Related Clinical Problems, 25*(1), 13–19.

De Alwis, A. (2014). Fitness to plead in Sri Lanka. *Sri Lanka Journal of Psychiatry*, *5*(1).

De Alwis, A., & Fernando, N. (2013). The insanity defense and the assessment of criminal responsibility in Sri Lanka. *Sri Lanka Journal of Psychiatry, 4*(2).

De Alwis, L. (2017). Development of civil commitment statutes (laws of involuntary detention and treatment) in Sri Lanka: A historical review. *Medico-Legal Journal of Sri Lanka, 5*(1), 22–31.

De Alwis, L. A. (2019). Historical origins of the insanity defense in Sri Lanka and India. *Sri Lanka Journal of Psychiatry, 10*(2), 4. https://doi.org/10.4038/sljpsyc.v10i2.8211

De Alwis, L. A. P., Seneviratne, V. L., Mendis, T. S. S., & Abhayanayaka, C. (2024). Laws relating to the disposal of forensic patients in Sri Lanka and suggestions for reform. *Sri Lanka Journal of Legal Studies, 1*(2), 89–113.

De Silva, W. I., & De Silva, R. (2023). Growth and structural changes of Sri Lankan population during coming decades with special reference to youth and elderly. *Sri Lanka Statistical Review, 2*(1), 1–21.

Deivanayagam, T. A., Ní Chobhthaigh, S., Devakumar, D., Patel, K., & Rannan-Eliya, R. P. (2024). Mental health prevalence, healthcare use and access between 2018 and 2022 in Sri Lanka: An analysis of survey data. *Global Health Research*, 1–16. https://doi.org/10.3310/HJWA5078

Department of Census and Statistics (DCS) and Ministry of Health, Nutrition and Indigenous Medicine. (2017). *Sri Lanka Demographic and Health Survey 2016* (p. 16). Department of Census and Statistics (DCS) and Ministry of Health, Nutrition and Indigenous Medicine. https://www.statistics.gov.lk/Resource/en/Health/DemographicAndHealthSurveyReport-2016-Contents.pdf

Department of Census and Statistics, Sri Lanka. (2024). *Statistical Pocket Book 2024*. Department of Census and Statistics, Sri Lanka. https://www.statistics.gov.lk/Publication/PocketBook2024

Department of Prisons. (2024). *Prison Statistics of Sri Lanka 2024* (No. Vol 43; p. 124). Department of Prisons. http://prisons.gov.lk/web/wp-content/uploads/2024/05/prison-statistics-2024.pdf

Deseau, A., Levai, A., & Schmiegelow, M. (2019). *Access to Justice and Economic Development: Evidence from an International Panel Dataset* (p. 45) [Discussion Paper]. Institute of Economic and Social Research, Catholic University of Louvain (UCLouvain). https://sites.uclouvain.be/econ/DP/IRES/2019009.pdf

Directorate of Mental Health. (2023). *Trends in Mental health problems based on Government hospital admissions 1996-2013*. National Data - Directorate of Mental Health. https://mental-health.health.gov.lk/index.php?option=com_content&view=article&id=22&Itemid=159&lang=en#mental-health-disorders

Dissabandara, L. O., Dias, S. R., Dodd, P. R., & Stadlin, A. (2009). Patterns of substance use in male incarcerated drug users in Sri Lanka. *Drug and Alcohol Review, 28*(6), 600–607.

Dissanayake, T. N. (2017). *Patterns of heroin use and risk behaviors among prisoners in Colombo, Sri Lanka* [Chulalongkorn University]. https://digital.car.chula.ac.th/cgi/viewcontent.cgi?article=1997&context=chulaetd

Fernando, N., Suveendran, T., & de Silva, C. (2017). Decentralizing provision of mental health care in Sri Lanka. *WHO South-East Asia Journal of Public Health, 6*(1), 18–21.

Hapangama, A., Dasanayake, D., Kuruppuarachchi, K., Pathmeswaran, A., & De Silva, H. (2021). *Substance use disorders and their correlates among inmates in a Sri Lankan prison.*

Human Rights Commission of Sri Lanka. (2020). *Prison Study by the Human Rights Commission of Sri Lanka* (p. 863). Human Rights Commission of Sri Lanka. https://www.hrcsl.lk/wp-content/uploads/2020/01/Prison-Report-Final-2.pdf

Human Rights Watch. (2024, March 1). *Sri Lanka: Events of 2023*. World Report 2024: Sri Lanka. https://www.hrw.org/world-report/2024/country-chapters/sri-lanka

K v. Pindorissa, 29 N.L.R. 385 (High Court 1927).

Ministry of Health (MoH). (2025). *Health Institutions In Sri Lanka* [Government]. Ministry of Health. https://www.health.gov.lk

Ministry of Justice. (2024). *Annual Performance Report 2023* (No. Expenditure Head Nos.110 & 228; p. 95). Ministry of Justice, Prison Affairs and Constitutional Reforms. https://www.moj.gov.lk/images/pdf/progress_report/2022/Performance-Report-2023-Eng.pdf

Nadaraja, T. (1972). *The legal system of ceylon in its historical setting*. EJ Brill.

Office of the United Nations High Commissioner for Human Rights (OHCHR). (2021, 01). *Sri Lanka on alarming path towards recurrence of grave human rights violations – UN report.* OHCHR. https://www.ohchr.org/en/press-releases/2021/01/sri-lanka-alarming-path-towards-recurrence-grave-human-rights-violations-un

Office of the United Nations High Commissioner for Human Rights (OHCHR). (2025). *Ratification Status for Sri Lanka.* UN Human Rights Office. https://tbinternet.ohchr.org/_layouts/15/TreatyBodyExternal/Treaty.aspx?CountryID=164

R v. Prichard, 7 Car & P (England and Wales High Court (King's Bench Division) 1836). https://www.bailii.org/ew/cases/EWHC/KB/1836/1.html

Raja, S., Wood, S. K., de Menil, V., & Mannarath, S. C. (2010). Mapping mental health finances in Ghana, Uganda, Sri Lanka, India and Lao PDR. *International Journal of Mental Health Systems*, *4*, 1–14.

Rajapaksa, L., De Silva, P., Abeykoon, P., Somatunga, L., Sathasivam, S., Perera, S., Fernando, E., De Silva, D., Perera, A., & Perera, U. (2021). *Sri Lanka Health System Review* (No. Vol. 10 No. 1 2021; Health Systems in Transition, p. 254). World Health Organization Regional Office for South-East Asia. https://iris.who.int/bitstream/handle/10665/342323/9789290228530-eng.pdf?sequence=1

Rajapakse, T. (2017). A review of the changing patterns of suicide and deliberate self-harm in Sri Lanka. *Sri Lanka Journal of Psychiatry, 8*(1).

Satkunanathan, A. (2021). *A broken system: Drug control, detention and treatment of people who use drugs in Sri Lanka* (p. 168). Harm Reduction International.

Suranga, M. A., & Vidanapathirana, J. (2022). Suicides among prison inmates in Sri Lanka: Prevalence and associated factors of suicidal behavior. *MedNEXT Journal of Medical and Health Sciences, 3*(2).

Wickramatilake, C., De Silva, B., Nanayakkara, T., Nanayakkara, R., & Gayashani, K. (2023). General health characteristics, psychological stress of inmates and living environment of a main prison in Sri Lanka. *Sri Lanka Journal of Medicine, 32*(1).

World Bank Group. (2013). *Sri Lanka—Justice sector review* (Legal and Judicial Sector Assessment No. 77662; p. 71). The World Bank Group South Asia region poverty reduction and economic management. https://documents.worldbank.org/en/publication/documents-reports/documentdetail/255751468164662812/sri-lanka-justice-sector-review

World Health Organization. (2021). *Mental Health Atlas 2020* (p. 136). World Health Organization. https://www.who.int/publications/i/item/9789240036703.

World Health Organization. (2022). *Addressing mental health in Sri Lanka* (p. 20). World Health Organization. Regional Office for South-East Asia. https://www.who.int/publications/i/item/9789290210221

World Health Organization. (2025). *Suicide rates*. The Global Health Observatory. https://www.who.int/data/gho/data/themes/mental-health/suicide-rates

World Population Review. (2025). *Incarceration Rates by Country 2024*. World Population Review. https://worldpopulationreview.com/country-rankings/incarceration-rates-by-country

Chapter 7
Forensic Psychiatry and Prison Mental Health in Other South Asian Countries (Afghanistan, Bhutan, and the Maldives)

Sujita Kumar Kar, Arpit Parmar, and S. M. Yasir Arafat

Abstract South Asian countries have similarities in many aspects of socioeconomic status. At the same time, there are variations in language, religion, local culture, health care delivery, and legal structure. Afghanistan, Bhutan, and the Maldives are three countries with relatively small population sizes compared to India, Pakistan, and Bangladesh. There are similarities in several aspects of mental health services in countries, such as inadequate services and human resources, along with local challenges like conflict in Afghanistan and the geography of the Maldives. Forensic psychiatry and prison mental health are largely neglected in these countries. In this chapter, we aim to discuss geographical characteristics, forensic psychiatry, and prison mental health services in Afghanistan, Bhutan, and the Maldives based on the available literature.

Keywords Forensic psychiatry · Prison · Mental health · Afghanistan · Bhutan · The Maldives

S. K. Kar (✉)
Department of Psychiatry, King George's Medical University, Lucknow, India

A. Parmar
Department of Psychiatry, All India Institute of Medical Sciences, Bhubaneswar, India

S. M. Y. Arafat
Department of Psychiatry, Bangladesh Specialized Hospital, Dhaka, Bangladesh

Senior Research Fellow, Biomedical Research Foundation, Dhaka, Bangladesh

A. Parmar et al. (eds.), *Forensic Psychiatry and Prison Mental Health in South Asia*, South Asian Perspectives in Mental Health and Psychology,
https://doi.org/10.1007/978-981-96-7206-6_7

1 Forensic Psychiatry and Prison Mental Health in Afghanistan

Afghanistan belongs to the category of a low-income country in South Asia (World Bank, 2025). As per the latest report, the population of Afghanistan was 41,454,761 by 2023 (World Health Organization, 2025a). As per the recently available information (by 2021), 21.8% of the Gross Domestic Product (GDP) was spent on health (World Health Organization, 2025a). Collective violence and legal intervention are the most common causes of death in Afghanistan (121.8 deaths per 100,000 population), which is more common among males than females (World Health Organization, 2025a). The suicide rate in the country is 4.1 per 100,000 population, whereas the mortality due to homicide is 8.5 per 100,000 population, latest by 2019 (World Health Organization, 2025a). As per the Afghanistan Health Profile 2015 by the WHO report, the estimated prevalence of mental illnesses in Afghanistan is 6.7% of the total burden of diseases (WHO EMRO, 2015). The annual prevalence of cannabis use is 4.3%, and opiates is 2.7%, whereas that of cocaine and amphetamine is 0.1% each (WHO EMRO, 2015). A national study from Afghanistan reports a significant level of mental stress in Afghans, with 26% having impairments (Ministry of Public Health, 2023). As per a recent report published in The Lancet Psychiatry, 85% of people from Afghanistan have witnessed or experienced a significant traumatic event, which indicates the devastating and widespread impact of war, terrorism, and disaster (Noroozi et al., 2024). Psychological distress is experienced by nearly half of the Afghans (Noroozi et al., 2024). A recent study conducted on 4445 individuals from 8 provinces (a nationally representative population recruited through multistage sampling) from Afghanistan reports that nearly 61% of the population who participated in the study had experienced collective violence with respect to war (Kovess-Masfety et al., 2021). This study also reported that nearly 80% of people are staying in very dangerous areas, which increases the risk of trauma and subsequent mental health morbidity (Kovess-Masfety et al., 2021). Children and adolescents are one of the major vulnerable groups for trauma and abuse (Cameron et al., 2021; Jobson et al., 2024). More than 70% of Afghan children have been exposed to physical violence during the past year, as found in research (O'Leary et al., 2018; Shoib et al., 2022). Despite this fact, the events are frequently underreported in the country by various strata of the community (O'Leary et al., 2018).

As per the report of the World Health Organization (WHO), by 2004, there were only two psychiatrists, 61 doctors, 37 nurses, and 40 other personnel working on mental health in Afghanistan (World Health Organization, 2006). Despite political turmoil, there have been initiatives taken by the government of Afghanistan at different times to improve healthcare delivery, including mental health (Shoib et al., 2024; Alemi et al., 2023; Ministry of Public Health, 2023; Saeedzai et al., 2023). Several policies have been drafted and revised from time to time to enhance mental healthcare in Afghanistan (Ministry of Public Health, 2023). In the current scenario, almost all Basic Package of Health Services (BPHS) and Emergency Package of

Health Services (EPHS) provide psychosocial services related to mental health (Ministry of Public Health, 2023). Recently, the government of Japan has supported Afghanistan with a donation of 500,000 USD for strengthening the essential health services in the country during the ongoing humanitarian crisis (World Health Organization, 2025b).

Since 1987, Afghanistan has had its own mental health legislation, action plan, and policy to address mental health issues. Figure 7.1 highlights the major objectives of the National Mental Health Program of Afghanistan.

The mental health action plan of Afghanistan emphasizes the protection of the rights of people with mental illness and their caregivers, the least restrictive care, voluntary and involuntary care, legislative control and monitoring of admission procedures and mental health care practices, and guardianship issues with reference to mental health issues (World Health Organization, 2006). In Afghanistan, a national mental health strategy (NMHS) was initiated in 2011, developing a five-year vision statement lasting from 2011 to 2015 (Ministry of Public Health, 2023). The national mental health strategy emphasizes the objectives of the national mental health program and additionally gives importance to:

- Prevention of mental illnesses
- Promotion of mental health
- Dealing with stigma and discrimination associated with mental health issues
- Addressing the mental health issues associated with crisis/emergency and disaster
- Expansion of outreach community mental health services
- Protection of the rights of people with mental illness
- Strengthening suicide prevention activities by integrating it into other programs
- Empowerment of people with mental illnesses and their caregivers

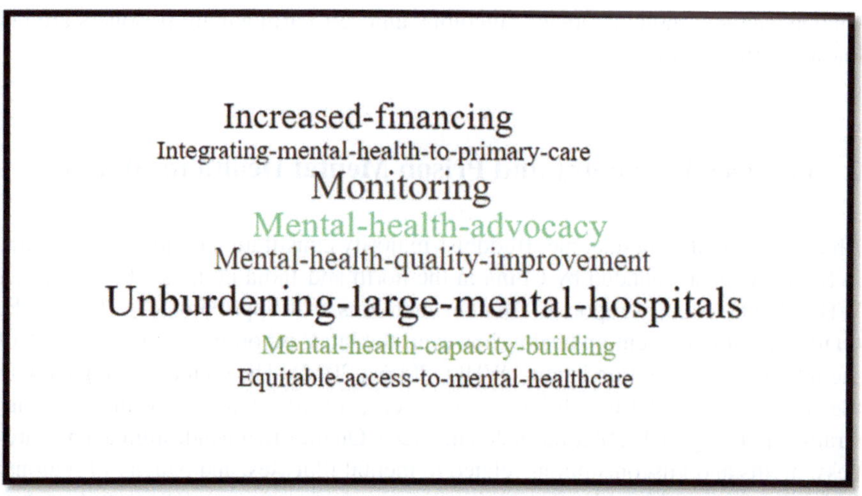

Fig. 7.1 Major objectives of the National Mental Health Program of Afghanistan

Drug use and trafficking are significant matters of concern in Afghanistan (Cottler et al., 2014; Hall & Degenhardt, 2014; Nafeh et al., 2022). Opioid use resulted in multiple medical morbidities and premature death in Afghanistan (Hall & Degenhardt, 2014). Injecting drug abuse is another serious issue among Afghans, which is particularly more prevalent in urban areas (mostly in and around Kabul) and among men (more than 95%) (Nafeh et al., 2022). Risky behavior is often seen among individuals using substances, particularly injecting drugs (Nafeh et al., 2022). A close association has been reported between drug use, trafficking, and organized crime (Bewley-Taylor, 2013; Bove & Elia, 2013; Mutasem, 2021; Shaw, 2006; Stepanova, 2012). Intimate partner violence (IPV) is another matter of concern in Afghanistan. Nearly 56% of Afghan women encounter some or other form of physical, emotional, or sexual violence by their intimate partners (Shinwari et al., 2022).

There is a paucity of published research on the forensic mental health aspects in Afghanistan as the country struggles with basic mental healthcare services amidst the socio-political crisis (Mohd Saleem et al., 2021). After an extensive search, we did not find any published, freely available literature on mental capacity assessment, mental health of criminals, and marriage with respect to mental illness referring to Afghanistan.

It has 251 prisons (34 provincial prisons, 187 district detention centers, and 30 juvenile corrections centers). There are 19,000 prisoners with an incarceration rate of 45 per 100,000 population and a 180% occupancy rate. Among the prisoners, 31.3% are in the pre-trial stage, and 4.2% are females (World Prison Brief, 2025, January 2024 data).

Prison health and mental health services in prison are largely neglected in Afghanistan (Michael, 2014). Little is known about psychiatric morbidity among prisoners and the current status of prison mental health. We did not find information about self-harm and suicidal behavior among prisoners in Afghanistan. The rates of suicide, suicidal thoughts, plans, attempts, and self-harm among prisoners are not known in the country.

2 Forensic Psychiatry and Prison Mental Health in Bhutan

Bhutan is a small, low-income, Buddhist-majority constitutional monarchy country in South Asia, surrounded by China in the north and India in the south. An earlier WHO-AIMS country report of Bhutan mentions that approximately 10% of the GDP in Bhutan is spent on health; however, the latest report mentions that 4.5% of the total GDP is spent on health (WHO, 2006a, 2022). The country struggles with the scarcity of mental health human resources, infrastructures, and financial constraints (Pelzang, 2012; Sharma & Joshi, 2024). On the other hand, stigma, unawareness, myths and misconceptions related to mental illnesses, and paucity of regional research on mental health are additional matters of concern in Bhutan (Arafat & Kar, 2024; Sharma & Joshi, 2024). As per the report of the Annual Health Bulletin

2020, Ministry of Health, Royal Government of Bhutan, there is an increasing trend of psychiatric disorders between 2016 and 2020 (WHO, 2022). Though there is no recent data available regarding the prevalence of mental health issues in Bhutan after 2020 (Arafat & Kar, 2024), but, considering the significant impact of COVID-19 on mental health, it is expected that the mental health issues in Bhutan must have been higher than what has been reported in 2020. There is no systematically conducted research to estimate the treatment gaps for mental illnesses in Bhutan to date. As per the latest available information, there are four psychiatrists, nine mental health nurses, seven occupational therapists, and 18 clinical counsellors in Bhutan by 2022 (WHO, 2022).

The Bhutanese government introduced the country's first-ever mental health policy in 1997 as a component of Bhutan's 8th five-year plan (WHO, 2006a). Figure 7.2 highlights the major objectives of the national mental health policy of Bhutan.

Admission of patients with mental illnesses in Bhutan can be voluntary as well as involuntary (Pelzang, 2012). As of now, there is no mental health legislation in Bhutan (Pelzang, 2012; WHO, 2022). Not having a dedicated mental health law gives flexibility and freedom to choose treatment for mental health by the patients and their caregivers (WHO, 2022). The other existing legislation covers some aspects of mental health (rights of persons with mental illness and the legal provisions for them) (WHO, 2022). The Bhutan penal code emphasizes providing treatment to an individual who has a mental illness and commits a crime (WHO, 2022). Bhutan formulated the Narcotic and Psychotropic Drugs Abuse Act in 2013, which has undergone multiple amendments subsequently. It has the intention to facilitate treatment and rehabilitation of patients with substance use disorder (WHO, 2022). Hard drugs like opioids, which are used in certain medical preparations (e.g., morphine, buprenorphine, pentazocine, and codeine), are also banned in Bhutan for

Fig. 7.2 Highlights of national mental health policy in Bhutan

therapeutic use (Nirola, 2024). Bhutan has also developed a suicide prevention policy for effective prevention of suicide (WHO, 2022).

Currently, there is a notable shortage of published research on forensic mental health in Bhutan. This deficiency arises as the country struggles to establish and enhance basic mental healthcare services for its population. Despite conducting a thorough search, we were unable to find any freely accessible literature on crucial topics such as mental capacity assessment, the mental health challenges faced by prisoners, and the implications of mental illness within the context of marriage in Bhutan. This scarcity of resources underscores an urgent need for further exploration and scholarship in these important areas, essential for improving our understanding of forensic mental health and advancing mental health services in the country.

It has seven prisons (six for adults, one for minors), 1119 prisoners, and an incarceration rate of 145 per 100,000. Of these, 4.3% are females (World Prison Brief, 2025, December 2014 data).

Little is known about psychiatric morbidity among prisoners and the current status of prison mental health. We did not find information about self-harm and suicidal behavior among prisoners in Bhutan. The rates of suicide, suicidal thoughts, plans, attempts, and self-harm among prisoners are not known in the country.

3 Forensic Psychiatry and Prison Mental Health in the Maldives

The Maldives consists of a chain of tiny islands in the Indian Ocean. Low population density, small size of islands, and rising sea levels around the island increase the ecological vulnerability (WHO, 2006b). There is no recent epidemiological study conducted over the past 12 years to estimate the burden of mental illnesses in the Maldives population. The previous surveys report that about 29% of people in the Maldives have some form of mental health issue (WHO Country Office for Maldives, 2017). Drug use is also a significant problem, but the drug users are centered around the Male area (WHO Country Office for Maldives, 2017). Traditional healers and religious healers still play a major role in providing mental healthcare in the community.

As per an earlier report, 6.7% of the GDP is spent on health in the Maldives. The government of the Maldives introduced a National Mental Health Policy in 2015, setting a ten-year goal (2025–2025) for the nation (WHO Country Office for Maldives, 2017). The major objectives of the national mental health policy in the Maldives are summarized in Fig. 7.3.

Additionally, the policy has identified certain key areas of attention (drug addiction, capacity building, quality enhancement, comprehensive mental healthcare development, and leadership in mental health) (WHO Country Office for Maldives, 2017). The Maldives does not have a dedicated mental health legislation; however,

Fig. 7.3 Objectives of national mental health policy in the Maldives

other laws in the country also partly deal with mental health. The country is in the process of drafting a dedicated mental health legislation in coordination with various stakeholders (Ministry of Health, 2022). The Ministry of Health in the Republic of the Maldives has developed a "Central and Regional Mental Health Services Development Plan 2022–2025" for bringing out reformation in mental healthcare in the country (Ministry of Health, 2022). In collaboration with UNICEF, the government of The Maldives has launched a National Mental Health Communications Strategy and Campaign. This initiative, led by the Health Protection Agency (HPA), aims to encourage social and behavioral change regarding current perceptions and attitudes toward mental health. It aligns with national efforts to improve mental health awareness and support (UNICEF, The Maldives, 2022). In the Republic of Maldives, a document was drafted in 2024 under the name of "National Standard for Forensic Medical Services in the Maldives," which mostly deals with the forensic medicine operational and documentation process (Ministry of Health, 2024). This document does not mention anything related to forensic psychiatry.

There is no forensic inpatient facility in the Maldives (Ministry of Health, 2024). There is a paucity of published research on forensic mental health issues in the Maldives, where the country is facing challenges with basic mental healthcare services. Migration of mental health professionals to other countries is also a challenge in providing mental healthcare. After conducting an extensive search, we found no freely available literature on mental capacity assessments, the mental health of criminals, or the impact of mental illness on marriage in the context of the Maldives.

It has 11 prisons, 1700 prisoners, an incarceration rate of 314 per 100,000 population, and a 125% occupancy rate. Of the prisoners, 14.3% are in the pre-trial stage, and 4.3% are females (World Prison Brief, 2025).

Little is known about psychiatric morbidity among prisoners and the current status of prison mental health. We did not find information about self-harm and suicidal behavior among prisoners in the Maldives. The rates of suicide, suicidal thoughts, plans, attempts, and self-harm among prisoners are not known in the country.

4 Conclusion

We attempted to overview the forensic psychiatry and prison mental health in Afghanistan, Bhutan, and the Maldives based on available literature. There is scant research and evidence in these countries, perhaps due to a lack of priority and focus on this neglected area of mental health, as there are other health priorities. However, a prudential judgment is warranted when considering the findings, as there may be evidence in vernacular language. This chapter may be considered a baseline overview that may open further avenues of research and attention to the field.

References

Alemi, Q., Panter-Brick, C., Oriya, S., Ahmady, M., Alimi, A. Q., Faiz, H., Hakim, N., Sami Hashemi, S. A., Manaly, M. A., Naseri, R., Parwiz, K., Sadat, S. J., Sharifi, M. Z., Shinwari, Z., Ahmadi, S. J., Amin, R., Azimi, S., Hewad, A., Musavi, Z., et al. (2023). Afghan mental health and psychosocial well-being: Thematic review of four decades of research and interventions. *BJPsych Open, 9*(4), e125. https://doi.org/10.1192/bjo.2023.502

Arafat, S. M. Y., & Kar, S. K. (Eds.). (2024). *Access to mental health care in South Asia: Current status, potential challenges, and ways out*. Springer Nature. https://doi.org/10.1007/978-981-99-9153-2

Bewley-Taylor, D. (2013). Drug trafficking and organised crime in Afghanistan: Corruption, insecurity and the challenges of transition. *The RUSI Journal, 158*(6), 6–17. https://doi.org/10.1080/03071847.2013.869719

Bove, V., & Elia, L. (2013). Drugs and violence in Afghanistan: A panel var with unobserved common factor analysis. *Defence and Peace Economics, 24*(6), 535–554. https://doi.org/10.1080/10242694.2012.723157

Cameron, C. M., O'Leary, P. J., Lakhani, A., Osborne, J. M., de Souza, L., Hope, K., Naimi, M. S., Khan, H., Jawad, Q. S., & Majidi, S. (2021). Violence against children in Afghanistan: Community perspectives. *Journal of Interpersonal Violence, 36*(5–6), 2521–2540. https://doi.org/10.1177/0886260518760610

Cottler, L. B., Ajinkya, S., Goldberger, B. A., Ghani, M. A., Martin, D. M., Hu, H., & Gold, M. S. (2014). Prevalence of drug and alcohol use in urban Afghanistan: Epidemiological data from the Afghanistan National Urban Drug Use Study (ANUDUS). *The Lancet Global Health, 2*(10), e592–e600. https://doi.org/10.1016/S2214-109X(14)70290-6

Hall, W. D., & Degenhardt, L. (2014). Afghanistan has a sizeable problem with opioid use. *The Lancet Global Health, 2*(10), e557–e558. https://doi.org/10.1016/S2214-109X(14)70299-2

Jobson, L., McAvoy, D., & Ahmadi, S. J. (2024). Psychological problems in the context of political violence in Afghan children. *Current Psychiatry Reports, 26*(5), 222–228. https://doi.org/10.1007/s11920-024-01496-2

Kovess-Masfety, V., Keyes, K., Karam, E., Sabawoon, A., & Sarwari, B. A. (2021). A national survey on depressive and anxiety disorders in Afghanistan: A highly traumatized population. *BMC Psychiatry, 21*(1), 314. https://doi.org/10.1186/s12888-021-03273-4

Michael, M. (2014). Prison health as public health in Afghanistan? A policy analysis of the on-going reform process. *Public Health, 128*(5), 478–481. https://doi.org/10.1016/j.puhe.2014.01.007

Ministry of Health. (2022, March). *Central and Regional Mental Health Services Development Plan 2022-2025*. Republic of Maldives. chrome-extension://efaidnbmnnnibpcajpcglclefindmkaj/https://health.gov.mv/storage/uploads/NAq7Loeg/opbcrit8.pdf

Ministry of Health. (2024). *National Standard for Forensic Medical Services in the Maldives*. Republic of Maldives. chrome-extension://efaidnbmnnnibpcajpcglclefindmkaj/https://health.gov.mv/storage/uploads/EoAjylw9/zae5c6sf.pdf

Ministry of Public Health. (2023). *National Strategy for Mental Health 2019-2023*. Mental health and substance abuse department. https://moph.gov.af/sites/default/files/2019-09/Mental%20Health%20Staregy%202019-2023.pdf

Mohd Saleem, S., Shoib, S., Dazhamyar, A. R., & Chandradasa, M. (2021). Afghanistan: Decades of collective trauma, ongoing humanitarian crises, Taliban rulers, and mental health of the displaced population. *Asian Journal of Psychiatry, 65*, 102854. https://doi.org/10.1016/j.ajp.2021.102854

Mutasem, M. H. (2021). *Drug trafficking in Afghanistan: Criminalization, investigation and prosecution* [PhD Thesis, Staats-und Universitätsbibliothek Hamburg Carl von Ossietzky]. https://ediss.sub.uni-hamburg.de/handle/ediss/9023

Nafeh, F., Fusigboye, S., & Sornpaisarn, B. (2022). Understanding injecting drug use in Afghanistan: A scoping review. *Substance Abuse Treatment, Prevention, and Policy, 17*(1), 65. https://doi.org/10.1186/s13011-022-00491-1

Nirola, D. K. (2024). Current perspectives on substance use disorder in Bhutan. In S. M. Y. Arafat & S. K. Kar (Eds.), *Current perspectives on substance use disorders in South Asia: Public mental health aspects* (pp. 63–69). Springer Nature. https://doi.org/10.1007/978-981-97-6619-2_4

Noroozi, A., Lara, M. D., & Abouzeid, A. (2024). Drug policies and responses in Afghanistan. *The Lancet Psychiatry, 11*(2), 90–91. https://doi.org/10.1016/S2215-0366(23)00390-5

O'Leary, P., Cameron, C. M., Lakhani, A., Osborne, J. M., de Souza, L., Hope, K., Naimi, M. S., Khan, H., Jawad, Q. S., & Majidi, S. (2018). Violence against children in Afghanistan: Concerns and opportunities for positive change. *Child Abuse & Neglect, 76*, 95–105. https://doi.org/10.1016/j.chiabu.2017.10.010

Pelzang, R. (2012). Mental health care in Bhutan: Policy and issues. *WHO South-East Asia Journal of Public Health, 1*(3), 339–346.

Saeedzai, S. A., Blanchet, K., Alwan, A., Safi, N., Salehi, A., Singh, N. S., Abou Jaoude, G. J., Mirzazada, S., Majrooh, W., Jan Naeem, A., Skordis-Worral, J., Bhutta, Z. A., Haghparast-Bidgoli, H., Farewar, F., Lange, I., Newbrander, W., Kakuma, R., Reynolds, T., & Feroz, F. (2023). Lessons from the development process of the Afghanistan integrated package of essential health services. *BMJ Global Health, 8*(9), e012508. https://doi.org/10.1136/bmjgh-2023-012508

Sharma, P., & Joshi, D. (2024). Access to mental health care in Bhutan: Current status, potential challenges, and ways out. In S. M. Y. Arafat & S. K. Kar (Eds.), *Access to mental health care in South Asia: Current status, potential challenges, and ways out* (pp. 57–69). Springer Nature. https://doi.org/10.1007/978-981-99-9153-2_4

Shaw, M. (2006). Drug trafficking and the development of organized crime in post-Taliban Afghanistan. *Introduction and Overview, 189*.

Shinwari, R., Wilson, M. L., Abiodun, O., & Shaikh, M. A. (2022). Intimate partner violence among ever-married Afghan women: Patterns, associations and attitudinal acceptance. *Archives of Women's Mental Health, 25*(1), 95–105. https://doi.org/10.1007/s00737-021-01143-2

Shoib, S., Essar, M. Y., Saleem, S. M., Legris, Z., & Chandradasa, M. (2022). The children of Afghanistan need urgent mental health support. *The Lancet, 399*(10329), 1045–1046. https://doi.org/10.1016/S0140-6736(22)00155-6

Shoib, S., Hussaini, S. S., Nazari, S. K., & Saeed, F. (2024). Mental Healthcare in Afghanistan. In S. M. Y. Arafat & S. K. Kar (Eds.), *Access to mental health care in South Asia*. Springer. https://doi.org/10.1007/978-981-99-9153-2_2

Stepanova, E. (2012). Illicit drugs and insurgency in Afghanistan. *Perspectives on Terrorism, 6*(2), 4–18.

UNICEF The Maldives. (2022). *Government of Maldives and UNICEF launch National Mental Health Communications Strategy and Campaign*. https://www.unicef.org/maldives/press-releases/government-maldives-and-unicef-launch-national-mental-health-communications-strategy

WHO. (2006a). *WHO-AIMS Report on Mental Health System in Bhutan*. World Health Organization. https://cdn.who.int/media/docs/default-source/mental-health/who-aims-country-reports/bhutan_who_aims_report.pdf?sfvrsn=f082a3c5_3

WHO. (2006b). *WHO-AIMS report on mental health system in Maldives* (pp. 1–19). WHO Regional Office for South-East Asia. https://apps.who.int/iris/bitstream/handle/10665/206158/B0768.pdf

WHO. (2022). *Addressing mental health in Bhutan*. https://www.who.int/publications/i/item/9789290210153

WHO Country Office for Maldives. (2017). *National Mental Health Policy 2015-2025*. https://health.gov.mv/storage/uploads/EoAjylw9/zae5c6sf.pdf

WHO EMRO. (2015). *WHO EMRO | Afghanistan Health Profile 2015. World Health Organization - Regional Office for the Eastern Mediterranean.*. http://www.emro.who.int/afg/who-in-afghanistan/

World Bank. (2025). *World Bank Country and Lending Groups*. https://datahelpdesk.worldbank.org/knowledgebase/articles/906519-world-bank-country-and-lending-groups. Accessed 26 February 2025

World Health Organization. (2006). *WHO-Aims report on mental health system in Afghanistan* (pp. 1–19). WHO and Ministry of Public Health.

World Health Organization. (2025a). *Afghanistan*. Datadot. https://data.who.int/countries/004

World Health Organization. (2025b, February). *WHO EMRO | Afghanistan | Countries*. World Health Organization - Regional Office for the Eastern Mediterranean. http://www.emro.who.int/countries/afg/index.html

World Prison Brief. (2025). *World Prison Brief Data*. Retrieved February 26, 2025, from https://www.prisonstudies.org/world-prison-brief-data

Chapter 8
Mental Health Rehabilitation Services After Release from Prison and the Risk of Reoffending in South Asia

Amit Khanna , Harmanpreet Kaur, Prerna Sharma, Pravin Yanavar, and Rajesh Kumar

Abstract This chapter examines the critical issue of mental health rehabilitation services for prisoner's post-release in South Asia, a region grappling with overcrowding, outdated criminal justice systems, and a high prevalence of mental health disorders among inmates. The chapter illustrates the challenges faced by former prisoners with mental illness upon reintegration into society, including securing basic necessities, rebuilding social ties, and the heightened risk of recidivism. It analyzes the current state of prison mental health services across South Asian countries, highlighting the scarcity of resources and the need for comprehensive aftercare programs. It also highlights the complex relationship between mental illness and recidivism, discussing risk factors and the importance of tailored interventions. Finally, it reviews various psychosocial interventions, including Cognitive Behavioral Therapy, mindfulness techniques, Motivational Enhancement Therapy, and Expressive Art Therapies, that have demonstrated effectiveness in improving mental health outcomes and facilitating successful reintegration, emphasizing the need for a multi-stakeholder approach to address this pressing issue.

Keywords Mental health rehabilitation · Prisoners · Aftercare facilities · Mental health morbidity in prisons · Recidivism · Psychological interventions for prisoners

---

A. Khanna (✉) · H. Kaur
Department of Psychiatry, Institute of Human Behaviour and Allied Sciences (IHBAS), New Delhi, India

P. Sharma
Department of Clinical Psychology, Institute of Human Behaviour and Allied Sciences (IHBAS), New Delhi, India

P. Yanavar
Department of Psychiatric Social Work, Institute of Human Behaviour and Allied Sciences (IHBAS), New Delhi, India

R. Kumar
Department of Psychiatry, Indira Gandhi Institute of Medical Sciences, Patna, Bihar, India

A. Parmar et al. (eds.), *Forensic Psychiatry and Prison Mental Health in South Asia*, South Asian Perspectives in Mental Health and Psychology,
https://doi.org/10.1007/978-981-96-7206-6_8

1 Introduction

South Asia, a culturally and geographically distinct region, encompasses around 11 countries (Bangladesh, Bhutan, Democratic People's Republic of Korea, India, Indonesia, Maldives, Myanmar, Nepal, Sri Lanka, Thailand, and Timor-Leste) in the low- to middle-income bracket, constituting a quarter of the global population. More than 13% of the population has a psychiatric morbidity, with one-third of all suicides in the world concentrated in this region. People living within this geographically distinct region are struggling not just with communicable and noncommunicable diseases but with natural calamities, high population burden, falling incomes, and poor access to healthcare facilities with even more sparse mental healthcare establishments (Arafat & Kar, 2024).

India is the most populous country in the world, and this region now, with its immense population burden, has high rates of crime, which leads to overcrowding in prisons (National Crime Records Bureau, 2023). As per the report, Indian prisons are far exceeding their capacity, housing 573,220 inmates with a capacity of only 436,266 inmates. Most South Asian countries rely on incarceration (carceral culture) as the main solution to social problems. The criminal justice system is outdated and focused on punitive measures rather than reformation and rehabilitation. The change to a reformative system of correctional facilities is slowly being realized, and this became more evident in the aftermath of the COVID-19 pandemic, which forced governments to evacuate all correctional facilities, which, as a result of overcrowding, had become hotbeds for the spread of the infection. As a consequence, various governments and countries have had to rethink the rules governing incarceration, especially for petty crimes and unnecessary delays in obtaining bail, particularly for mentally ill prisoners charged with low-level misdemeanors (Basu, 2023).

Other South Asian countries, like Bangladesh, Indonesia, Nepal, and Sri Lanka, also suffer from a similar gestalt of issues as in India, ranging from high psychiatric disease morbidity to overcrowding and poor access to healthcare. Bangladesh's prisons are overburdened to twice their capacity, while Nepal's operate at over 150% capacity (Arafat & Kar, 2024). Indonesian prison health15000care is also grappling with harsh prison environments, along with an increasing crime and disease burden (Arafat & Kar, 2024). Pakistan's prisons are even more overcrowded, housing three times the number of inmates they were designed for, with many awaiting trial (Basu, 2023). In Sri Lanka, the situation is even more challenging in the aftermath of the recent civil unrest. Further, women in prisons in this region experience additional vulnerabilities, including stigma, intrusive surveillance, and gender-based violence. Overall, violence is a major concern in prisons across the South Asia region (Basu, 2023). Consensus has been established through systematic reviews and meta-analyses of mental illness in prisoners in low- to middle-income countries, which have found much higher rates of psychiatric disorders in the prison population as compared to the general population (Baranyi et al., 2019; Fazel & Seewald, 2012; Fazel & Danesh, 2002).

Prison is inherently a bleak environment that can have a detrimental effect on the well-being of people living and working within its confines. Prisons are generally considered unhealthy places (Viggiani, 2007). So, managing mental health issues such as stress and anxiety in a jail setting presents unique challenges due to the restricted environment and the nature of incarceration. If statistics from India are considered, then, as per the current data, at least 450,000 undertrial prisoners are lodged in various prisons in India, constituting around 75.8% of the total prison population in the region, meaning a significant majority of prisoners in India are awaiting trial and are an at-risk population for developing mental health issues (National Crime Records Bureau, 2023).

The intersection of mental illness and incarceration is a complex one with far-reaching consequences. The prevalence of mental health problems in prisons has been three to five times higher than in the general population (Fazel & Danesh, 2002). Among prisoners, the common mental health problems include anxiety, depression, suicide, and sleep and substance use disorders (Brinded et al., 2001). Studies report that environmental factors in prison include overcrowding, poor hygiene, abuse, poor quality of food, lack of activity, drug use, and forced solitude. Individual factors such as guilt over committing the crime, shame, and a sense of poor social support can all worsen prisoners' mental health (Møller et al., 2007). Undetected and undertreated mental health and substance use disorders among prisoners are a clear and present public health problem (Uche & Princewill, 2015). Most studies report poor access to treatment for these issues in prisons, leading to a complex conundrum of problems (Fazel & Danesh, 2002).

The South Asian region is specifically grappling with an overburdened judicial and prison system, leading to prisoners experiencing social isolation due to prolonged confinement, separating them from their communities, families, and friends. Placements in unfamiliar environments foster loneliness, despair, and hopelessness. Poor conditions in prisons, including unsanitary environments and inadequate infrastructure for both mental and physical healthcare, further exacerbate these issues. Adapting to these conditions and the resulting frustration and deprivation can lead to various psychological disorders, including PTSD and related issues like decreased self-confidence and self-esteem (Jain & Team SACJ, 2021).

Mental health rehabilitation encompasses all measures to help disabled individuals develop the emotional, social, and intellectual skills needed to live, learn, and work in the community with the least amount of professional support (Rössler, 2006). This task can be even more daunting for imprisoned individuals after their release, as most of their societal ties have been fractured. The term "After-Care" refers to the programs and services organized for the rehabilitation of inmates from correctional institutions. After-care has two connotations. In its narrow sense, it is somewhat like probation, i.e., the released person is placed under the care of a probation officer who performs the role of a social worker. In its wider sense, after-care implies all efforts to enable the prisoner to overcome all the various social, economic, and psychological problems faced after release (Banamali, 2019).

While the West is implementing aftercare interventions for prisoners, South Asian countries are still struggling to assess and intervene to reduce mental health morbidity in persons while they are in prison. Although the importance of aftercare interventions is well recognized in principle and in Law, there is a huge gap in the services that are actually available in most South Asian countries. This chasm in aftercare services is mostly bridged by non-governmental organizations rather than taken up by the national health or legal systems of the respective countries (Singh & Bajpai, 2016). Especially among women, the mental health challenges they face escalate further after release from prison as compared to men. Living with a psychiatric diagnosis, psychological trauma suffered during the course of imprisonment, substance use disorders, limited access to mental health medications and services, challenges of motherhood, lack of support systems, unmet basic needs, and criminalized behaviors all contribute to hindrances in the rehabilitation and restoration of the mentally ill persons back into the community (Stanton et al., 2016).

It is essential to bridge this gap in services else to stop a never-ending chain of crime and recidivism while people grapple with their mental health issues. With a lack of systematic research in this area, this chapter aims to understand the existing conditions of mental health and rehabilitation in prison setups across the South Asian region.

2 From Prison to Progress

2.1 Incarceration and Mental Health in South Asian Countries

Prisoners, based on their psychological distress trajectories, fall into five categories: consistently low, consistently moderate, increasing, decreasing, and consistently high distress. Factors like mood disorders, anxiety, self-harm, and substance abuse are linked to higher levels of distress. Women are more likely to experience fluctuating distress levels, while men are at a higher risk of consistently high distress. Only a quarter of those with severe distress access mental health services post-release, often with limited contact time (Thomas et al., 2016). Interestingly, severe mental health disorders such as schizophrenia and depression, even though in higher proportion in the general population in low- to middle-income countries, are less often reported in the prison population. Higher cases of alcohol and substance use disorders are found in the prison population at intake than in the general population but end up having a better prognosis during the course of imprisonment as a natural consequence of the incarceration process itself (Baranyi et al., 2019).

Self-harm and suicidal behaviors are one of the foremost causes of morbidity in the prison population. The rates are as high as 5–6% in men and up to 20–24% in women, as compared to 1% in the general population (Favril et al., 2020). Further, there is an increased risk of violence and victimization in prison settings. Male prisoners with mental disorders are more likely to experience sexual victimization (1 in

12 vs. 1 in 33 without a disorder), with even higher rates for women (23% vs. 8% without a disorder) (Fazel et al., 2016).

Indian prisons are overcrowded, with an occupancy rate exceeding 130%. While there are some dedicated facilities for women and transgender individuals, the majority of prisoners are male. Uttar Pradesh, Bihar, and Madhya Pradesh have the highest number of inmates. Mental health services within Indian prisons are grossly inadequate. The scarcity of mental health professionals, with only one per 16,789 inmates, highlights the urgent need for increased support. Poor prison conditions and high rates of unnatural deaths, including suicide and homicide, further exacerbate the mental health crisis among inmates. Suicide is a major concern in Indian prisons, with rates doubling over the past two decades. Substance use disorders and severe mental illnesses like schizophrenia are prevalent among inmates. Factors like coping difficulties, interpersonal issues, and substance use contribute to these problems.(Arafat et al., 2024).

Tihar Prison, the largest prison facility in India, spanning 400 acres, offers the best of facilities for prisoners, ensuring that their mental health needs are met. Courts regularly seek mental health assessments, wherein indicated, including suitable rehabilitation after the end of the jail term. Prisoners are engaged in weaving, bakeries, cooking oil production, carpentry, and similar semi-skilled tasks, with the hope of being able to utilize them after release from prison. It has famously come to be called *TJ's*, which has brought about a change in the perception of prison setups and reduced the stigma of being in prison. This public-private partnership has brought about significant change over the years in the overall mental health and well-being of prisoners but has not been systematically researched as an aftercare model (https://tiharprisons.delhi.gov.in/).

The Mental Healthcare Act of 2017 offers a ray of hope in India; the Law has been a major advancement towards the care of mentally ill persons, being patient-centric and ensuring the protection of rights during the period of hospitalization. Section 103, MHA, 2017, specifically deals with the transfer of mentally ill prisoners to mental health facilities for treatment. While the Act guarantees the right of a person with mental illness to live within the community, which is the first step towards planning and developing aftercare and rehabilitation facilities, it does not specifically address the issue for prisoners (Mental Health Care Act, 2017).

As in India, Bangladesh too, with a population of approximately 170 million, has a legal and judicial system rooted in British colonial rule. While several laws, including the Mental Health Act, address prison mental health, the country lacks adequate resources and infrastructure (Ahmed et al., 2024).

Limited mental health services are provided by NGOs, primarily focusing on substance abuse and stress management. Prisoners with suspected mental illness are often sent to nearby hospitals, where they receive free medication and outpatient care. However, a comprehensive system for identifying, assessing, and treating mental disorders within prisons needs attention, especially following the recent civil unrest. Several studies have examined mental health among referred prisoners in Bangladesh, revealing high prevalence rates of psychiatric disorders, often exceeding 90%. Psychotic disorders and depression are common diagnoses. However, studies are limited in scope, and more research is needed to represent the broader prison population (Arafat et al., 2024).

Mental health systems in prisons in Sri Lanka, Indonesia, and Nepal are not far behind and struggle with similar issues of overcrowding and overburdened judicial and police systems, making the treatment and aftercare of mentally ill persons in prisons difficult and strained.

In contrast to the West, most South Asian countries have very limited research documenting mental health issues among prisoners and in aftercare, leading to a huge treatment gap and unmet mental health needs. Concerted action in the near future may perhaps help prevent this from becoming an emerging public health emergency. There is a notable absence of comprehensive, nationwide prison mental health assessments, with growing concerns related to suicide in prison setups. The key challenges include a lack of awareness, inadequate collaboration, and a dearth of formal mental health services. Addressing these issues requires increased recognition of the importance of prison mental health, enhanced training for professionals, and the establishment of a comprehensive system for identifying, assessing, and treating mental disorders within prisons (Arafat et al., 2024; Baranyi et al., 2019).

2.2 The Importance of Aftercare and Rehabilitation

The period immediately following a former prisoner's release is often one of the most difficult times in their life. Imprisonment disrupts the social fabric of the individual. The longer the individual has been incarcerated, the more challenging the process of reintegration becomes. The repetitive nature of prison life may leave them unprepared to handle the complexities of living in freedom. Relationships with family and friends get broken, finances get exhausted, and the stigma of having been imprisoned often lingers, making it difficult to secure employment and pursue personal growth. Many struggle with self-confidence and independence, similar to the recovery process after a serious injury. For successful reintegration, they often require strong support systems and rehabilitation services. The goal of rehabilitation is to facilitate a smooth transition from prison to community life through comprehensive support. This includes providing financial assistance, material resources, and psychological counseling. Additionally, it involves assisting with employment, securing housing, reconnecting with family, and resolving debt issues (Singh & Bajpai, 2016).

Most South Asian countries, including India, currently lack a legal framework to support prisoners after their release, leaving a significant gap in their rehabilitation process. There is a long history of attempts to incorporate aftercare services for all released prisoners in India in the last century, but it has not achieved the momentum it should have, largely due to societal resistance and stigma. However, the exigency to implement the aftercare reforms is well recognized as a means to bring about a change in the system, with ongoing efforts to bridge the gap between the prison and the community through the police, correctional officers, legal aid officials, NGOs, and voluntary agencies (MoHA, GOI, 2016).

Systematic research on the lives of prisoners after release in India and other South Asian countries is very limited and mostly difficult in view of the lack of coordination between various judicial and quasi-judicial organizations. Some studies done on small prisoner sample sizes have been hugely informative about the factors affecting social reintegration in the Indian context. Seven factors, namely, training programs at prisons, visits by family members, availing parole, financial assistance, help from NGOs, the role of probation officers, and duration of stay in prison, affect the overall social re-integration of the prisoner back into society. Upon adequate social reintegration, at least four factors, namely, economic independence/stability of income, good relationship with family, good relationship with the community, and membership in informal groups, are reflective of the success of the process of social reintegration. Of these, of utmost importance are the healthy relationships with the family and community, which the prisoner, after release, can establish, and which determine a successful social reintegration (Santhosh & Mathew, 2021).

Vocational training, which is provided by most prison setups in an archaic and rudimentary fashion, has not been found to be an effective resource that the prisoners can use after their release in the community (Varghese & Raghavan, 2019). Given the agricultural background of most South Asian countries, prisoners from rural backgrounds are better accepted and successfully reintegrated back into society than other male counterparts from urban backgrounds; hence, the aftercare planning needs to begin at inception into the prison setup and be individualized to the needs and strengths of the person (Santosh, 2019).

Aftercare rehabilitation is the statutory responsibility of the Department of Prisons and Correctional Services. From the initial stages of incarceration, prison officers assist inmates in planning their rehabilitation and provide guidance and counseling services. This includes facilitating legal assistance and legal aid, maintaining family ties, and fostering community acceptance. Police officers, especially at the grassroots level, receive training to support released prisoners during their reintegration into society. State-level teams of trained officers are appointed to evaluate, monitor, and coordinate rehabilitation activities. These officers work closely with voluntary organizations specializing in aftercare services. There is a felt need for an increased number of aftercare institutions with well-equipped infrastructure and technical resources to fulfill responsibilities effectively (Santhosh & Mathew, 2021).

The effectiveness of prison reform is intrinsically linked to the professionalism and motivation of prison personnel. Selecting officers based on their humane outlook, integrity, and respect for prisoners is essential. Offering attractive remuneration can help recruit and retain qualified individuals for these roles. Moreover, penal policymakers and judges must shift focus from punitive measures to reformation and rehabilitation. Alternatives to imprisonment, such as probation, fines, and community corrections, need to be prioritized to reduce the prison population and facilitate smoother reintegration of former prisoners into society. However, in spite of the efforts in the right direction, there appears to be a disconnect between the prison systems and the community, with a lack of adequate research in the area of aftercare rehabilitation, especially for mentally ill persons after completion of their prison tenure (Ahmed, 2012).

At least in juvenile facilities, aftercare mental health rehabilitation is well documented in law in India and followed in principle as per provisions of section 44 of the Act (Juvenile Justice Care and Protection of Children Act, 2016). This is primarily done through various NGOs working in the field of mental health rehabilitation after the end of the jail term. Unlike aftercare facilities for adults, there is coordination between various child and adolescent-centric services in rehabilitating the juvenile in conflict with the law.

Given the complexities and the social and economic context of the Indian and other South Asian countries, comprehensive measures need to be taken, highlighting the need for a multi-stakeholder approach to ensure a humane and effective rehabilitation process for released prisoners, fostering the reintegration of mentally ill persons into the community and reducing recidivism in crime.

2.3 Mental Illness and Recidivism: Prevalence, Predictors, and Contributing Factors

Recidivism, a key concept in criminal justice, describes the tendency of individuals to re-engage in criminal behavior, typically after experiencing sanctions or interventions for prior offenses. Recidivism is frequently measured by criminal acts leading to rearrest, reconviction, or re-incarceration (with or without a new sentence) within a defined period after release (e.g., three years). The tendency to fall back into crime has myriad social, economic, and institutional factors. Individuals with a history of having a troubled childhood, poor educational backgrounds, poor social and economic backgrounds, and engagement in substance use have a very high rate of relapse into committing crime. Substance abuse happens to be the most important personal factor in promoting recidivism in crime. At the Institutional level, failure of the organization to provide institutional rehabilitation and support during imprisonment is an important reason for recidivism in most countries in the Indian subcontinent (Jayanti, 2023).

In India, the conviction rate is 57%, while the case pendency rates have increased to 91.2 percent with a recidivism rate of around 5–8%. The rate of recidivism in India, as compared to the West, has been found to be low not because of any high-grade institutional support, which is protective in preventing relapse, but because of low conviction rates. As such, there is a dearth of literature on recidivism rates in undertrials, and hence, no true measures are available (Jayanti, 2023).

A significant portion of incarcerated individuals have mental health diagnoses. Incarcerated individuals with mental health diagnoses have higher recidivism rates. One study found that 75% of those with diagnoses had prior arrests. Another showed a 9% greater chance of rearrest after one year of release, increasing to 15% after five years. Those with severe diagnoses have a 4% higher likelihood of rearrest compared to those with milder conditions (Sahlin, 2018). Treating mental illness in incarcerated individuals remains crucial due to its high prevalence, legal mandates, and potential to reduce disciplinary issues, enhance rehabilitation, and improve post-release outcomes beyond just recidivism(Cohen et al., 2024).

Studies examining recidivism risk factors in "mentally disordered offenders" found substance abuse, pro-criminal attitudes, and criminal personality to be strong predictors, while clinical variables had minimal impact. One study showed parolees with severe personality disorder (SPD) had higher risk levels in employment/education, family/marriage, pro-criminal attitudes, and antisocial personality. Notably, substance abuse and antisocial companions were particularly strong predictors of recidivism for those with SPD. These findings indicate that while system-involved individuals with mental disorders share risk factors with others, they often exhibit higher levels of these factors and are especially vulnerable due to substance abuse and negative peer influences (Andrews & Bonta, 2010). Unfortunately, personality disorders are less researched in India (Narayanan & Rao, 2018), and more research is needed in this area to comment on the possibility of specific personality types being predictors of recidivism.

It is of foremost importance to provide continued aftercare services linked with the prison systems, which provide mental health and substance abuse interventions to persons after release from prison. Individual risk assessment, personalized treatment protocols, and tertiary-level social support services through community and NGO services have a protective effect in reducing recidivism in persons released from prisons (Young et al., 2018). Preemptive planning of aftercare services while the person is in prison can offer protection to those at risk of developing first-episode psychosis after release from prison and reduce the risk of recidivism (Chowdhury et al., 2022).

Community programs employ diverse strategies to reduce recidivism among justice-involved individuals with serious mental illness. These "jail diversion" approaches, such as mental health courts, specialized probation/parole, and conditional release programs, often use legal incentives to ensure adherence to required treatments and services rather than simply transferring individuals from the justice system to mental healthcare (Lambert, 2016).

2.4 Interventions for Mentally Ill Prisoners to Improve Outcomes and Strategies for Post-Incarceration Reintegration

In light of the above findings, psychosocial intervention matters for improving mental health outcomes while the person is serving his sentence in prison. The interventions can be focused on symptom management, significant concerns around incarcerated individuals' risk of self-harm, enhanced reintegration in the form of skill development, reducing recidivism, and ultimately improving prison climate with the aim of reducing violence and enhancing staff-inmate relationships. Psychosocial interventions for mental health problems and substance use disorder are interpersonal or informational activities, techniques, or strategies that target biological, behavioral, cognitive, emotional, interpersonal, social, or environmental factors to improve health functioning and well-being (Thekkumkara et al., 2022).

There have been several attempts to investigate the different types of psychosocial interventions for individuals with mental illness in prison setups. A limited number of studies have focused on evaluating psychosocial interventions in prison settings. Most of the interventions were tested in prisoners with substance use disorder alone or in those with dual diagnoses and in high-income countries. Most studies have been conducted in Western countries, and very few studies have been from lower- and middle-income countries, especially India, which has the current prevalence of mental illnesses ranging from 21% to 33% among prisoners, excluding substance use disorders. Substance use disorder among the prisoners ranged from 47.1% to 56.4% (Yoon et al., 2017).

The key components of psychosocial interventions include early identification and assessment of mental health conditions essential for appropriate care, individualized treatment plans tailored to the specific needs of each individual given their unique vulnerabilities, evidence-based therapeutic interventions like cognitive behavioral therapy and motivational interviewing that can address underlying psychological issues, and peer support programs to provide social support and a reduced feeling of isolation. A comprehensive aftercare plan can facilitate a smooth transition upon release and reduce the risk of relapse. It may include ensuring regular follow-ups for mental health concerns, enhanced accessibility of healthcare systems, and collective efforts of stakeholders to reduce stigma and discrimination so that reintegration happens while preserving the dignity of the individual who had served the sentence (Thomas et al., 2016).

A systematic review of 21 Randomized Control Trials (RCTs) conducted in the West showed significant improvement post-intervention in prisoners receiving the motivational intervention, interpersonal therapy, cognitive behavior therapy, positive psychology intervention, music therapy, and acceptance and commitment therapy on primary outcome measures such as symptom severity of depression, anxiety, and substance abuse. Positive effects were observed on secondary outcome measures such as motivation, aggression, follow-up rates, and recidivism. There is a dearth of literature that addresses the effectiveness of various psychological interventions conducted in prison settings for managing mental illnesses and substance use disorders (McIntosh et al., 2021). Such studies are the need of the hour in countries such as India and other South Asian countries in view of the public health impact of mental illness and substance use disorders in prisoners and the lives they lead thereafter.

In another comprehensive systematic review, the randomized controlled trials (RCTs) used non-pharmacological interventions alone or in combination with pharmacological interventions for managing mental illness and SUDs in prison/correctional settings. The review mentioned that the intervention group underwent different therapies such as motivation enhancement therapy (MET), seeking safety program, cognitive behavior therapy (CBT), interpersonal therapy (IPT), acceptance and commitment therapy (ACT), cognitive behavioral suicidal prevention therapy (CBSP), group interpersonal psychotherapy, music therapy, art therapy, group psychological intervention, and mindfulness-based relapse prevention intervention. The average duration of intervention in the studies ranged from 10 min to 120 min, with the frequency of sessions being one per week to six per week over a period of 1 month to 6 months. The follow-up period ranged from 1 month to 12 months. No differences were found between the group and individual therapy or different treatment types, except for cognitive behavioral and mindfulness-based therapies, which had a larger effect size than any other therapy (Yoon et al., 2017). This finding has been consistently reported in the past as well (Lipsey et al., 2007).

Since substance use and mental disorders are mostly present together among incarcerated individuals, therapies can target both conditions or can be used for a specific single condition as well. Before utilizing the more sophisticated models of therapy, which require trained professionals, a low-intensity psychoeducational program can lead to improved insight and understanding of one's mental disorder and is more suited for implementation in correctional facilities (McIntosh et al., 2021).

2.4.1 Cognitive Behavioral Therapy

The mainstay of Cognitive Behavioral Therapy (CBT) is to build cognitive skills and replace distorted cognitions that might be more prevalent in such individuals, for example, rationalizing one's thoughts and actions for the need for self-preservation, displacement of blame, and maladaptive schemas of dominance and entitlement, with noncriminal thought patterns (Forrester et al., 2014).

Cognitive behavioral therapy (CBT), largely considered the gold standard treatment for depression and anxiety, as well as personality disorder, reduces forensic psychiatric symptoms in patients. The therapist facilitates individuals to recognize negative or maladaptive thought patterns and encourages exploring alternative perspectives in order to develop more realistic, balanced thinking patterns. Cognitive skill programs aimed at reducing violence risk and aggressive behavior have proved beneficial in correctional facilities. Such skill programs focus on changing maladaptive behaviors that perpetuate mental health problems and teach problem-solving skills and social skills. These strategies equip individuals with practical tools to manage stress, regulate emotions, and improve interpersonal relationships within and outside the prison. These skills become particularly important when individuals have to transition back into the community (Gold et al., 2014).

Psychological therapies based on CBT or mindfulness approaches can improve mental health outcomes for prisoners when compared with providing no intervention at all. Collaborative working between justice delivery agencies, psychologists, and health professionals needs to be encouraged to provide fruitful avenues for both ex-prisoners' mental and social outcomes (Qiu et al., 2017).

2.4.2 Mindfulness and Meditation

Transcendental Meditation (TM), through simple meditation and yoga, addresses mental health, particularly trauma, especially among female offenders, and plays an important role in dealing with stress and anxiety across all ages. There is a strong need to teach mindfulness techniques to prisoners, which can help them develop awareness of their thoughts and emotions without judgment; this can ultimately reduce their stress and improve their coping mechanism while being incarcerated and as a lifestyle in the aftercare. Along with mindfulness, regular meditation practice can promote emotional regulation and reduce anxiety among prisoners (Bouw et al., 2019).

2.4.3 Motivation Enhancement Therapy

Motivational Enhancement Therapy (MET) is designed to increase motivation for change and help individuals make positive decisions about their substance use and eventually reduce relapse. There is a strong linkage between criminal behavior and the use of substances. Hence, such individuals are subjected to more stigma and discrimination, which further worsens their recovery. Offering empathy, acceptance, and a supportive environment is a prerequisite for MET. It urges individuals to identify long-term goals and values that would drive them once they are reintegrated in the community, and then the therapist helps the individual identify the discrepancy between the substance use behavior and long-term goals (Miller et al., 1994).

This discrepancy can motivate the individual to change. When the individual develops the motivation to change in varying degrees across sessions in therapy, the therapist ensures that self-efficacy is built upon. Once the individual develops a sense of belief in their ability to change, more realistic and achievable goals can be set. The therapist focuses on exploring the ambivalence associated with readiness for change and rolls with resistance by offering empathy and understanding rather than confrontation. A concrete plan for change to achieve recovery goals is made collaboratively with the individual (Miller et al., 1994).

These interventions for substance use disorders reduce craving, the risk associated with substance use, harmful use, and drug-related criminal activity, and improve follow-up rates. Addressing substance use through MET can contribute to lower rates of reoffending. Reducing recidivism can further improve psychosocial well-being and overall quality of life (Thekkumkara et al., 2022). Brief intervention programs have been found to be successful in prison setups for alcohol and drug use and are practical and simple for implementation in prison setups (Owens & McCrady, 2016). Further, interventions delivered by prisoners themselves have also been found to be as effective as those delivered by trained therapists (Forsberg et al., 2011).

For prisoners with opioid dependence, buprenorphine/naloxone treatment effectively aids in community re-entry and reduces post-release hospitalization, mortality, and recidivism in crime among incarcerated individuals with substance addiction. Patient navigation programs help overcome healthcare barriers post-incarceration. Comprehensive treatments addressing substance use and multiple behavioral issues can effectively meet the complex needs of incarcerated individuals and improve aftercare outcomes (Sanjanaa et al., 2024).

2.4.4 Expressive Art Therapies

Expressive Art Therapy (EAT) is a combination of various modalities like visual arts, music, drama, and dance/movement, which can facilitate emotional expression, self-awareness, and healing in prisoners with mental illness. Given the fact that their physical environment is restricted and the possibility of experiencing life in a real social context is limited, such therapies can provide the ground for emotional release and expression. EATs can provide a safe space for individuals to express themselves, especially for those who struggle with verbal communication. Emotional release can reduce stress and anxiety. Self-awareness is enhanced by engaging in creative activities, and individuals can gain insights into their own thoughts, feelings, and behaviors. EATs improve self-esteem and social connection since they can foster social interaction and a sense of belonging. It's a medium to develop healthier ways of coping with stress. Studies on music therapy to engage prisoners with depressive and anxiety disorders and associated problems found that compared with standard care in prison, anxiety and depression in the music therapy group decreased significantly after 20 sessions, and self-esteem improved substantially among the participants (Rowe et al., 2007).

Art-based interventions have also been shown to decrease the levels of anxiety, depression, and anger and increase social interaction and medication compliance among prisoners with schizophrenia (South et al., 2016). However, more research is needed to know of its effectiveness for other populations, such as female prisoners and adolescent delinquents, and investigate different outcomes (e.g., social skills, aggression management, impulse control, empathy) relating to psychosocial well-being, behaviors, and cognitive functions.

2.4.5 Peer-Led Interventions

Most studies have been conducted in higher-income or upper-middle-income countries, and there is an absence of published studies from lower and middle-income countries such as India. There is a poor ratio of dedicated mental health professionals to prisoners in low- middle-income countries. Thus, alternative systems that utilize existing resources need to be explored. One such cost-effective approach could be through training and using peers (prisoners who are ready to engage in voluntary activities) to screen and provide simple problem-solving skills to prisoners with mental health and substance use disorders under the supervision of prison staff, which has been shown to significantly reduce aggression, violence, and substance use in prison (Perry et al., 2021). The models need to be culturally adapted and tested in the prison settings in India and the South Asian region.

3 Prisoner-Vocational and Educational Training Programs

Educational and job training programs are essential for lowering the rate of reoffending and helping former prisoners successfully reenter society, particularly by securing employment. Vocational training improves rehabilitation, fosters creativity, and leads to better outcomes. Occupational therapists who provide intervention have proven effective in improving skills and reducing negative incidents among women with intellectual and developmental disabilities. They need to be included in teams of professionals providing justice services (Sanjanaa et al., 2024).

4 Recent Reformative Directions in Correctional Facilities

The Indian prison system, still largely governed by the outdated 1894 Prisons Act, faces challenges in achieving modern reformative goals. While modern systems prioritize offender reformation and reintegration, as advocated by Mahatma Gandhi, India's progress has been slow despite numerous reform recommendations and international standards. Over the past decade, India has developed rehabilitation policies, including a significant ₹4000 crore investment in 2016 to transform prisons into reformation centers. The Delhi Prison Rules (2018) promote modernized infrastructure and improved conditions, with plans for 200 new prisons, prioritizing reintegration, legal aid, research, and NGO support. A key component of these reforms is prisoner education, encompassing schooling programs, vocational training, and work opportunities designed to reduce recidivism. Jail manuals mandate schooling with trained staff and adequate resources, even allowing some prisoners to attend external schools. State advisory groups oversee prisoner needs and provide skills training for future livelihood opportunities. Crucially, effective rehabilitation hinges on post-release care, including aftercare and follow-up services that provide ex-convicts with essential support in finding employment and housing, facilitating their successful reintegration into society (Dubey & Agarwal, 2021).

Norway, in the European Union, perhaps, has set the benchmark in terms of prison management and mental health recuperation. Norway's highly regarded prison system offers a compelling model for reducing recidivism and upholding human rights. In contrast to punitive models, Norway prioritizes inmate well-being through smaller, community-based facilities resembling comfortable homes rather than large, impersonal prisons common in South Asia and elsewhere. Even for serious offenses, maximum sentences are relatively short (generally under 21 years, extendable to 30), with most sentences being less than a year. Inmates engage in skill-building activities and maintain strong social connections through family visits and conjugal rights, facilitating their reintegration into society. These reforms have resulted in a remarkably low recidivism rate of approximately 25% and a decrease in pre-existing mental health issues. However, the substantial cost (up to $100,000 per prisoner) poses a challenge even for Western nations. Adopting these reforms, or even some of the individual components, to the context of South Asian countries would require a significant and systematic overhaul of the existing prison systems and laws (Jayanti, 2023).

5 Future Directions

Protecting prisoners' mental health is crucial throughout their sentences and trials. Governments and judicial organizations must recognize the need for legal reforms and ensure their effective implementation to promote inclusivity and appropriate treatment for those with mental health conditions. Imprisonment can leave individuals not only without job skills but also with lasting physical and mental health problems that hinder their future employability. Therefore, the state must prioritize improvements that benefit prisoners struggling with mental health (Jain & Team SACJ, 2021).

- Increased Research and Data Collection: Systematic research on the specific mental health needs of prisoners in South Asia is crucial. This includes collecting reliable data on prevalence rates of different disorders, evaluating the effectiveness of culturally adapted interventions, and tracking long-term outcomes of rehabilitation programs. More research is needed on the effectiveness of existing programs like the Tihar Jail model and rigorous evaluation of their impact.
- Policy Reform and Implementation: Governments must prioritize policy reforms that promote rehabilitation and mental healthcare within prisons. This includes increasing funding for mental health services, improving prison conditions, and implementing alternatives to incarceration for non-violent offenders. Crucially, existing legal frameworks for mental healthcare within prisons need effective implementation and enforcement.
- Capacity Building and Training: Addressing the severe shortage of mental health professionals in prisons requires significant capacity building. This involves training prison staff in basic mental health awareness and providing specialized training for mental health professionals working in correctional settings. Teleconsultation and collaborations with external mental health facilities can also help bridge the gap.

- Focus on Aftercare and Reintegration: Comprehensive aftercare programs are essential for successful reintegration of former prisoners with mental health issues. These programs should provide ongoing mental health support and assistance with housing and employment and facilitate connections with community-based resources. Research into effective aftercare models and their long-term impact on recidivism is also crucial.
- Addressing Stigma and Discrimination: Reducing the stigma associated with mental illness and incarceration is vital for improving access to care and promoting successful reintegration. Public awareness campaigns and community-based programs can play a key role in challenging negative stereotypes and fostering a more supportive environment for former prisoners.
- Regional Collaboration and Knowledge Sharing: Sharing best practices and research findings across South Asian countries can accelerate progress in addressing the mental health crisis in prisons. Regional collaborations can also facilitate the development of culturally relevant interventions and policies.

By fortifying the gains achieved so far and continuing efforts to integrate mental health and judicial services, South Asian nations can move towards a more humane and effective approach to aftercare, one that prioritizes the mental health and well-being of prisoners and promotes their successful reintegration into society.

6 Conclusion

The state of mental health within South Asian prisons presents a significant and multifaceted crisis. Overcrowding, inadequate resources, outdated punitive systems, and a lack of trained mental health professionals contribute to a high prevalence of mental health disorders among inmates, exceeding rates in the general population. This situation is further exacerbated by poor prison conditions, social isolation, and the inherent stresses of incarceration. While legal frameworks for mental healthcare exist in some countries, their implementation is often lacking. Studies consistently demonstrate the effectiveness of psychosocial interventions like CBT, DBT, and mindfulness-based therapies in improving mental health outcomes and reducing recidivism.

These interventions are underutilized in the region. Furthermore, the transition from prison to the community is particularly challenging for individuals with mental health issues, highlighting the critical need for comprehensive aftercare programs and support systems. Addressing this crisis requires a multi-pronged approach involving increased investment in mental health services, improved prison conditions, greater collaboration between justice and health professionals, and a shift towards reformative and rehabilitative practices. Prioritizing the mental health of prisoners is not only a matter of human rights but also a crucial step toward reducing recidivism and promoting successful reintegration into society.

References

Ahmed, M. R. (2012). Criminal justice system aftercare and rehabilitation of released prisoners, an Indian perspective. *Journal of the National Human Rights Commission India, 11*, 1–10. Retrieved January 26, 2025, from https://nhrc.nic.in/sites/default/files/nhrc_journal_2012.pdf

Ahmed, A., Bose, P. K., & Arafat, S. Y. (2024). Forensic psychiatry in Bangladesh. In *Mental health in Bangladesh: From bench to community* (pp. 167–183). Springer Nature Singapore.

Andrews, D. A., & Bonta, J. (2010). Rehabilitating criminal justice policy and practice. *Psychology, Public Policy and Law, 16*(1), 39–55. https://doi.org/10.1037/a0018362

Arafat, S. M. Y., & Kar, S. K. (2024). Epidemiology of psychiatric disorders and overview of access to mental health care in South Asia. In S. M. Y. Arafat & S. K. Kar (Eds.), *Access to mental health care in South Asia*. Springer. https://doi.org/10.1007/978-981-99-9153-2_1

Arafat, S. M. Y., Kar, S. K., Abhayanayake, C., Sharma, P., & Marthoenis, M. (2024). Prison mental health in South-East Asia: A narrative review. *Brain and Behavior, 14*(8), e70004. https://doi.org/10.1002/brb3.70004

Banamali B, (2019). *Rehabilitation of released prisoners in India through after-care programmes and services: An analysis*. https://thelawbrigade.com/wp-content/uploads/2019/05/Banamali-1.pdf

Baranyi, G., et al. (2019). Severe mental illness and substance use disorders in prisoners in low-income and middle-income countries: A systematic review and meta-analysis of prevalence studies. *The Lancet Global Health, 7*(4), e461–e471.

Basu, D. K., (2023). *South Asia's overcrowded prisons: Lock-up culture needs to give way to reformation and empathy*. South Asia Monitor. Retrieved December 1, 2024, from https://www.southasiamonitor.org/spotlight/south-asias-overcrowded-prisons-lock-culture-needs-give-way-reformation-and-empathy

Bouw, N., Huijbregts, S. C. J., Scholte, E., & Swaab, H. (2019). Mindfulness-based stress reduction in prison: Experiences of inmates, instructors, and prison staff. *International Journal of Offender Therapy and Comparative Criminology, 63*(15–16), 2550–2571. https://doi.org/10.1177/0306624X19856232

Brinded, P. M. J., Simpson, A. I. F., Laidlaw, T. M., Fairley, N., & Malcolm, F. (2001). Prevalence of psychiatric disorders in New Zealand prisons: A national study. *Australian & New Zealand Journal of Psychiatry, 35*(2), 166–173. https://doi.org/10.1046/j.1440-1614.2001.00885.x

Chowdhury, N. Z., Wand, H., Albalawi, O., Adily, A., Kariminia, A., et al. (2022). Mental health service contact following release from prison or hospital discharge in those with psychosis. *Frontiers in Psychiatry, 13*, 1034917. https://doi.org/10.3389/fpsyt.2022.1034917

Cohen, T. R., Fronk, G. E., Kiehl, K. A., Curtin, J. J., & Koenigs, M. (2024). Clarifying the relationship between mental illness and recidivism using machine learning: A retrospective study. *PLoS One, 19*(2), e0297448. https://doi.org/10.1371/journal.pone.0297448

Dubey, D., & Agarwal, V. (2021). Overview of correctional reform in India: A "different" approach to offender rehabilitation. In *Global perspectives on reforming the criminal justice system* (pp. 162–181). IGI Global.

Favril, L., Yu, R., Hawton, K., & Fazel, S. (2020). Risk factors for self-harm in prison: A systematic review and meta-analysis. *Lancet Psychiatry, 7*(8), 682–691. https://doi.org/10.1016/S2215-0366(20)30190-5

Fazel, S., & Danesh, J. (2002). Serious mental disorder in 23,000 prisoners: A systematic review of 62 surveys. *The Lancet, 359*(9306), 545–550. https://doi.org/10.1016/S0140-6736(02)07740-1

Fazel, S., & Seewald, K. (2012). Severe mental illness in 33,588 prisoners worldwide: Systematic review and meta-regression analysis. *The British Journal of Psychiatry, 200*(5), 364–373. https://doi.org/10.1192/bjp.bp.111.096370

Fazel, S., Hayes, A. J., Bartellas, K., Clerici, M., & Trestman, R. (2016). The mental health of prisoners: A review of prevalence, adverse outcomes, and interventions. *The Lancet Psychiatry, 3*(9), 871–881. https://doi.org/10.1016/S2215-0366(16)30142-0

Forrester, A., MacLennan, F., Slade, K., Brown, P., & Exworthy, T. (2014). Improving access to psychological therapies in prisons. *Criminal Behaviour and Mental Health, 24*, 163.

Forsberg, L. G., Ernst, D., Sundqvist, K., & Farbring, C. A. (2011). Motivational interviewing delivered by existing prison staff: A randomized controlled study of effectiveness on substance use after release. *Substance Use & Misuse, 46*, 1477–1485. https://doi.org/10.3109/10826084.2011.591880

Gold, C., Assmus, J., Hjørnevik, K., Qvale, L. G., Brown, F. K., et al. (2014). Music therapy for prisoners: Pilot randomised controlled trial and implications for evaluating psychosocial interventions. *International Journal of Offender Therapy and Comparative Criminology, 58*(12), 1520–1539. https://doi.org/10.1177/0306624X13498693

Government of National Capital Territory of Delhi. (2018). The Delhi Prison Rules, 2018, F.9/87/2018/HG/5980, October 1, 2018, Delhi Gazette (Extraordinary).

Jain, M., & Team SACJ. (2021, January 31). *Mental health of prisoners in India: An analysis*. The Society for Advancement of Criminal Justice. https://www.nujssacj.com/post/mental-health-of-prisoners-in-india-an-analysis

Jayanti, M. (2023). Recidivism in India: An analytical study. *International Journal of Law Management and Humanities*. Retrieved February 16, 2025, from https://www.ijlmh.com/wp-content/uploads/Recidivism-in-India-An-Analytical-Study.pdf

Juvenile Justice (Care and Protection of Children) Act, 2015, Act No. 2 of 2016, India code. https://www.indiacode.nic.in/handle/123456789/2148.

Lambert, J. S. (2016). Preventing criminal recidivism through mental health and criminal justice collaboration. *Psychiatric Services, 67*(11), 1206–1212. https://doi.org/10.1176/appi.ps.201500384

Lipsey, M. W., Landenberger, N. A., & Wilson, S. J. (2007). Effects of cognitive-behavioral programs for criminal offenders. *Campbell Systematic Reviews, 9*(6), 1–27.

McIntosh, L. G., Janes, S., O'Rourke, S., & Thomson, L. D. G. (2021). Effectiveness of psychological and psychosocial interventions for forensic mental health inpatients: A meta-analysis. *Aggression and Violent Behavior, 58*, 101551. https://doi.org/10.1016/j.avb.2021.101551

Mental Health Care Act, 2017, Act No. 10 of 2017, India code. https://www.indiacode.nic.in/handle/123456789/2249.

Miller, W. R., Zweben, A., DiClemente, C. C., & Rychtarik, R. G. (1994). *Motivational enhancement therapy manual: A clinical research guide for therapists treating individuals with alcohol abuse and dependence (NIH Publication No. 94-3723)*. National Institute on Alcohol Abuse and Alcoholism.

Ministry of Home Affairs (MoHA), Government of India (GOI), Model Prison Manual 2016. https://www.mha.gov.in/sites/default/files/2024-12/PrisonManualA2016_20122024

Møller, L., Stöver, H., Jürgens, R., Gatherer, A., & Nikogosian, H. (2007). *Health in prisons: A WHO guide to the essentials in prison health (EUR/07/5063925)*. World Health Organization, Regional Office for Europe. https://iris.who.int/handle/10665/107829

Narayanan, G., & Rao, K. (2018). Personality disorders in the Indian culture: Reconsidering self-perceptions, traditional society and values. *Psychological Studies, 63*(1), 32–41. https://doi.org/10.1007/s12646-017-0437-3

National Crime Records Bureau. (2023). *Prison statistics India 2022*. National Crime Records Bureau. https://ncrb.gov.in/uploads/nationalcrimerecordsbureau/custom/psiyearwise2022/1701613297PSI2022ason01122023.pdf

Owens, M. D., & McCrady, B. S. (2016). A pilot study of a brief motivational intervention for incarcerated drinkers. *Journal of Substance Use and Addiction Treatment, 68*, 1–10. https://doi.org/10.1016/j.jsat.2016.05.005

Perry, A. E., Waterman, M. G., Dale, V., Moore, K., & House, A. (2021). The effect of a peer-led problem-support mentor intervention on self-harm and violence in prison: An interrupted time series analysis using routinely collected prison data. *EClinicalMedicine, 32*, 100702. https://doi.org/10.1016/j.eclinm.2020.100702

Qiu, H. Z., Ye, Z. J., Liang, M. Z., Huang, Y. Q., Liu, W., et al. (2017). Effect of an art brut therapy program called go beyond the schizophrenia (GBTS) on prison inmates with schizophrenia in mainland China-a randomized, longitudinal, and controlled trial. *Clinical Psychology & Psychotherapy, 24*(5), 1069–1078. https://doi.org/10.1002/cpp.2069

Rössler, W. (2006). Psychiatric rehabilitation today: An overview. *World Psychiatry, 5*(3), 151–157.

Rowe, M., Bellamy, C., Baranoski, M., et al. (2007). A peer-support, group intervention to reduce substance use and criminality among persons with severe mental illness. *Psychiatric Services, 58*(7), 955–961.

Sahlin, J. (2018). *The prison problem: Recidivism rates and mental health*. GoodTherapy.org Therapy Blog. https://www.goodtherapy.org/blog/prison-problem-recidivism-rates-mentalhealth-0520187

Sanjanaa, G. A., Chandran, Y., & Krishna, N. S. (2024). Community reintegration for prison inmates through multimodal service delivery approach: A systematic review. *International Journal of Multidisciplinary Research & Reviews, 3*, 129–141. https://doi.org/10.56815/IJMRR.V3.I1.2024/129-141

Santhosh, R., & Mathew, E. (2021). Social reintegration of released prisoners: An empirical analysis from two Indian states. *International Annals of Criminology, 59*(2), 200–222. https://doi.org/10.1017/cri.2021.18

Singh, R., & Bajpai, G. S. (2016). *After-care and rehabilitation of released prisoners*. Human Rights and Criminal Justice, Ministry of Human Resource and Development, GOI. Retrieved February 13, 2025, from https://epgp.inflibnet.ac.in/epgpdata/uploads/epgp_content/S001608/P001812/M027785/ET/1521116258et.pdf

South, J., Woodall, J., Kinsella, K., & Bagnall, A. M. (2016). A qualitative synthesis of the positive and negative impacts related to delivery of peer-based health interventions in prison settings. *BMC Health Services Research, 16*(1), 525. https://doi.org/10.1186/s12913-016-1753-3

Stanton, A. E., Kako, P., & Sawin, K. J. (2016). Mental health issues of women after release from jail and prison: A systematic review. *Issues in Mental Health Nursing, 37*(5), 299–331. https://doi.org/10.3109/01612840.2016.1154629

Thekkumkara, S. N., Jagannathan, A., Muliyala, K. P., & Murthy, P. (2022). Psychosocial interventions for prisoners with mental and substance use disorders: A systematic review. *Indian Journal of Psychological Medicine, 44*(3), 211–217. https://doi.org/10.1177/02537176211061655

Thomas, E. G., Spittal, M. J., Heffernan, E. B., Taxman, F. S., Alati, R., et al. (2016). Trajectories of psychological distress after prison release: Implications for mental health service need in ex-prisoners. *Psychological Medicine, 46*(3), 611–621. https://doi.org/10.1017/S0033291715002123

Uche, N., & Princewill, S. (2015). Clinical factors as predictors of depression in a Nigerian prison population. *J Psychiatry, 19*(1), 1–6.

Varghese, J., & Raghavan, V. (2019). Restoration of released prisoners to society: Issues, challenges and further ways; insights from Kerala, India. *International Annals of Criminology, 57*(1–2), 61–74. https://doi.org/10.1017/cri.2020.5

Viggiani, D. N. (2007). *Unhealthy prisons: Exploring structural determinants of prison health*. Sociology of Health & Illness. Retrieved January 25, 2025, from https://onlinelibrary.wiley.com/doi/10.1111/j.1467-9566.2007.00474.x

Yoon, I. A., Slade, K., & Fazel, S. (2017). Outcomes of psychological therapies for prisoners with mental health problems: A systematic review and meta-analysis. *Journal of Consulting and Clinical Psychology, 85*(8), 783–802. https://doi.org/10.1037/ccp0000214

Young, J. T., Heffernan, E., Borschmann, R., Ogloff, J. R. P., Spittal, M. J., et al. (2018). Dual diagnosis of mental illness and substance use disorder and injury in adults recently released from prison: A prospective cohort study. *Lancet Public Health, 3*(5), e237–e248. https://doi.org/10.1016/S2468-2667(18)30052-5

Chapter 9
Suicide: A Forensic Psychiatry Perspective from South Asia

Natarajan Varadharajan, Sandesh Venu, Sabaresh Pandiyan, Gokul Raj, and Vikas Menon

Abstract Suicide represents a significant public health crisis and a complex forensic issue within the diverse sociocultural and legal contexts of South Asia. This chapter explores the prevalence of suicide in correctional facilities, as well as the increased vulnerabilities faced by juveniles and women. It highlights the importance of psychological autopsies in identifying contributing factors and informing policy, while also addressing sociocultural phenomena such as suicide pacts and media-induced copycat behaviours. Systemic challenges, including stigmatised mental health discourse, the criminalisation of suicidal behaviours, and insufficient prevention frameworks, shape the landscape of suicide in the region. Although recent efforts towards decriminalisation and improved forensic investigations have emerged, critical gaps persist. This chapter advocates for interdisciplinary strategies that integrate forensic insights with socio-legal considerations, aiming to promote systemic reforms and evidence-based interventions that reduce suicide rates and safeguard vulnerable populations.

Keywords Suicide · Forensic psychiatry · South Asia · Correctional settings · Suicide prevention

N. Varadharajan · G. Raj · V. Menon (✉)
Department of Psychiatry, Jawaharlal Institute of Postgraduate Medical Education and Research (JIPMER), Puducherry, India

S. Venu
Department of Psychiatry, Pondicherry Institute of Medical Sciences (PIMS), Kalapet, Puducherry, India

S. Pandiyan
Department of Psychiatry, Mahatma Gandhi Medical College and Research Institute (MGMCRI), Pillayarkuppam, Puducherry, India

A. Parmar et al. (eds.), *Forensic Psychiatry and Prison Mental Health in South Asia*, South Asian Perspectives in Mental Health and Psychology,
https://doi.org/10.1007/978-981-96-7206-6_9

1 Introduction

Suicide is a pervasive global public health issue, claiming more than 700,000 lives annually and causing profound familial, social, and economic consequences (Bertuccio et al., 2024). This issue is exacerbated in South Asia by socio-economic disparities, cultural stigmas, and legal challenges. Forensic psychiatry offers a unique lens to analyse suicide's complexities in this region, particularly within correctional settings, where suicide rates are alarmingly high (Favril et al., 2022; Mundt et al., 2024).

Juveniles and women are disproportionately affected, with juveniles in Sri Lanka's justice system reporting self-harm rates as high as 43%, and Indian prisons recording suicide rates 11 times higher than the national average (Hettiarachchi et al., 2018; Math et al., 2011). Psychological autopsies, a crucial forensic tool, provide valuable insights into the contributing factors of suicide, guiding both judicial decisions and preventive strategies (Isometsä, 2001; Menon et al., 2020e).

Despite advancements in understanding, significant gaps remain in mental health infrastructure, suicide prevention strategies, and decriminalisation efforts. Low- and middle-income countries (LAMICs) within South Asia face unique challenges, including overburdened health systems, widespread inequities, and a considerable treatment gap for mental health disorders (Arafat & Kar, 2024). Addressing these issues requires interdisciplinary strategies integrating forensic, cultural, and policy-driven perspectives (Mishara & Weisstub, 2016; WHO Policy Brief on the Health Aspects of Decriminalization of Suicide and Suicide Attempts, 2023).

This chapter aims to explore these critical dimensions, focusing on the epidemiological patterns of suicide, the vulnerabilities of specific populations, and the role of forensic psychiatry in mitigating this crisis. By synthesising forensic and socio-legal insights, this chapter seeks to inform more effective, context-specific interventions to reduce suicide and its devastating impact across South Asia.

2 Theories of Suicide from a Forensic Perspective

The risk factors outlined below can be understood through the bio-psychosocial framework (Menon, 2020c) and various suicide theories, including those by Joiner (Van Orden et al., 2010), Durkheim (Taylor, 1982), and the three-step theory (Klonsky et al., 2021) (Table 9.1).

Table 9.1 Theories of suicide and its association with risk factors

Durkheim's theory Suicide is influenced by the social structure of a group or class of individuals, depending on the levels of social integration and regulation	
Egoistic suicide (minimal social integration)	Marginality/Isolation in the society (for family)/prison, uncertainty with parole, and isolation in special cells leading to a lack of belonging and connectedness with society
Altruistic suicide (excessive social integration)	Shame/burden brought on to family
Anomic suicide (minimal social regulation)	Socioeconomic factors (financial loss, unemployment due to imprisonment, loss of loved ones) and those with chronic physical and mental illness
Fatalistic suicide (excessive social regulation)	Prison environments (authoritarian environment, staff insensitivity, hostility and bullying, isolation in special cells, and lack of privacy) can also lead to a sense of entrapment with no hope for a future without suffering.
Interpersonal theory	
Perceived burdensomeness	Socioeconomic factors (financial loss, unemployment due to imprisonment, loss of loved ones) and those with chronic physical and mental illness
Thwarted belongingness	Marginality/isolation in the society (for family)/prison, uncertainty with parole, and isolation in special cells leading to a lack of belonging and connectedness with society
Three-step theory	
Pain, hopelessness, connection, and suicide capability	Marginality/isolation in the society (for family)/prison, uncertainty with parole, and isolation in special cells leading to a feeling of being left alone or entrapment
Bio-psychosocial theory	
Biological	Genetic predisposition to suicidal behaviour which may be mediated by increased prevalence of impulsivity and aggression
Psychological	Prison-environment-related experiences, personality-related factors (intolerance to uncertainty/aggression), isolation, guilt
Social	Socioeconomic factors highlighted earlier

3 Epidemiology of Suicide in Prisons and Correctional Settings

Prison suicide is a major global public health concern, as suicide rates among incarcerated individuals are consistently higher than those in the general population. A meta-analysis across 20 countries estimates the pooled prevalence of suicide attempts during incarceration at 8.6% for men (95% CI: 6.1–11.2) and 12.2% for women (95% CI: 7.1–17.2) (Favril et al., 2022). Additionally, the worldwide incidence of suicide rates in prisons ranges from 24 to 89 per 100,000 person-years for both sexes (22–86 for men and 25–107 for women) (Mundt et al., 2024).

South Asia (SA) is home to approximately 25% of the world's population as of 2021. Nearly 920,000 people in SA were held in prisons, 7.8% of the world prison population as of 2019 (UNODC-KOSTAT, 2022). Prisons in SA are burdened with inadequate infrastructure, severe overcrowding, lack of adequate staff training, and dismal living conditions in many facilities (UNODC, 2024). These harsh conditions may lead to unmet psychological needs among inmates, increasing the risk of mental health crises.

As of 2019, the crude suicide mortality rate in SA was 11.2 per 100,000 population (World Bank, 2019). Although, suicide is widely recognised as a compelling problem in SA, there is a limited focus on suicide within prison settings, where prisoners face unique challenges. This lack of attention persists despite significant media coverage, as demonstrated by the newspaper excerpts below, highlighting how the issue remains underexplored and inadequately addressed in the region (Box 9.1).

Box 9.1 Excerpts from Newspapers Highlighting Suicides in Prisons and Correctional Settings

Suicide major cause of unnatural deaths among prisoners in India: SC committee tells apex court—The Hindu; August 2023

NHRC flags cases of self-harm, suicides in prisons—The Indian express; June 2023

Sri Lankan prisons have seen a disturbing rise in deaths among inmates, nearly 50 from suicide—Asia News; April 2024

Bangladesh's overcrowded prisons see almost one death of inmate daily with 859 deaths, including 12 suicides—New Age; January 2023

Suicide by youth in police custody raises concern over mental health of inmates—The Kathmandu Post; July 2020

3.1 Bangladesh

In Bangladesh, the data on suicides among prisoners primarily comes from news reports. Between January 2020 and September 2022, there were 12 suicides recorded among 859 inmate deaths. In 2020, seven suicides occurred out of 250 deaths, while in 2021, two suicides were reported among 375 deaths (Rashid, 2023). This data likely under-represents the issue, as there is no publicly available information on suicidality among prisoners in Bangladesh.

3.2 India

The data on suicide rates in Indian prisons are inconsistent but indicate a troubling and persistent upward trend over the years. On average, approximately three inmates died daily in Indian prisons, a figure that rose to about five deaths per day in 2014, with at least two of these deaths attributed to suicide (Sawant, 2018). Over the past two decades, there has been a concerning increase in suicide rates among inmates in Indian prisons, which have doubled from 12.12 per 100,000 inmates in 2001 to

24.23 per 100,000 inmates by 2019. This figure is twice the national average, underscoring the significant vulnerability of this population (Gowda et al., 2021). Between January 1, 2015, and December 31, 2019, suicides accounted for 6.24% of all deaths reported in Indian prisons (Gowda et al., 2021). Recent data from 2022 report that suicide accounted for 74.8% of all unnatural deaths among prison inmates in India, making it the leading cause of such deaths (NCRB, 2022). Hanging was the most common method, followed by poisoning and self-inflicted injuries.

The 2011 Bangalore Prison Mental Health Study, the most extensive of its kind in India, screened 5000 prisoners and revealed a suicide rate of 119 per 100,000, which is 11 times higher than the national average (Math et al., 2011). These findings align with global trends, with Nordic and Western European countries reporting rates exceeding 100 suicides per 100,000 prisoners, emphasising the heightened vulnerability to suicide within prison populations across different regions (Fazel et al., 2017).

3.3 *Nepal*

Suicidal behaviours among prisoners in Nepal vary significantly across studies. Suicide attempts during incarceration were reported to range from 0.9% (Jhumka Regional Prison, the largest prison in eastern Nepal) to 7.27% in Gandaki Province (Shrestha et al., 2017). Between 2.3% and 4.3% of prisoners reported having suicidal ideations (Shrestha et al., 2017; Mahato et al., 2023). Notably, Bhusal et al. (2024) found that prisoners who had previously attempted suicide were four times more likely to have depression while incarcerated.

3.4 *Pakistan*

A study conducted among Pakistani juvenile offenders found that 30.8% of the male participants reported having thoughts of suicide since entering prison, while 31.6% said they would consider taking their own lives if given the opportunity. The study suggested that having a strong emotional connection with other criminals (in-group ties) is a significant factor in reducing suicidal thoughts (Shagufta et al., 2015). Additionally, an analysis of custodial deaths in Karachi from 2005 to 2010 revealed that out of 61 deaths, 7 (11.5%) were classified as suicides (Mirza et al., 2012).

3.5 *Sri Lanka*

The Human Rights Commission of Sri Lanka in 2018 reported that 11% of male and 7% of female inmates had attempted self-harm, whereas 7% of men and 4% of women reported suicide attempts. Longer prison sentences have been found to correlate with increased rates of depression, self-harm, and suicide attempts, especially among inmates serving indefinite sentences, including those held under the Prevention of Terrorism Act (HRCL, 2019). A cross-sectional study conducted in an institutional setting with 1730 inmates found that 22.7% had suicidal behaviour (95% CI: 20.7%–24.7%) (Suranga & Vidanapathirana, 2022). Among youth in Sri Lanka's juvenile justice system, self-harm and suicidal behaviours were alarmingly high, with 43% reporting a lifetime history of self-harm, 25% expressing suicidal intent, and 65% acting impulsively (Hettiarachchi et al., 2018).

3.6 Bhutan

No public data is available.

3.7 Maldives

No public data is available.

3.8 Afghanistan

No public data is available.

Across South Asian countries, suicide-related data within prison settings show inconsistencies, often reflecting underlying systemic challenges. Common factors contributing to these disparities have not been systematically studied, but the probable causes might be inconsistent reporting practices, lack of standardised monitoring systems, and variations in prison infrastructure and resources. Studies related to suicide in prison from SA are given in Table 9.1.

4 Epidemiology of Prison Suicide in Special Population

Suicide among juveniles and females in prison is an area that has not been subjected to a lot of research and emphasis in SA. Despite the growing awareness of mental health issues within correctional settings, there remains a significant gap in studies focusing on suicide in these vulnerable groups.

4.1 Offenders Who Are Minors

Young individuals are considered particularly vulnerable to suicide due to the complex interplay of individual, environmental, and psychological factors (Balaji et al., 2023). International data indicates that youth in the juvenile justice system who died by suicide were more likely to be older and male gender, irrespective of their incarceration status (Ruch et al., 2019).

In India, the Juvenile Justice Act was enacted to address children's developmental and psychological well-being in conflict with the law, aiming for their social reintegration and rehabilitation (Snehil & Sagar, 2020). However, there is no publicly available data on suicide in offenders who are minors from India. A study from Sri Lanka revealed over 43% of young individuals detained in certified schools had engaged in self-harm at least once during their lives, with one-third initiating it after detention, in line with global data (Hettiarachchi et al., 2018). A similar study from Pakistan revealed one-third of the juveniles experienced suicidal ideation while incarcerated (Shagufta et al., 2015) (Table 9.1).

4.2 Women

The level of female criminality has been rising over the past decade in India, and the percentage increase is almost the same as the increase in male criminality (SPRF, 2020). One study from India showed that 83.3% of female prisoners showed some form of diagnosable psychological distress (Nirmala et al., 2000). The Bangalore Prison study reported that 16.7% of women inmates had a current major depressive episode, 1.5% had engaged in deliberate self-harm, and 2% had a history of lifetime suicidal attempts (Math et al., 2011).

The majority of female forensic patients in one study were young adults from nuclear families, with most having mood disorders, schizophrenia, or other psychotic disorders (Gowda et al., 2019). The NHRC monograph from India reports that the average suicide rate for female inmates is 34.6 per 100,000, which is twice that of male inmates (16.12 per 100,000). Female inmates who are awaiting trial attempt suicide more frequently than women in the general population and even their male counterparts in prison (NHRC, 2014).

A study of female inmates at the Central Prison of Kathmandu, Nepal, found that 13% had suicidal ideation during imprisonment, compared to 4.3% before detention. Additionally, 6.5% had attempted suicide during imprisonment, while 4.3% had attempted suicide before detention (Regmi et al., 2019). No other publicly available data could be found from other countries (Table 9.2).

Table 9.2 Studies related to suicide in prison and correctional homes in South Asia

Studycountry	Study design	Population	Sample size (n)	Assessment method	Suicide risk/ideations/ attempts n (%)	Other key findings
Ayirolimeethal et al. (2014), India	Cross-sectional	UTP and CTP	255	MINI plus	High suicidal risk in nearly 7 (4%) inmates	A significant association between suicide risk and psychosis, mood and anxiety disorders
Math et al. (2011), India	Cross-sectional	UTP and CTP	5024	MINI plus	Lifetime suicide attempt UTP = 65(1.7) CTP = 13(1.1)	More than seven out of every 100 inmates had deliberate self-harm, and two out of every 100 had attempted suicide in the past. Approximately 2 to 3 out of every 100 UT prisoners are at risk of self-harm while incarcerated.
Bardale and Dixit (2015), India	Post mortem examination based retrospective study	UTP and CTP	173	NA	Suicide attempt = 14(8.09)	71.42% of deaths were noted in police lock-ups, while 28.57% were recorded in prison. Hanging was the common method, followed by poisoning.
Raha et al. (2018), India	Cross-sectional	UTP and CTP	80	C-SSRS	Suicide ideation Females = 12(30) Male = 4(10)	The prevalence of depression was 62.5% in males and 85% in females. Depression, insomnia, and suicidality were significantly correlated with longer incarceration, convict status, medical illness, substance abuse, and the increased age of their children among female inmates.
Patel and Vankar (2024), India	Cross-sectional	UTP and CTP	140	MSSI	Moderate suicidal ideation in the last 48 hours = 10(7.1) Suicidal ideation at any point in life = 58(41.4)	Minimal depressive symptoms in 57.9% of inmates and 9.3% had moderate to severe symptoms. Non-convicted inmates residing in urban areas reported significantly more depressive symptoms compared to their counterparts.

Shrestha et al. (2017), Nepal	Cross-sectional	Inmates (>3 months in prison)	434	CES-D	Suicide ideation = 10(2.3) Suicide attempt = 4(0.9)	The prevalence of depression among the inmates was 35.3%. Depression was significantly associated with suicidal ideation (OR = 4.44, 95%CI = 1.13–17.44, p = 0.038).
Bhusal et al. (2024), Nepal	Cross-sectional	Prisoners from eight districts	223	BDI-II	Suicide ideation = 29(13) Suicide attempts = 16(7.2)	18% of inmates were found to have depression. Inmates with health issues (aOR = 2.39), suicidal ideation during incarceration (aOR = 4.37), and prior suicide attempts (aOR = 7.97) had a statistically significant correlation with depression.
Mahato et al. (2023), Nepal	Cross-sectional	Aged 18-75, with ≥3 months in prison and no release within six months	352	CES-D 20	Suicide ideation = 15(4.3)	Prevalence of depression among the inmates was 54.3%. Depression was significantly associated with prior occupation, substance abuse, length of incarceration, cell population density, familial support, social support, and suicidal ideation during imprisonment.
Mirza et al. (2012), Pakistan	Cross-sectional	Retrospective analysis of custodial deaths autopsied in Karachi from 2006–10	61	NA	Suicide attempts (custodial death by suicide) = 7(11.5)	Hanging was the most common method of suicide.

(continued)

Table 9.2 (continued)

Studycountry	Study design	Population	Sample size (n)	Assessment method	Suicide risk/ideations/ attempts n (%)	Other key findings
Minors						
Shagufta et al. (2015), Pakistan	Cross-sectional	Male prisoners from age 11–18 years	415	BDI-II	Suicide ideation = 127(30.8)	The shared identity among offenders who are minors could help prevent suicidal ideation. Therefore, separating and isolating young offenders may be detrimental.
Hettiarachchi et al. (2018) SriLanka	Cross-sectional	Both male and female aged 12–16	181	No instruments used; based on oral report	Lifetime history of self-harm = 77(43) Self-harm ideations at some point in life time = 107(59)	A study found high levels of substance abuse, bullying victimization, parental incarceration, and exposure to suicide in inmates who are minor
Women						
Regmi et al. (2019), Nepal	Cross-sectional	Female inmates selected through random sampling	92	BDI	Suicidal ideation before detention = 9(9.8) Suicidal ideation in imprisonment = 12(13) Suicidal attempt before detention = 4(4.3) Suicidal attempt in imprisonment = 6(6.5)	40.2% had symptoms of depression. No correlation was found between the level of depression and the prisoners'socio-demographic factors, imprisonment-related factors, or substance use.

UTP, under trial prisoner; *CTP*, convicted prisoner; *MINI-Plus*, Mini-International Neuropsychiatric Interview-Plus; *C-SSRS*, Columbia Suicide Severity Rating Scale; *aOR*, adjusted odds ratio; *CES-D 20*, The Centre for Epidemiological Studies–Depression 20; *BDI-II*, Beck Depression Inventory-II; *BDI*, Beck Depression Inventory; *MSSI*, modified suicide ideation scale; NA, not applicable

5 Suicide in Healthcare Settings

In resource-limited settings, addressing suicidal behaviours is a complex challenge that requires a holistic approach to overcome societal and systemic barriers. The situation becomes particularly difficult when patients present with active suicidal and homicidal thoughts, but hospitalisation is not feasible due to their refusal or lack of acknowledgement of suicidal behaviour in existing frameworks. The absence of family support for care and financial expenses would add another layer of complexity. While community engagement could theoretically offer support, it often risks further stigmatisation and bullying due to pervasive negative social attitudes (Arafat, 2021b). On the other hand, admitting a patient at risk of suicide in a hospital places a significant duty of care on healthcare professionals, requiring them to monitor the patient and ensure their safety closely. Beyond routine clinical management, addressing issues of foreseeability through comprehensive suicide risk assessment and timely intervention is essential. A breach of this duty—whether through acts of commission or omission—may result in harm to the patient, with the most severe consequence being in-hospital suicide. Recognised as a 'sentinel event', in-hospital suicide is a critical hospital safety issue that is often deemed preventable. Despite its importance, data on inpatient suicides remain limited, with most studies originating from Western countries. A meta-analysis by Walsh et al. (2015) found a pooled estimate of 147 psychiatric inpatient suicides per 100,000 admissions. However, information on inpatient suicide rates in South Asian countries is scarce, with a few studies from India reporting rates between 10 and 20 per 100,000 admissions (Bose et al., 2016; Dahale et al., 2017; Khanra et al., 2016), significantly lower than those observed in Western populations. The higher rates in Western countries may reflect publication bias, while the lower rates in South Asian countries could stem from a lack of high-quality data and the absence of structured reporting platforms or guidelines for adverse incidents. Even when hospitals implement policies for reporting events such as medication errors, reporting often remains inconsistent. Another suggested protective factor in South Asian hospitals is the norm of requiring family members to stay with hospitalised patients, which may help reduce the risk of in-hospital suicide (Dahale et al., 2017).

6 Inpatient Suicide and Medical Negligence

Failure to protect the admitted patients from harming themselves would be considered a breach of duty of care, implying Medical Negligence (Rupasinghe, 2015). It is one of the most common reasons for lawsuits in psychiatry (Ajdacic-Gross et al., 2009). There is a dearth of data related to inpatient-related suicide and related malpractice suits worldwide, restricted to a few studies published in Western countries (Sabe et al., 2021).

In recent years, there has been a global rise in the number of malpractice cases against mental health professionals and an increasing number of court rulings favouring patients. While suicide is a relatively uncommon basis of litigation in South Asian countries, it remains the leading cause of medical lawsuits and the highest financial settlement in the United States.

A few reasons for malpractice suits are

1. Failure to properly diagnose or assess suicide risk.
2. Failure to implement adequate protective measures. Psychiatrists may be held liable if they fail to take adequate protective measures against a patient's suicide in accordance with the accepted practices. Neglecting or overlooking a patient's suicidal tendencies in the treatment plan can lead to legal consequences.
3. Early discharge of the patient, particularly when it is not supported by sound professional judgement.
4. Failure to commit decisions regarding whether to commit a patient must be based on a comprehensive history, thorough examination, and sound clinical judgement. If a psychiatrist overlooks significant suicidal intent or fails to account for it in the treatment plan, the liability increases proportionally to the level of risk ignored.

6.1 Individual Doctor vs Hospital Liability

Regarding the liability of the hospitals, Psychiatrists must recognise that malpractice claims related to inpatient suicides can be directed against both the psychiatrist and the hospital, particularly if the psychiatrist holds staff privileges or has hospital privileges. Individual cases from South Asian countries suggest that the doctor, as well as the hospital, are bound to pay compensation to the family members following the death of the patient. (Subhas Chandra Sarkar vs Dr. D. J. Shee on 26 September, 2022) A key consideration in these cases is foreseeability. Hospital staff are responsible for conducting thorough evaluations and providing appropriate monitoring, even if the patient is under the private care of a psychiatrist. Hospitals are typically not held liable if proper surveillance and procedures are followed. However, current legal and psychiatric perspectives suggest that an overly restrictive environment for suicidal patients can be just as harmful as an overly permissive one. Psychiatrists must carefully weigh the benefits of treatment against the risks of granting freedom. The concept of calculated risk is no longer accepted in these cases (D'Souza & Sousa, 2021). An essential element of effective risk management and high-quality clinical care in professional psychiatric practice is understanding the legal system and current legal perspectives on the standard of care.

7 Risk Factors of Suicide in Prison Settings

The *National Human Rights Commission of India* (NHRC) identifies two key factors contributing to suicide in prisons, including the detrimental characteristics of the prison environment and various crisis situations. Psychological stressors, social and environmental challenges, physical and resource limitations, including hostility and bullying, and healthcare and staff-related issues collectively create a hostile and isolating atmosphere in prisons that exacerbates mental health struggles and increases the risk of suicide. On the other hand, the domains contributing to crisis situations in prisons include substance use, mental health challenges, physical health issues, trauma, and emotional and social stressors (Table 9.3). (National Human Rights Commission India & Jain, 2014). Various risk factors associated with suicide in prisons are given in Table 9.4.

8 Role of Psychological Autopsy: A South Asian Perspective

Psychological autopsy (PA) is a post-mortem investigative method that reconstructs the mental state of the deceased through thorough, structured informant interviews and record reviews, aiming to uncover intent, contributing factors, and missed intervention opportunities related to death (Isometsä, 2001).

8.1 Types of Psychological Autopsy

A selective review of the methods, ethical considerations, and standardisation practices of PA in India categorised PA into two distinct types (Saini, 2017):

Table 9.3 Factors contributing to the prison environment (NHRC, 2014)

Suicide	Crisis situations
1. Authoritarian environment	1. Recent substance use
2. Lack of control over the future	2. Recent loss of spouse/loved one/ home/finances
3. Isolation	3. Guilt and shame related to the offence
4. Hostility and bullying	4. History of being raped/assaulted
5. Feelings of shame	5. Underlying physical health issues
6. Unpleasant noises and odours in prison contribute to negative feelings	6. Reaching an emotional breaking point
7. Fear about prison	7. Current mental illness
8. Lack of privacy and	
9. Overcrowding	
10. Staff insensitivity	
11. Lack of adequate mental health care	
12. Uncertainty about parole	

Table 9.4 Studies related to risk factors for suicide in prison and correctional homes in SA

Specific risk factors	Major findings
Socio-demographic factors	Young prisoners (Gupta & Girdhar, 2012) Advanced age (Patel & Vankar, 2024) Both male and female sex (Suranga & Vidanapathirana, 2022; Gupta & Girdhar, 2012; Hettiarachchi et al., 2018 Missing family (Suranga & Vidanapathirana, 2022) Childhood experiences of violence or neglect (Suranga & Vidanapathirana, 2022) History of sexual abuse (Hettiarachchi et al., 2018)
Clinical factors	History of any psychiatric morbidity, prior suicide attempts, poor coping with stressors (Sawant, 2018) Depressive symptoms, high psychological distress, and suicidal ideation in the past (Patel & Vankar, 2024; Suranga & Vidanapathirana, 2022) Psychosis, mood and anxiety disorders (Ayirolimeethal et al., 2014) Exposure to self-harm in the past (Hettiarachchi et al., 2018)
Substance use	Any substance use history (Sawant, 2018; Math et al., 2011; Hettiarachchi et al., 2018) Substance use disorder was the most common diagnosis (47.1%) in a study, but no association with suicide risk was found (Ayirolimeethal et al., 2014).
Medical conditions	Any coexisting medical illness (Sawant, 2018)
Trial status-related factors	Under trial detainees (Gupta & Girdhar, 2012) Impending release, sentencing, first 24 h of confinement (Sawant, 2018) Higher number of court cases (Suranga & Vidanapathirana, 2022)
Institutional factors	Holidays, change of cell, decreased staff supervision (Sawant, 2018) The negative impact of imprisonment on life (Patel & Vankar, 2024) Stigma (Suranga & Vidanapathirana, 2022)

1. Suicide Psychological Autopsy (SPA): This PA is performed when death is clearly a suicide, aiming to identify the psychosocial factors involved.
2. Equivocal Death Psychological Autopsy (EDPA): This investigation is conducted when the manner of death is uncertain, helping to determine if it was accidental, suicide, or homicide.

EDPA is particularly relevant in forensic investigations, where it resolves ambiguities in the manner of death, thereby aiding medico-legal and judicial processes.

8.2 *Forensic Applications of Psychological Autopsy (Murthy et al., 2010; Saini, 2017)*

1. Assisting Medical Investigators with Equivocal Deaths: PA can determine whether the death was accidental, suicide, or homicide in equivocal death scenarios like drug-related deaths, autoerotic asphyxia, self-induced asphyxia, vehicular deaths, suicide by cop, and staged death scenes.

Examples

(a) A case study by Puranik et al. on EDPA investigated a girl's death initially deemed suicide, while the family suspected homicide. The study found that the history and circumstantial behaviours were not typically associated with suicide. The authors concluded that the possibility of homicide could not be completely ruled out (Puranik et al., 2015).
(b) Another case study into the death of a 29-year-old medical graduate found hanging in a hotel room initially raised suspicions of homicide due to the presence of multiple ligature loops around his neck. However, a PA, combined with a post-mortem examination and crime scene analysis, conclusively determined the death to be a suicide (Padubidri et al., 2015).

2. Criminal Cases: To find the circumstances of the crime and identify potential suspects. It can also help determine whether the death was a suicide or homicide, especially in cases where the evidence is ambiguous.

   Examples

   (a) A PA study in the Indian Army revealed that military service was not a primary factor for suicide. Instead, the suicides were predominantly linked to identifiable psychosocial stressors (Sinha et al., 2021). PA can be used in military contexts where ambiguous evidence exists, such as distinguishing between accidental firearm discharge and intentional suicide.
   (b) A study from Cuttack, Orissa, in India, utilised additional evidence, including suicide notes and circumstantial details provided by the police and magistrate, to identify gender-specific risk factors, demonstrating how PA can uncover previously unidentified risk factors in criminal investigations (Bastia & Kar, 2009).
   (c) A study in Pakistan utilised records from police stations and hospital forensic departments, which provided a list of suicide cases based on medico-legal autopsies. By integrating PA findings with these medico-legal autopsies, the nature of death can be more accurately confirmed, aiding criminal investigations in distinguishing suicides from other causes of death (Ali & Saleem, 2024).

3. Institutional Care: PA in jails and prisons helps in understanding the factors contributing to inmate suicides and taking necessary precautions.
4. Worker's Compensation and Product Liability Cases: In worker's compensation cases, PAs can help determine if the deceased's employer was responsible for their suicide.

   Similarly, in product liability cases, PAs evaluate if the use of a specific product played a role in the suicide.
5. Insurance Claims: PAs can help establish whether the death was a suicide, which can be crucial in insurance claim disputes.
6. Medical Malpractice: In malpractice cases, including suicide, PA can help to establish whether the doctor's negligence was a proximate cause of the suicide.

8.3 Studies on Psychological Autopsy in Forensic Settings

There is a paucity of PA studies in SA, with existing research largely focusing on suicide risk factors within the general population, overlooking marginalised groups, such as prison inmates and individuals in forensic settings. A similar trend has been observed with most Indian studies focusing on SPA to assess risk factors associated with suicide rather than determining the mode of death in equivocal cases (Arafat et al., 2022; Menon et al., 2020e).

A review analysing PA studies in Muslim-majority countries, such as Afghanistan, Pakistan, and Bangladesh, highlighted the identification of suicidal risk factors while offering limited insight into forensic aspects (Arafat et al., 2021a).

8.4 Challenges in Conducting Psychological Autopsy

Various challenges encountered in conducting PA studies in the South Asian context, as exemplified by the Dhaka suicide study, highlight issues common in low-resource settings across the region and offer valuable insights for similar research (Arafat et al., 2021a, 2021b, 2021c; Arafat, 2021a, 2021b).

- Challenges in Obtaining Suicide Data: The absence of a central suicide database, inadequate liaison with the police, incomplete records and limited collaboration with forensic departments due to minimal research attention
- Conducting Interviews: The criminalisation of suicide in many countries, combined with the associated social stigma, often results in low response rates for interviews with the next of kin.
- Accessing Documents: Access to key documents such as suicide notes, post-mortem reports, and medical records is often restricted. Police may withhold suicide notes, and post-mortem reports are frequently inaccessible due to procedural limitations. Additionally, irregular consultation patterns and poorly implemented referral systems hinder access to medical information.
- Diagnosing Psychiatric Morbidity: Limited mental health literacy, low awareness of mental illness, and stigma make it difficult to identify psychiatric disorders in suicide cases.

8.5 Recommendations for Psychological Autopsy Reviews in Correctional Settings

The NHRC India advocates for a mortality-morbidity evaluation process for every completed suicide and serious suicide attempt in jails. This process should include a PA addressing the subsequent facets if resources permit (National Human Rights Commission India & Jain, 2014).

1. A comprehensive analysis of the conditions pertaining to the incident
2. Recognition of possible contributing elements
3. A critical evaluation of prison procedures relevant to the incident
4. Assessment of staff training
5. Review of medical and mental health services involving the victim
6. Proposals for modifications to policy, training, the physical environment, medical or mental health services, and operational processes to avert future events

8.6 Legal Status of Psychological Autopsy

PAs are emerging in Indian forensics and gaining recognition in legal proceedings. Despite challenges regarding the admissibility of these reports, they can serve as valuable investigative tools and corroborative evidence. Although there is limited judicial precedent for their use in India, psychological autopsies may be admissible in court under Section 293 of the Code of Criminal Procedure (CrPC), pending judicial scrutiny. Unfortunately, we could not locate any publicly available documents regarding the legal status of psychological autopsies in other countries.

9 Suicide Pacts

A suicide pact is a mutual agreement between two people to die at the same time and, usually, in the same place. The decision to enter into a suicide pact is typically made jointly, with both individuals deciding together from the outset. The plan is usually kept secret, potentially for weeks or months leading up to the chosen date (Cohen, 1961).

Sathyavathi (1975), based on a study on suicide pacts in Bangalore, reported that suicide pacts can be categorised into two main types: **usual** and **unusual** (Sathyavathi, 1975)

1. **Usual Suicide Pacts**:

   These involve individuals in pre-existing, socially expected relationships, such as husband-wife pairs or romantic partners.
2. **Unusual Suicide Pacts**:

   These occur between individuals whose relationships are not typically associated with suicide pacts, such as friends or siblings.

Crime scene analysis is indispensable for reconstructing events and validating findings, such as ruling out foul play and corroborating post-mortem results, to distinguish between different manners of death, such as suicide pacts and dyadic deaths (homicide-suicide). In resource-constrained settings like India, the development of improved crime scene investigation protocols and the enhancement of forensic expertise in cases of suicide pacts are essential (Devraj et al., 2022).

9.1 Studies on Suicide Pacts

Studies on suicide pacts are mainly based on case reports. Suicide pacts are a relatively rare phenomenon, particularly in India, which accounts for 2.5% of the total number of suicides (Dhawane & Bardale, 2011). It was found to be more prevalent among women than expected based on general population statistics. In Sri Lanka, such incidents are estimated to occur in approximately 1 per 5000 post-mortem examinations, predominantly among married, middle-aged couples (Senanayake, 2016). The most common suicide methods employed in pacts are

1. Hanging
2. Drowning
3. Jumping from a height
4. Shooting
5. Poisoning
6. Self-immolation

9.2 Key Factors in Suicide Pacts

Several factors contribute to suicide pacts, going beyond the demographic characteristics of the individuals involved.

Dysfunctional Relationships and Marriages: Both are important contributors to suicide pacts in India. Factors such as the dowry system and the pressures of arranged marriages often play a role, particularly among young women (Behera et al., 2014; Latha, 1996; Sathyavathi, 1975). A case report from Nepal highlights an inter-caste relationship between a couple that led them to a suicide pact (Atreya et al., 2018).

Poverty, Debt, and Unemployment: Poverty, debt, and unemployment are often intertwined factors contributing to suicide pacts, particularly among couples (Latha, 1996; Sathyavathi, 1975).

COVID-19 Pandemic: Multiple cases of suicide pacts and behaviours have been reported as secondary to the psychological impact of the COVID-19 pandemic (Griffiths & Mamun, 2020). One study describes a triadic suicide pact involving a family struggling with economic hardship during the pandemic in India (Mamun, 2021). Similarly, in Bangladesh, a suicide pact involving a mother and son reported during the pandemic was linked to challenges with online learning (Mamun et al., 2023).

Psychiatric Disorders: The prevalence of psychiatric disorders in suicide pacts from South Asia is not well defined, particularly based on accounts from survivors. A case report from Nepal describes a couple with emotionally unstable personality traits and depressive disorder in one spouse who attempted suicide as part of a pact (Risal, 2017).

One case report, where a mother drowned her three daughters and then herself, possibly due to the stress of not having a son (Ateriya et al., 2019). This is relevant in societies like India, where the strong preference for male children can put immense pressure on mothers of daughters.

A study observed suicide among medical students, residents, and physicians in India and identified nine suicide pacts over a ten-year period. On average, each pact resulted in 2.4 deaths, with financial difficulties emerging as a primary contributing factor for suicide pacts in the medical fraternity (Chahal et al., 2022).

Research on suicide pacts remains limited. While this phenomenon is rare, it is influenced by various socio-economic, psychological, and cultural factors in South Asia. There remains a gap in understanding suicide pacts related to emerging concerns, such as cyberbullying and internet suicides, where individuals, often strangers, negotiate their pact through the internet (Rajagopal, 2004). Further research is essential to explore these contemporary issues in the context of suicide pacts in SA.

10 Media Reporting of Prisoner's Suicide

Media coverage of suicide has a significant impact on public attitudes and can greatly affect vulnerable individuals. Sensationalism or including explicit details can lead to imitating suicidal behaviours, while responsible reporting can encourage help-seeking behaviours, reduce stigma, and support prevention efforts (Menon et al., 2018; Niederkrotenthaler et al., 2010). In South Asian countries, there are notable differences in how suicidal behaviours are reported in the general population, often in violation of WHO media guidelines. Many countries in this region either lack specific guidelines or face challenges with their implementation and monitoring (Arafat et al., 2020, 2021a, 2021b, 2021c).

Prisoner suicides often draw significant attention from the public, administrators, and politicians, which can result in sensationalised media coverage. This coverage may worsen the stigma associated with mental health issues in correctional facilities. Also, poor-quality media reporting of prisoner suicides reinforces stigma, fuels public misinformation, and exacerbates mental health issues among inmates. In South Asia, only one study from India has examined media reporting on prisoner suicides, analysing coverage from 2011 to 2021. The study revealed that nearly half of the news reports used sensational language and headlines. Over one-third of these reports included photographs of the deceased. Contrary to the WHO media reporting guidelines, most of the news articles mentioned the name, gender, method, and location of the suicide either in their headlines or within the content. This trend was observed more frequently in media coverage of suicides in incarcerated individuals compared to studies on the general population in India (Arafat et al., 2021b; Ayub et al., 2023; Menon et al., 2020b). Only about 16.67% of the reports addressed the mental health issues faced by the deceased, and fewer than 10% provided educational information about suicide prevention (Kar et al., 2022).

It is time to establish guidelines and create a national media monitoring agency to address the ongoing gaps in following suicide reporting guidelines in each South Asian country. Through consistent monitoring, engagement, and training of media professionals, such an agency might play a transformative role in improving the quality of reporting, thereby contributing to suicide prevention efforts (Menon et al. 2021a, 2021b).

11 The Intersection of Suicide and Law in South Asia

Suicide is intricately linked to a complex array of social, economic, cultural, and psychological factors. These include the violation of fundamental human rights, limited access to essential resources, and significant life stressors such as job loss, academic pressures, relationship breakdowns, and discrimination (Bose et al., 2023; WHO Policy Brief on the Health Aspects of Decriminalization of Suicide and Suicide Attempts, 2023). Consequently, individuals who attempt suicide often endure profound psychological stress arising from these various challenges. Subjecting these individuals or their family members to legal proceedings only exacerbates their stress and is unjustified (Vadlamani & Gowda, 2019). Despite this, many countries still have laws that impose punishment of varying degrees on suicide attempters (Mishara & Weisstub, 2016). This section provides an essential overview of the legal status of suicide and suicidal behaviours, emphasising the importance of awareness and understanding in this sensitive area. The text also provides a concise overview of national suicide prevention policies in relation to correctional settings in various countries where such information is available.

A review by Mishara and Weisstub (2016), pointed out that out of 192 countries worldwide, 45 countries (20 follow the Islamic or Sharia Law) still have punishments for suicide attempters, which includes all the South Asian countries except Maldives, Nepal, and Bhutan (Mishara & Weisstub, 2016; Tandon & Nathani, 2018). Historically, religious institutions viewed suicide as a sin, which led to the implementation of laws that punished individuals who attempted it. These laws were believed to have a utilitarian purpose by reducing the number of suicide attempts. However, empirical evidence does not support the notion that such laws effectively lower suicide rates. In fact, countries that have not decriminalised suicide are experiencing rising rates (29%) of suicides and suicide attempts, particularly among females (a 40% increase compared to male prisoners) (Lew et al., 2022; Wu et al., 2022). Additionally, there is no data indicating that suicide rates increase after decriminalisation; in fact, the evidence suggests the opposite (Mishara & Weisstub, 2016).

There are some important implications of criminalising suicide attempts highlighted in Box 9.2 (Bose et al., 2023; WHO Policy Brief on the Health Aspects of Decriminalization of Suicide and Suicide Attempts, 2023; Wu et al., 2022).

Box 9.2 Implications of Criminalizing Suicide Attempts

1. Fear of legal repercussions/punitive actions
2. Stigmatization towards the victim
3. Discrimination surrounding suicide
4. Exclusion and marginalization of individuals and families
5. Violates key human rights, such as freedom from discrimination & access to essential health and social services
6. Delay in treatment-seeking
7. Under-reporting of data
8. Hinders governments from initiating appropriate suicide preventive measures
9. Failure to recognise the role of sociocultural and economic factors
10. Increases suicide rates in the country

The majority of SA countries maintain similar legislation concerning attempted suicide, as well as the abetment, assistance, or encouragement of such acts. These laws were established during the British colonial period. Notably, Britain itself decriminalised suicide in 1961, rendering these regulations in South Asia somewhat antiquated (Bose et al., 2023; Ranjan et al., 2014) (Table 9.4).

11.1 India

In this regard, Section 309 of the Indian Penal Code (IPC), formed under the colonial era, states that an attempt to die by suicide is a criminal offence and is unjust and discriminatory against persons attempting suicide. Similarly, the other sections related to abetment of suicide were 109, 116, 306, and 309 (The Indian Penal Code 1860) (Table 9.4).

Data from the National Crime Records Bureau (NCRB) and multiple studies done on persons attempting to die by suicide to delineate the clinical and sociodemographic profile clearly indicate the presence of various stressors like relationship issues, family problems, financial issues, etc. Subjecting such persons to legal litigations would further augment their stress and is unwarranted. Rather, the focus should be on providing necessary mental health interventions by professionals (Vadlamani & Gowda, 2019).

The fight towards decriminalisation of suicide began in the early 1970s with the Law Commission of India's recommendation to remove the attempt to suicide from the IPC, which eventually made its way to the mental health care bill in 2013 (Ranjan et al., 2014).

Later, in the Mental Health Care Act (MHCA) of 2017, section 115 mentioned the decriminalisation of suicide attempts, superseding Section 309 of IPC. The Act emphasised the government's responsibility to ensure the provision of care, treatment, and rehabilitative services to reduce future suicidal attempts. A key aspect of India's National Suicide Preventive Strategy, 2022, is the training of lawyers and police personnel to ensure the effective implementation of Section 115, which decriminalises attempted suicide. This includes capacity building in psychosocial support, such as psychological first aid, which shifts the focus from punitive measures to providing care and rehabilitation for individuals who attempt suicide (Government of India, 2017; Ministry of Health and Family Welfare, Government of India, 2022).

Bharatiya Nyaya Sanhita Act (BNSA), enacted by the Indian Parliament on December 21, 2023, was a remarkable change and paradigm shift in the Indian legislature. In line with MHCA 2017, it adopted a more compassionate approach towards suicide-related attempts. It removed 309 IPC from the legislature but introduced section 226. The onus of responsibility was on the authorities to establish that an attempt was not motivated by severe stress but rather constituted an effort to coerce a public servant, as delineated in Section 226 of the BNSA.

When deciding whether to register a patient who has attempted suicide as a medico-legal case (MLC), the medical officer should use their judgement based on several factors: the suspicion of foul play, the patient's capacity to consent, and their medical stability. If there is no suspicion of foul play, the patient has intact capacity, and they are medically stable, the decision to register as an MLC will depend on the patient's report. This marks a significant shift from previous practices, where MLC registration was mandatory. The change reflects a more compassionate approach to mental health crises.

The BNSA has commendably removed outdated terms like 'lunatic' and 'insane'. However, the term 'person of unsound mind' still raises concerns, as it perpetuates stigma against individuals with mental illness. Table 9.4 provides a comparative overview of the IPC and the current BNSA to facilitate better understanding.

11.2 Pakistan

Suicide is prohibited in Islam, and hence, in Muslim-majority countries like Pakistan, Bangladesh, and Afghanistan, it is a criminal offence. But, after sustained efforts, Pakistan has managed to decriminalise suicide.

In response to challenges related to suicide, the Sindh Mental Health Authority, led by Dr. Karim Ahmed Khawaja in 2017, initiated a campaign for the decriminalisation of suicide attempts. The Taskeen Health Initiative, in collaboration with the Pakistan Mental Health Coalition (PMHC), launched a nationwide advocacy campaign in September 2021 titled 'Mujrim Nahin Mareez' ('Patients, not criminals'). This campaign aimed to shift the perception of suicide from a criminal act to a public health issue, emphasising stigma reduction and accurate reporting of suicide statistics. Senator Shahadat Awan became involved in this effort, introducing a bill to amend the Pakistan Penal Code in September 2021. With support from Taskeen, the bill was passed by the Senate in May 2022 and signed into law in December.

This legislative reform has enabled the establishment of a suicide hotline in Pakistan and improved the accuracy of suicide data reporting (Pakistan Penal Code (Act XLV of 1860); WHO Policy Brief on the Health Aspects of Decriminalization of Suicide and Suicide Attempts, 2023).

Recognising that suicidal behaviours are sensitive and stigmatised in conservative Islamic countries like Pakistan is crucial. Islam strongly condemns suicide, making discussions about its decriminalisation delicate. While it is important to address the negative impacts of criminalisation, we must also consider the protective role of religion, a viewpoint common among opponents of decriminalisation. Advocates should present a balanced case that includes religious, social, political, psychological, and medical perspectives. Identifying thoughtful figures is vital, given the influence of religious leaders in these societies. However, there is a risk of backlash from the religious community, as evidenced by past challenges in the Sharia Court in Pakistan (Chan et al., 2024).

11.3 Bangladesh

Bangladesh inherited the Penal Code Act of 1860, which was formed by the British Raj for India after its liberation in 1971. Therefore, it follows the same laws as for India (same as IPCs) listed in the table. Although the new MHCA 2018 has been enacted, suicide decriminalisation still remains ignored (The Penal Code, 1860 | 306. Abetment of Suicide) (Table 9.5).

11.4 Sri Lanka

Sri Lanka adopted the Indian Penal Code; however, it revoked the criminalisation of suicide attempts (Penal Code Ordinance No 02 of 1883-Section 302) in 1998 by the Presidential committee, becoming the first country in the Indian subcontinent to take this significant step forward (Ceylon, 1885) (Table 9.5).

There is no mention of specific information related to suicide and correctional settings from the Sri Lankan suicide prevention policy (Presidential Committee on Prevention of Suicide, Sri Lanka, 1997).

11.5 Nepal

The Muluki Ain is Nepal's General Code that outlines all civil and criminal laws. Notably, it does not include any provisions that criminalise, define, or punish suicide. However, it does reference the procedural investigation of all homicides and suspicious suicides. While suicide is not considered illegal, it is often reported by

Table 9.5 Laws related to suicide

Law or act	Description
India	
IPC Section 109	Whoever abets any offence shall, if the act abetted is committed in consequence of the abetment, and no express provision is made by this Code for the punishment of such abetment, be punished with the punishment provided for the offence
IPC Section 116	Whoever abets an offence punishable with imprisonment shall, if that offence be not committed in consequence of the abetment, be punished with imprisonment of any description provided for that offence for a term which may extend to one-fourth part of the longest term provided for that offence; or with such fine as is provided for the offence, or with both
IPC Section 305	Abetment of suicide of child or insane person—If any person under 18 years of age, any insane person, any delirious person, any idiot, or any person in a state of intoxication, commits suicide, whoever abets the commission of such suicide, shall be punished with death or imprisonment for a term not exceeding 10 years, and shall also be liable to fine
IPC Section 306/ Section 108 BNSA 2023	If any person dies by suicide, whoever abets the commission of such suicide, shall be punished with imprisonment of either description for a term which may extend to 10 years, and shall also be liable to fine
IPC Section 309	Whoever attempts to commit suicide and does any act towards the commission of such offence shall be punished with simple imprisonment for a term which may extend to 1 year or with fine, or with both
Section 115 of MHCA 2017	Notwithstanding anything contained in Section 309 of the IPC, any person who attempts to die by suicide shall be presumed, unless proved otherwise, to have severe stress and shall not be tried and punished under the said Code
Section 105	Abetment of suicide of child or a person with mental illness with death or imprisonment for life, imprisonment of 10 years and fine
Section 106	Abetment of suicide imprisonment of 10 years or fine
Section 107 of the BNSA 2023	Abetment of suicide of child or person of unsound mind—If any child, any person of unsound mind, any delirious person or any person in a state of intoxication, commits suicide, whoever abets the commission of such suicide, shall be punished with death or imprisonment for life, or imprisonment for a term not exceeding 10 years, and shall also be liable to fine
Section 226 of the BNSA 2023	Attempt to commit suicide to compel or restrain exercise of lawful power—Whoever attempts to commit suicide with the intent to compel or restrain any public servant from discharging his official duty shall be punished with simple imprisonment for a term which may extend to one year, or with fine, or with both, or with community service.
Bangladesh	
Section 109, 116, 305, 306, 309	Same as mentioned for India under the corresponding laws
Pakistan	
Section 107	Abetment of a thing
Sri Lanka	
Article 302	Attempt to Commit Suicide.
Article 299	Abetment of suicide—If any person commits suicide whoever abets the commission of such suicide shall be punished with death

(continued)

Table 9.5 (continued)

Law or act	Description
Afghanistan	
Article 397	Where a person instigates another to suicide and where the suicide is committed: Imprisonment for up to 7 years. Where the suicide is only initiated: Short imprisonment
Bhutan	
Article 150	A defendant shall be guilty of offence of complicity in suicide, if the defendant aids, abets, counsels or procures the suicide of another person
Article 151	The offence of complicity in suicide shall be a misdemeanour
Nepal	
Section 185	Prohibition on Abetment of Suicide states: (1) No one should provoke or generate a situation abate anyone to commit suicide or to create circumstances compelling someone to commit the same (2) Anyone found guilty under the clause is liable to a five-year jail sentence and Rs 50,000 fine
Maldives	
Section 113—Class 1 misdemeanour	It is an offence while keeping in possession or using or dealing with any poisonous substance that could endanger the life of one's own or another and commit any act in a manner likely to cause danger to any other person. A person guilty of this offence shall be subjected to imprisonment of either description not exceeding one year, or exile not exceeding one year or a fine.

IPC, Indian Penal Code; *BNSA*, Bharatiya Nyaya Sanhita Act; *MHCA*, Mental Health Care Act

health informants and publications as a 'criminal' and 'legal issue' (Benson & Shakya, 2008). However, when an individual survives after a suicidal attempt, it is invariably registered as a medico-legal case (Utyasheva et al., 2022). The proceedings with the family and victims are primarily handled by the police, with minimal input from clinicians (Hagaman et al., 2016; Marahatta et al., 2017; The National Penal (Code) Act, 2017 (Nepal)) (Table 9.5).

11.6 Afghanistan and Bhutan

There seems to be no punishment or penalty for those attempting suicide except for abetment to suicide in Bhutan and Afghanistan (NATLEX - Bhutan - Penal Code of Bhutan, 2004).

The Suicide Prevention Policy of 2019, Afghanistan, highlights the significance of intersectoral coordination among multiple departments, including the prison health department. It aims to integrate with the mental health strategy to deliver training for staff working with women in major prisons. This training will focus on providing psychosocial support related to gender-based violence, which may have an indirect impact on suicide rates. (Islamic Republic of Afghanistan, Ministry of Public Health, DG of Diseases Control & Prevention, Primary Health Care Directorate, Mental Health Department, 2019).

In Bhutan, the recent five-year action plan (2018–2023) emphasizes the need to develop accredited courses for suicide prevention and to train police personnel in suicide prevention and forensic investigations (Ministry of Health, Bhutan, 2021).

11.7 Maldives

In Maldives, Section 113 defines suicidal attempts; individuals would be subjected to imprisonment/exile or a fine (Maldives Penal Code, 2004) (Table 9.5).

The Maldives National Mental Health Policy 2015–2025 stresses the need to address mental health issues in correctional facilities and calls for training prison officers in crisis support and psychosocial interventions for effective prevention, promotion, and identification of mental health problems. But, there is no specific national suicide prevention strategy which is available (Ministry of Health, Maldives, 2017).

Despite laws being in place, it is not often that individuals attempting suicide are penalised, but it's an area that deserves further study. It is also important to consider the decriminalisation of suicide in countries that currently view suicide attempts through a criminal lens.

12 Suicide Prevention in the Prison Population

As per WHO, 'Suicide is a significant public health problem worldwide, but with appropriate efforts, it is preventable' (World Health Organization: WHO, 2024). The United Nations initially encouraged individual countries to develop a National Suicide Prevention Strategy through a key document titled 'Prevention of Suicide: Guidelines for the Formulation and Implementation of National Strategies', which was published in the early 1990s. Following this, WHO published a guiding framework for countries to establish suicide prevention strategies through their report on 'Public Health Action for the Prevention of Suicide: A Framework' in 2013, which aimed to reduce national suicide rates in member states by 10% till 2020 by following a number of strategies such as identifying stakeholders, undertaking situational analysis, assessing the requirement and availability of resources, achieving political commitment, addressing stigma and increasing awareness' (Arafat et al., 2024). Particular emphasis is placed on high-risk populations such as prisoners, young pregnant women, the elderly, Indigenous people and armed forces in suicide prevention. Among the Southeast Asian countries, Sri Lanka (Presidential Committee on Prevention of Suicide, Sri Lanka, 1997), Bhutan (Ministry of Health, Bhutan, 2021), India (Ministry of Health and Family Welfare, Government of India, 2022), and Afghanistan (Islamic Republic of Afghanistan, Ministry of Public Health, DG of Diseases Control & Prevention, Primary Health Care Directorate, Mental Health

Department, 2019) have formulated a national suicide prevention strategy, whereas Nepal, Pakistan and Maldives are yet to do so.

Important strategies for vulnerable populations that can be used for prisoners or those admitted to forensic psychiatry settings are (Fig. 9.1):

1. Gatekeeper training, i.e., professionals who frequently come in contact with the vulnerable group to be trained to recognise the risk factors of suicide.
2. Mobilising communities, NGOs, governmental, community health or social services
3. Survivors reaching out to the prison population
4. Responsible media reporting

A few strategies suggested by some national commission reports are (WHO Policy Brief on the Health Aspects of Decriminalization of Suicide and Suicide Attempts, 2023; Ahmed & Mahboob, 2021; Islamic Republic of Afghanistan, Ministry of Public Health, DG of Diseases Control & Prevention, Primary Health Care Directorate, Mental Health Department., 2019; Ministry of Health, Bhutan, 2021):

1. Screening of all prisoners for suicide risk by prison staff during intake and identification of high-risk groups
2. Training of prison staff in signs of suicide risk and precautions
3. Effective communication between the arresting officer, prison staff and the inmate
4. Establishment of suicide-safe cell
5. Adequate monitoring of suicidal inmates
6. Providing adequate social support
7. Maintaining a healthy prison environment
8. Administrative review regarding adverse events
9. Standardised record-keeping

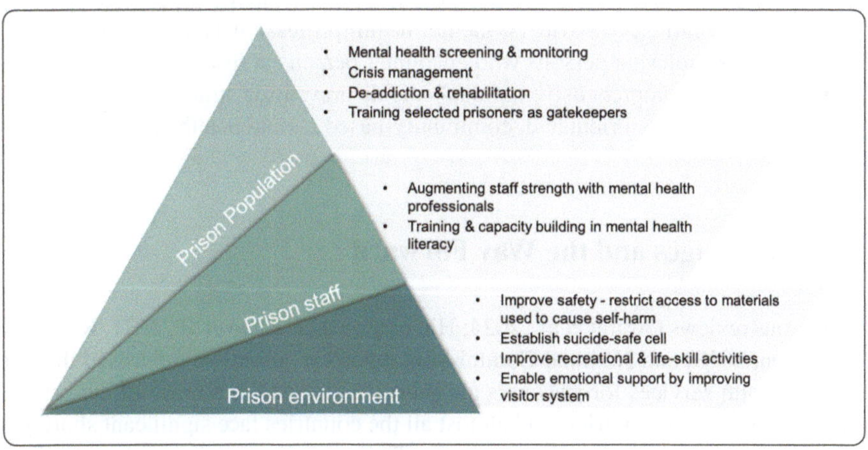

Fig. 9.1 Strategies for suicide prevention in prisons

Additionally, countries that have recently decriminalised suicide must continue to implement strategies to raise awareness about this legislative change, as many tend to be unaware of such laws (Kattimani et al., 2015). A comprehensive, multi-sectoral approach is essential, involving collaboration among the judiciary, law enforcement, media, and other relevant sectors. By changing this perspective, reformed laws could.

- Save lives and reduce the distress experienced by individuals and their families
- Challenges stigma surrounding mental health, promoting a deeper understanding of emotional struggles
- Openness leads to better data collection on suicides, informing effective interventions

WHO has formulated key recommendations in a policy brief on the health aspects of the decriminalisation of suicide and suicidal attempts (WHO Policy Brief on the Health Aspects of Decriminalization of Suicide and Suicide Attempts, 2023) (Box 9.3),

Box 9.3 WHO Recommendations on the Decriminalisation of Suicide and Suicidal Attempts

-
- Identify and repeal legislation and policies that criminalise suicide and suicide attempts
- Engage with relevant stakeholders to understand and dispel moral, cultural or religious justifications for criminalisation or those based on the notion of punishment as a deterrent to suicide.
- Organise an advocacy campaign
- Build and budget for a 'post-decriminalization'/"transition' awareness programme specifically to train first responders, including police, emergency health care providers, mental health professionals, peer supporters and other relevant persons who encounter persons at risk of suicide
- Develop a comprehensive national suicide prevention strategy
- Establish rights-orientated, community-based mental health services

13 Challenges and the Way Forward

Numerous reviews (Arafat et al., 2024; Hill et al., 2022; Khan et al., 2021; Rabiya & Raghavan, 2018) and National Commission reports repeatedly emphasised that the mental health services for prisoners are pretty inadequate in almost all the prisons of Southeast Asian countries, and almost all the countries face significant shortages of mental health professionals in prisons. The screening for mental health disorders is largely absent. The inmates requiring specialised mental health services are often referred to external hospitals. The services are fragmented between ministries,

	Current status	Recommendations
Dedicated Mental Health Staff	Limited mental health professionals	Increase recruitment and training of mental health professionals Integrate teleconsultation services
Screening for Mental Disorders	No formal screening strategy or structured mental health assessments	Implement regular and standardized mental health screenings at intake and periodically during incarceration.
Training for Prison Staff	Lack of awareness of prison staff regarding mental health issues	Provide mandatory, training for prison staff to identify, manage, and support inmates with mental health issues
Infrastructure and safety	Overcrowded prisons Inadequate infrastructure for mental health care	Improve healthcare infrastructure Establish dedicated treatment spaces Eliminate potential suicide hotspots
Forensic Psychiatry services	Limited to no forensic psychiatry units	Establish dedicated forensic psychiatric units

Fig. 9.2 Current status of prisons' mental health services in South Asian countries and recommendations for improvement

leading to coordination challenges. External support is restricted to some NGOs that play an important role in substance abuse intervention programmes (Khan et al., 2021) (e.g., Dhaka Ahsania Mission in Bangladesh) and training of prison staff in emotional regulation and handling vulnerable groups in the prison population.

Moving forward, innovative models like teleconsultation (Agarwal et al., 2019) to bridge the gap in mental health care delivery services, adequate training of prison staff to identify and manage mental health issues, establishing a unified authority to oversee prison population, adequate training of prison staff to identify mental health issues, increasing the number of mental health professionals and improving healthcare infrastructure within prisons, and establishing dedicated forensic psychiatry units when needed are essential to improve the mental health care of prison populations (National Human Rights Commission India & Jain, 2014) (Fig. 9.2).

14 Conclusion

The forensic psychiatric perspective on suicide in South Asia emphasises the urgent need for systemic reforms. Vulnerable groups, including incarcerated individuals, minors, and women, are at greater risk due to insufficient mental health care and pervasive stigma. Although there have been strides made through initiatives like psychological autopsies and decriminalisation, significant gaps in prevention and reporting practices still exist. A coordinated approach is essential, prioritising enhanced mental health services in correctional facilities, culturally sensitive interventions, and efforts to reduce stigma. By fostering collaboration among legal, medical, and social systems, South Asia can create effective strategies to lower suicide rates and provide critical support to its most vulnerable populations.

References

Agarwal, P. P., Manjunatha, N., Gowda, G. S., Kumar, M. N. G., Shanthaveeranna, N., Kumar, C. N., & Math, S. B. (2019). Collaborative tele-neuropsychiatry consultation services for patients in central prisons. *Journal of Neurosciences in Rural Practice, 10*(1), 101–105. https://doi.org/10.4103/jnrp.jnrp_215_18

Ahmed, E., & Mahboob, Z. (2021). *Mental health awareness toolkit 2021 for prison authorities*. Penal Reform International, & Justice Project Pakistan.

Ajdacic-Gross, V., Lauber, C., Baumgartner, M., Malti, T., & Rössler, W. (2009). In-patient suicide—A 13-year assessment. *Acta Psychiatrica Scandinavica, 120*(1), 71–75. https://doi.org/10.1111/j.1600-0447.2009.01380.x

Ali, S. A.-Z., & Saleem, T. (2024). Psychological autopsies: Religious and spiritual factors for suicide in cases and controls. *Frontiers in Psychiatry, 15*, 1419669. https://doi.org/10.3389/fpsyt.2024.1419669

Arafat, S. M. Y. (2021a). Challenges of conducting psychological autopsy study in Bangladesh: Data enumerator's view. *Asian Journal of Psychiatry, 63*, 102760. https://doi.org/10.1016/j.ajp.2021.102760

Arafat, S. M. Y. (2021b). Practical challenges of addressing suicidal behaviors for a clinician in Bangladesh. *International Journal of Mental Health Addiction, 19*, 2175–2177. https://doi.org/10.1007/s11469-020-00310-3

Arafat, S. M. Y., & Kar, S. K. (2024). Epidemiology of psychiatric disorders and overview of access to mental health care in South Asia. In S. M. Y. Arafat & S. K. Kar (Eds.), *Access to mental health care in South Asia*. Springer. https://doi.org/10.1007/978-981-99-9153-2_1

Arafat, S. M. Y., Kar, S. K., Marthoenis, M., Cherian, A. V., Vimala, L., & Kabir, R. (2020). Quality of media reporting of suicidal behaviors in South-East Asia. *Neurology, Psychiatry and Brain Research, 37*, 21–26. https://doi.org/10.1016/j.npbr.2020.05.007

Arafat, S. M. Y., Khan, M. M., Menon, V., Ali, S. A., Rezaeian, M., & Shoib, S. (2021a). Psychological autopsy study and risk factors for suicide in Muslim countries. *Health Science Reports, 4*(4), e414. https://doi.org/10.1002/hsr2.414

Arafat, S. M. Y., Menon, V., Bascarane, S., Kar, S. K., & Kabir, R. (2021b). Variations in newspaper reporting of suicidal behavior in the WHO-South-East Asian region. *Journal of Public Health (Oxford, England), 43*(4), e684–e688. https://doi.org/10.1093/pubmed/fdaa139

Arafat, S. M. Y., Mohit, M. A., Mullick, M. S. I., Khan, M. A. S., & Khan, M. M. (2021c). Suicide with and without mental disorders: Findings from psychological autopsy study in Bangladesh. *Asian Journal of Psychiatry, 61*, 102690. https://doi.org/10.1016/j.ajp.2021.102690

Arafat, S. M. Y., Menon, V., Varadharajan, N., & Kar, S. K. (2022). Psychological autopsy studies of suicide in South East Asia. *Indian Journal of Psychological Medicine, 44*(1), 4–9. https://doi.org/10.1177/02537176211033643

Arafat, S. M. Y., Kar, S. K., Abhayanayake, C., Sharma, P., & Marthoenis, M. (2024). Prison mental health in South-East Asia: A narrative review. *Brain and Behavior, 14*(8), e70004. https://doi.org/10.1002/brb3.70004

Ateriya, N., Saraf, A., Kanchan, T., Meshram, V. P., Singh Shekhawat, R., & Setia, P. (2019). Filicide-suicide: An unusual variant of dyadic death. *The Medico-Legal Journal, 87*(1), 44–46. https://doi.org/10.1177/0025817218787392

Atreya, A., Shrestha, M., & Acharya, J. (2018). Inter-caste lovers' suicide pact—Case report from Nepal. *The Medico-Legal Journal, 86*(2), 103–106. https://doi.org/10.1177/0025817217730993

Ayirolimeethal, A., Ragesh, G., Ramanujam, J. M., & George, B. (2014). Psychiatric morbidity among prisoners. *Indian Journal of Psychiatry, 56*(2), 150–153. https://doi.org/10.4103/0019-5545.130495

Ayub, M., Rafiq, B., Tahir, S. M., Imran, N., Naveed, S., & Haider, I. I. (2023). Assessing the quality of media reporting of suicide deaths in Pakistan against international guidelines. *The International Journal of Social Psychiatry, 69*(2), 406–411. https://doi.org/10.1177/00207640221106683

Balaji, M., Mandhare, K., Nikhare, K., Shah, A. K., Kanhere, P., Panse, S., Santre, M., Vijayakumar, L., Phillips, M. R., Pathare, S., Patel, V., Czabanowska, K., & Krafft, T. (2023). Why young people attempt suicide in India: A qualitative study of vulnerability to action. *SSM - Mental Health, 3*, 100216. https://doi.org/10.1016/j.ssmmh.2023.100216

Bardale, R. V., & Dixit, P. G. (2015). Suicide behind bars: A 10-year retrospective study. *Indian Journal of Psychiatry, 57*(1), 81. https://doi.org/10.4103/0019-5545.148531

Bastia, B. K., & Kar, N. (2009). A psychological autopsy study of suicidal hanging from Cuttack, India: Focus on stressful life situations. *Archives of Suicide Research, 13*(1), 100–104. https://doi.org/10.1080/13811110802572221

Behera, C., Karthik, K., Singh, H., Deepak, P., Jhamad, A. R., & Bhardwaj, D. N. (2014). Suicide pact by drowning with bound wrists: A case of medico-legal importance. *The Medico-Legal Journal, 82*(1), 29–31. https://doi.org/10.1177/0025817213508676

Benson, J., & Shakya, R. (2008). Suicide prevention in Nepal: A comparison to Australia - A personal view. *Mental Health in Family Medicine, 5*(3), 177–182.

Bertuccio, P., Amerio, A., Grande, E., Vecchia, C. L., Costanza, A., Aguglia, A., Berardelli, I., Serafini, G., Amore, M., Pompili, M., & Odone, A. (2024). Global trends in youth suicide from 1990 to 2020: An analysis of data from the WHO mortality database. *eClinicalMedicine, 70*, 102506. https://doi.org/10.1016/j.eclinm.2024.102506

Bhusal, R., Anjali, P. C., Bhattarai, N., Mishra, D. K., Sapkota, S. K., Sharma, S., & Sapkota, K. P. (2024). Depression among inmates of Gandaki Province, Nepal: A cross-sectional study. *BMC Psychiatry, 24*(1), 446. https://doi.org/10.1186/s12888-024-05896-9

Bose, S., Khanra, S., Umesh, S., Khess, C. R. J., & Ram, D. (2016). Inpatient suicide in a psychiatric hospital: Fourteen years' observation. *Asian Journal of Psychiatry, 19*, 56–58. https://doi.org/10.1016/j.ajp.2015.12.004

Bose, P. K., Kushal, S. A., & Arafat, S. M. Y. (2023). Forensic and legal aspects of suicide in Bangladesh. In S. M. Y. Arafat & M. M. Khan (Eds.), *Suicide in Bangladesh* (pp. 17–30). Springer Nature. https://doi.org/10.1007/978-981-99-0289-7_2

Ceylon. (1885). *Penal code. In an ordinance to provide a general penal code for Ceylon.*

Chahal, S., Nadda, A., Govil, N., Gupta, N., Nadda, D., Goel, K., & Behra, P. (2022). Suicide deaths among medical students, residents and physicians in India spanning a decade (2010-2019): An exploratory study using online news portals and Google database. *The International Journal of Social Psychiatry, 68*(4), 718–728. https://doi.org/10.1177/00207640211011365

Chan, L. F., Ibrahim, N., Khamal, N. R., Panirselvam, R. R., Pereira, E. J., & Khan, M. (2024). A global call for decriminalization of attempted suicide. *Crisis, 45*(6), 383–388. https://doi.org/10.1027/0227-5910/a000974

Cohen, J. (1961). A study of suicide pacts. *Medico-Legal Journal, 29*(3), 144–151. https://doi.org/10.1177/002581726102900305

D'Souza, R., & Sousa, A. D. (2021). Ethical and legal issues in suicide. *Global Bioethics Enquiry, 9*(2), 64–69. https://doi.org/10.38020/GBE.9.2.2021.64-69

Dahale, A., Sherine, L., & Chaturvedi, S. K. (2017). In-patient suicide in psychiatry—An Indian experience. *Epidemiology and Psychiatric Sciences, 26*(5), 565–569. https://doi.org/10.1017/S2045796017000129

Devraj, N., Barman, S., & Sonar, V. D. (2022). Crime scene examination of a suicidal pact: A case report. *Cureus, 14*(11), e31981. https://doi.org/10.7759/cureus.31981

Dhawane, S. G., & Bardale, R. V. (2011). Dying together: A study of suicide pacts. *Journal of Forensic Medicine, Science and Law, 20*(1).

Favril, L., Shaw, J., & Fazel, S. (2022). Prevalence and risk factors for suicide attempts in prison. *Clinical Psychology Review, 97*, 102190. https://doi.org/10.1016/j.cpr.2022.102190

Fazel, P. S., Ramesh, T., & Hawton, P. K. (2017). Suicide in prisons: An international study of prevalence and contributory factors. *The Lancet Psychiatry, 4*(12), 946. https://doi.org/10.1016/S2215-0366(17)30430-3

Government of India. (2017). *The Mental Healthcare Act, 2017 (Act No. 10 of 2017)*. https://www.indiacode.nic.in/bitstream/123456789/2249/1/A2017-10.pdf

Gowda, G. S., Komal, S., Sanjay, T. N., Mishra, S., Kumar, C. N., & Math, S. B. (2019). Sociodemographic, legal, and Clinical profiles of female forensic inpatients in Karnataka: A retrospective study. *Indian Journal of Psychological Medicine, 41*(2), 138–143. https://doi.org/10.4103/IJPSYM.IJPSYM_152_18

Gowda, G. S., Shadakshari, D., Vajawat, B., Reddi, V. S. K., Math, S. B., & Murthy, P. (2021). Suicide in Indian prisons. *The Lancet Psychiatry, 8*(8), e19. https://doi.org/10.1016/S2215-0366(21)00233-9

Griffiths, M. D., & Mamun, M. A. (2020). COVID-19 suicidal behavior among couples and suicide pacts: Case study evidence from press reports. *Psychiatry Research, 289*, 113105. https://doi.org/10.1016/j.psychres.2020.113105

Gupta, A., & Girdhar, N. K. (2012). Risk factors of suicide in prisoners. *Delhi Psychiatry Journal, 15*, 45–49.

Hagaman, A. K., Maharjan, U., & Kohrt, B. A. (2016). Suicide surveillance and health systems in Nepal: A qualitative and social network analysis. *International Journal of Mental Health Systems, 10*, 46. https://doi.org/10.1186/s13033-016-0073-7

Hettiarachchi, L. V., Kinner, S. A., Tibble, H., & Borschmann, R. (2018). Self-harm among young people detained in the youth justice system in Sri Lanka. *International Journal of Environmental Research and Public Health, 15*(2), 209. https://doi.org/10.3390/ijerph15020209

Hill, K., Wainwright, V., Stevenson, C., Senior, J., Robinson, C., & Shaw, J. (2022). Prevalence of mental health and suicide risk in prisons in low- and middle-income countries: A rapid review. *Journal of Forensic Psychiatry & Psychology, 33*(1), 37–52. https://doi.org/10.1080/14789949.2021.2016891

HRCL. (2019). https://www.hrcsl.lk/documentation/reports/

Islamic Republic of Afghanistan, Ministry of Public Health, DG of Diseases Control & Prevention, Primary Health Care Directorate, Mental Health Department. (2019). *National Suicide Prevention Strategy (NSPS).*

Isometsä, E. T. (2001). Psychological autopsy studies—A review. *European Psychiatry: The Journal of the Association of European Psychiatrists, 16*(7), 379–385. https://doi.org/10.1016/s0924-9338(01)00594-6

Kar, S. K., Menon, V., Bascarane, S., Sharma, G., Ransing, R., Pattnaik, J. I., Mukherjee, S., Padhy, S. K., & Agarwal, V. (2022). Online media reporting of prisoner's suicide in India during 2011 to 2021. *Ethics, Medicine and Public Health, 22*, 100788. https://doi.org/10.1016/j.jemep.2022.100788

Kattimani, S., Sarkar, S., Mukherjee, A., & Mathan, K. (2015). What do suicide attempters think about legal status of suicide in India? *Indian Journal of Psychiatry, 57*(1), 103–104. https://doi.org/10.4103/0019-5545.148543

Khan, A. A., Ryland, H., Pathan, T., Ahmed, H. U., Hussain, A., & Forrester, A. (2021). Mental health services in the prisons of Bangladesh. *BJPsych International, 18*(4), 88–91. https://doi.org/10.1192/bji.2021.34

Khanra, S., Mahintamani, T., Bose, S., Khess, C. R. J., Umesh, S., & Ram, D. (2016). Inpatient suicide in a psychiatric hospital: A nested case-control study. *Indian Journal of Psychological Medicine, 38*(6), 571–576. https://doi.org/10.4103/0253-7176.194914

Klonsky, E. D., Pachkowski, M. C., Shahnaz, A., & May, A. M. (2021). The three-step theory of suicide: Description, evidence, and some useful points of clarification. *Preventive Medicine, 152*(Pt 1), 106549. https://doi.org/10.1016/j.ypmed.2021.106549

Latha, K. S. (1996). Suicide pact survivors: Some observations. *Medicine, Science, and the Law, 36*(4), 295–298. https://doi.org/10.1177/002580249603600404

Lew, B., Lester, D., Mustapha, F. I., Yip, P., Chen, Y.-Y., Panirselvam, R. R., Hassan, A. S., In, S., Chan, L. F., Ibrahim, N., Chan, C. M. H., & Siau, C. S. (2022). Decriminalizing suicide attempt in the 21st century: An examination of suicide rates in countries that penalize suicide, a critical review. *BMC Psychiatry, 22*, 424. https://doi.org/10.1186/s12888-022-04060-5

Mahato, S., Devkota, N., Kafle, B. R., Singh, M., & Dahal, H. R. (2023). Prevalence of depression and its associated factors among inmates. *Journal of Nepal Health Research Council, 21*(2), 232–237. https://doi.org/10.33314/jnhrc.v21i02.4617

Maldives Penal Code. (2004). [Translation]. In Translator (Trans.), *Maldives Penal Code* (Act Number 1/81, pp. 1–15).

Mamun, M. A. (2021). The first COVID-19 triadic (homicide!)-suicide pact: Do economic distress, disability, sickness, and treatment negligence matter? *Perspectives in Psychiatric Care, 57*(3), 1528–1531. https://doi.org/10.1111/ppc.12686

Mamun, M. A., Chandrima, R. M., & Griffiths, M. D. (2023). Mother and son suicide pact due to COVID-19-related online learning issues in Bangladesh: An unusual case report. *International Journal of Mental Health and Addiction, 21*(2), 687–690. https://doi.org/10.1007/s11469-020-00362-5

Marahatta, K., Samuel, R., Sharma, P., Dixit, L., & Shrestha, B. (2017). Suicide burden and prevention in Nepal: The need for a national strategy. *WHO South-East Asia Journal of Public Health, 6*(1), 45. https://doi.org/10.4103/2224-3151.206164

Math, S. B., Murthy, P., Parthasarathy, R., Kumar, C. N., & Madhusudhan, S. (2011). *Mental health and substance use problems in prisons. The Bangalore Prison Mental Health Study: Local lessons for national action.*

Menon, V., Subramanian, K., Selvakumar, N., & Kattimani, S. (2018). Suicide prevention strategies: An overview of current evidence and best practice elements. *International Journal of Advanced Medical and Health Research, 5*(2), 43. https://doi.org/10.4103/IJAMR.IJAMR_71_18

Menon, V., Arafat, S. M. Y., Akter, H., Mukherjee, S., Kar, S. K., & Padhy, S. K. (2020a). Cross-country comparison of media reporting of celebrity suicide in the immediate week: A pilot study. *Asian Journal of Psychiatry, 54*, 102302. https://doi.org/10.1016/j.ajp.2020.102302

Menon, V., Kaliamoorthy, C., Sridhar, V. K., Varadharajan, N., Joseph, R., Kattimani, S., Kar, S. K., & Arafat, S. Y. (2020b). Do Tamil newspapers educate the public about suicide? Content analysis from a high suicide union territory in India. *The International Journal of Social Psychiatry, 66*(8), 785–791. https://doi.org/10.1177/0020764020933296

Menon, V., Padhy, S. K., & Pattnaik, J. I. (2020c). Two to tango: Deconstructing the COVID-19 and suicidality conundrum from a biopsychosocial perspective. *Asian Journal of Psychiatry, 54*, 102400. https://doi.org/10.1016/j.ajp.2020.102400

Menon, V., Padhy, S. K., Ransing, R., Kar, S. K., & Arafat, S. Y. (2020d). Impact of celebrity suicide on population mental health: Mediators, media, and mitigation of contagion. *Indian Journal of Psychological Medicine, 42*(6), 588–590. https://doi.org/10.1177/0253717620962446

Menon, V., Varadharajan, N., Bascarane, S., Subramanian, K., Mukherjee, M., & Kattimani, S. (2020e). Psychological autopsy: Overview of Indian evidence, best practice elements, and a semi-structured interview guide. *Indian Journal of Psychiatry, 62*(6), 631. https://doi.org/10.4103/psychiatry.IndianJPsychiatry_331_20

Menon, V., Kar, S. K., Marthoenis, M., Arafat, S. Y., Sharma, G., Kaliamoorthy, C., Ransing, R., Mukherjee, S., Pattnaik, J. I., Shirahatti, N. B., Varadharajan, N., & Padhy, S. K. (2021a). Is there any link between celebrity suicide and further suicidal behaviour in India? *The International Journal of Social Psychiatry, 67*(5), 453–460. https://doi.org/10.1177/0020764020964531

Menon, V., Kar, S. K., Ransing, R., Arafat, S. Y., & Padhy, S. K. (2021b). National Media Monitoring Agency for reporting of suicide: An idea whose time has come? *Asian Journal of Psychiatry, 55*, 102516. https://doi.org/10.1016/j.ajp.2020.102516

Ministry of Health (Bhutan). (2021). *Suicide prevention in Bhutan—A five year action plan*. https://www.moh.gov.bt/wp-content/uploads/ict-files/2021/05/NSPP-Action-Plan.pdf

Ministry of Health and Family Welfare, Government of India. (2022). *National suicide prevention strategy*. Retrieved December 21, 2022, from https://main.mohfw.gov.in/sites/default/files/National%20Suicide%20Prevention%20Strategy.pdf

Ministry of Health, Maldives. (2017). *National Mental Health Policy 2015–2025*. https://health.gov.mv/storage/uploads/EoAjylw9/zae5c6sf.pdf

Mirza, F. H., Memon, A. A., Adil, S. E.-R., & Paryar, H. A. (2012). Audit of custodial deaths in Karachi—An autopsy-based study. *The Journal of the Pakistan Medical Association, 62*(8), 752–755.
Mishara, B. L., & Weisstub, D. N. (2016). The legal status of suicide: A global review. *International Journal of Law and Psychiatry, 44*, 54–74. https://doi.org/10.1016/j.ijlp.2015.08.032
Mundt, A. P., Cifuentes-Gramajo, P. A., Baranyi, G., & Fazel, S. (2024). Worldwide incidence of suicides in prison: A systematic review with meta-regression analyses. *The Lancet Psychiatry, 11*(7), 536–544. https://doi.org/10.1016/S2215-0366(24)00134-2
Murthy, V., Lakshman, V., & Gupta, M. (2010). Psychological autopsy-a review. *Journal of Punjab Academy of Forensic Medical Toxicology, 10*, 101–103.
National Human Rights Commission India, & Jain, S. K. (2014). *Suicide in prison: Prevention strategy and implication from human rights and legal points of view*. National Human Rights Commission. https://nhrc.nic.in/sites/default/files/SUICIDE%20IN%20PRISON%202014.pdf
NATLEX - Bhutan—Penal Code of Bhutan, 2004. (n.d.). Retrieved December 18, 2024, from https://natlex.ilo.org/dyn/natlex2/r/natlex/fe/details?p3_isn=87826
NCRB. (2022). *Prison Statistics* | National Crime Records Bureau. https://www.ncrb.gov.in/prison-statistics-india.html
Niederkrotenthaler, T., Voracek, M., Herberth, A., Till, B., Strauss, M., Etzersdorfer, E., Eisenwort, B., & Sonneck, G. (2010). Role of media reports in completed and prevented suicide: Werther v. Papageno effects. *The British Journal of Psychiatry: The Journal of Mental Science, 197*(3), 234–243. https://doi.org/10.1192/bjp.bp.109.074633
Nirmala, B. P., Reddy, N. V., & Kaliaperumal, V. G. (2000). Psychiatric morbidity among female prisoners. *Indian Journal of Psychological Medicine, 23*(2), 27–32. https://doi.org/10.1177/0975156420000207
Padubidri, J. R., Rao, D. S. J., Dutt, A., Shetty, B. S. K., & Boloor, A. (2015). Psychological autopsy- Unraveling the mystery of death. *Austin Journal of Forensic Science and Criminology, 2*(3), 1025.
Pakistan Penal Code (Act XLV of 1860). Retrieved December 18, 2024, from https://www.pakistani.org/pakistan/legislation/1860/actXLVof1860.html
Patel, D. J., & Vankar, G. K. (2024). A cross-sectional observational study of suicidal behavior among people in prison at Lajpore Central district jail, India. *The Journal of Forensic Psychiatry & Psychology, 36*(2), 1–14. https://doi.org/10.1080/14789949.2024.2412683
Presidential Committee on Prevention of Suicide, Sri Lanka. (1997). *National Policy and action plan on prevention of suicide*. Government of Sri Lanka.
Puranik, D., Paul, P., & Krishnamurthy, R. (2015). Application of equivocal death psychological autopsy for investigation: A case study. *International Journal of Indian Psychology, 2*(2). https://doi.org/10.25215/0202.063
Rabiya, S., & Raghavan, V. (2018). Prison mental health in India: Review. *Indian Journal of Social Psychiatry, 34*(3), 193. https://doi.org/10.4103/ijsp.ijsp_9_18
Raha, B., Sarma, S., & Phookun, H. R. (2018). A cross-sectional comparative study of insomnia, depression, and suicidality between male and female prisoners of Guwahati Central Jail. *Open Journal of Psychiatry & Allied Sciences, 9*(2), 136. https://doi.org/10.5958/2394-2061.2018.00027.7
Rajagopal, S. (2004). Suicide pacts and the internet. *British Medical Journal, 329*(7478), 1298–1299.
Ranjan, R., Kumar, S., Pattanayak, R. D., Dhawan, A., & Sagar, R. (2014). (De-) criminalization of attempted suicide in India: A review. *Industrial Psychiatry Journal, 23*(1), 4–9. https://doi.org/10.4103/0972-6748.144936
Rashid. (2023). *One prison inmate dies daily*. New Age. https://www.newagebd.net/article/192965/one-prison-inmate-dies-daily
Regmi, S., Shrestha, P., Gaihre, S., & Thagunna, N. S. (2019). Depression among female inmates in central prison of Kathmandu, Nepal. *Global Journal of Medicine and Public Health, 8*(1), 1–9.

Risal, A. (2017). Attempted suicide pact by married couple: A case study. *Journal of Psychiatrists' Association of Nepal, 5*(1), 49–52. https://doi.org/10.3126/jpan.v5i1.18332

Ruch, D. A., Sheftall, A. H., Schlagbaum, P., Fontanella, C. A., Campo, J. V., & Bridge, J. A. (2019). Characteristics and precipitating circumstances of suicide among incarcerated youth. *Journal of the American Academy of Child and Adolescent Psychiatry, 58*(5), 514–524.e1. https://doi.org/10.1016/j.jaac.2018.07.911

Rupasinghe, P. (2015). Medical negligence and doctor's liability; A critical review in present legal regime in Sri Lanka. In *Proceedings of 8th International Research Conference,* 260-265. http://ir.kdu.ac.lk/bitstream/handle/345/1394/law-043.pdf?sequence=1&isAllowed=y

Sabe, M., Kaiser, S., & Niveau, G. (2021). Suicide in psychiatry and medical liability: A case series. *International Journal of Law and Psychiatry, 74,* 101671. https://doi.org/10.1016/j.ijlp.2020.101671

Saini, V. (2017). Psychological autopsy—A way to revealing the enigma of equivocal death. *International Journal of Forensic Sciences, 2*(2). https://doi.org/10.23880/IJFSC-16000123

Sathyavathi, K. (1975). Usual and unusual suicide pacts in Bangalore - A report. *Indian Journal of Social Work, 36,* 173–180.

Sawant, N. S. (2018). Suicide in Indian prisoners. *Annals of Indian Psychiatry, 2*(1), 1. https://doi.org/10.4103/aip.aip_17_18

Senanayake, S. M. H. M. K. (2016). Suicide pacts in a district of Sri Lanka between year 2001 and 2014. *Medico-Legal Journal of Sri Lanka, 4*(1), 32. https://doi.org/10.4038/mljsl.v4i1.7335

Shagufta, S., Boduszek, D., Dhingra, K., & Kola-Palmer, D. (2015). Criminal social identity and suicide ideation among Pakistani young prisoners. *International Journal of Prisoner Health, 11*(2), 98–107. https://doi.org/10.1108/IJPH-06-2014-0018

Shrestha, G., Yadav, D. K., Sapkota, N., Baral, D., Yadav, B. K., Chakravartty, A., & Pokharel, P. K. (2017). Depression among inmates in a regional prison of eastern Nepal: A cross-sectional study. *BMC Psychiatry, 17*(1), 348. https://doi.org/10.1186/s12888-017-1514-9

Sinha, A., Gupta, S., Ray, M., Kumar, S., & Gupta, A. K. (2021). Lessons learned from psychological autopsies in armed forces. *Indian Journal of Psychological Medicine, 43*(2), 150–153. https://doi.org/10.1177/0253717620950254

Snehil, G., & Sagar, R. (2020). Juvenile justice system, juvenile mental health, and the role of MHPs: Challenges and opportunities. *Indian Journal of Psychological Medicine, 42*(3), 304–310. https://doi.org/10.4103/IJPSYM.IJPSYM_82_20

SPRF. (2020). *Female prisoners in India: The consequences of triple marginalisation.* https://sprf.in/female-prisoners-in-india-the-consequences-of-triple-marginalisation/

Suranga, M. A., & Vidanapathirana, J. (2022). Suicides among prison inmates in Sri Lanka: Prevalence and associated factors of suicidal behavior | *MedNEXT Journal of Medical and Health Sciences.* https://mednext.zotarellifilhoscientificworks.com/index.php/mednext/article/view/162

Tandon, R., & Nathani, M. K. (2018). Increasing suicide rates across Asia- A public health crisis. *Asian Journal of Psychiatry, 36,* A2–A4. https://doi.org/10.1016/j.ajp.2018.09.006

Taylor, S. (1982). *Durkheim and the study of suicide.* Retrieved August 8, 2024, from https://cir.nii.ac.jp/crid/1130282272828825600

The Indian Penal Code-1860. Government of India. (n.d.) Retrieved on December 18, 2024, from https://www.indiacode.nic.in/bitstream/123456789/2263/1/aA1860-45.pdf

The National Penal (Code) Act, 2017 (Nepal). (n.d.) *ADB's Law and Policy Reform Program.* Retrieved December 18, 2024, from https://lpr.adb.org/resource/national-penal-code-act-2017-nepal

The Penal Code, 1860 | 306. (n.d.). *Abetment of suicide.* Retrieved December 4, 2024, from http://bdlaws.minlaw.gov.bd/act-11/section-3137.html

UNODC. (2024). https://www.unodc.org/southasia/en/topics/frontpage/2009/crime-prevention-and-criminal-justice.html

UNODC-KOSTAT. (2022). https://coekostat.unodc.org/coekostat/en/news/new-publication_-regional-snapshot-4%2D%2D-prison-population-in-southern-asia.html

Utyasheva, L., Robertson, G., & Sharma, J. R. (2022). Perception of the criminality of attempted suicide in Nepal and its impact on suicide reporting. *International Journal of Law and Psychiatry, 83*, 101796. https://doi.org/10.1016/j.ijlp.2022.101796

Vadlamani, L. N., & Gowda, M. (2019). Practical implications of Mental Healthcare Act 2017: Suicide and suicide attempt. *Indian Journal of Psychiatry, 61*(Suppl 4), S750–S755. https://doi.org/10.4103/psychiatry.IndianJPsychiatry_116_19

Van Orden, K. A., Witte, T. K., Cukrowicz, K. C., Braithwaite, S. R., Selby, E. A., & Joiner, T. E. (2010). The interpersonal theory of suicide. *Psychological Review, 117*(2), 575–600. https://doi.org/10.1037/a0018697

Walsh, G., Sara, G., Ryan, C. J., & Large, M. (2015). Meta-analysis of suicide rates among psychiatric in-patients. *Acta Psychiatrica Scandinavica, 131*(3), 174–184. https://doi.org/10.1111/acps.12383

World Bank. (2019). *Health nutrition and population statistics* | DataBank. https://databank.worldbank.org/source/health-nutrition-and-population-statistics

WHO. (2023). *WHO policy brief on the health aspects of decriminalization of suicide and suicide attempts*. Retrieved December 2, 2024, from https://www.who.int/publications/i/item/9789240078796

World Health Organization. (2024). *Suicide*. WHO. Retrieved December 2, 2024, from https://www.who.int/news-room/fact-sheets/detail/suicide

Wu, K. C.-C., Cai, Z., Chang, Q., Chang, S.-S., Yip, P. S. F., & Chen, Y.-Y. (2022). Criminalisation of suicide and suicide rates: An ecological study of 171 countries in the world. *BMJ Open, 12*(2), e049425. https://doi.org/10.1136/bmjopen-2021-049425

Chapter 10
Substance Use and Forensic Psychiatry in South Asia

Roshan Bhad and Manmeet Kaur Brar

Abstract The South Asian region, home to approximately 22% of the global population, faces significant challenges related to substance use due to its proximity to major illicit drug-producing regions, the Golden Triangle and the Golden Crescent. This chapter explores the intersection of substance use and forensic psychiatry in South Asia across four key domains: (1) the legal framework surrounding the sale, production, and consumption of illicit substances; (2) the diverse policy responses to substance use in the region; (3) substance use in prison settings, including the implications for rehabilitation and recidivism; and (4) forensic assessments related to offenses committed under intoxication, including capacity evaluations and criminal responsibility. Given the high burden of substance-related offenses and the significant treatment gap, there is a pressing need for enhanced regional collaboration, such as under the SAARC Convention on Narcotic Drugs and Psychotropic Substances, to integrate psychiatric expertise into legal and policy frameworks. Strengthening forensic evaluations, improving access to addiction treatment within the criminal justice system, and fostering cross-border cooperation can help address the complex interplay of substance use, crime, and mental health in the region.

Keywords Addiction · Drug control · Forensic psychiatry · Policy · Substance use · Prison

---

R. Bhad (✉)
National Drug Dependence Treatment Centre (NDDTC), AIIMS, New Delhi, New Delhi, India
e-mail: roshan@aiims.edu

M. K. Brar
All India Institute of Medical Sciences (AIIMS), Jammu, Vijaypur, India

A. Parmar et al. (eds.), *Forensic Psychiatry and Prison Mental Health in South Asia*, South Asian Perspectives in Mental Health and Psychology,
https://doi.org/10.1007/978-981-96-7206-6_10

1 Introduction

The southern region of Asia, also known as South Asia, includes a group of eight nations, namely Afghanistan, Bangladesh, Bhutan, India, Maldives, Nepal, Pakistan, and Sri Lanka. South Asia is an important WHO region, accounting for over 21% of the global population, out of which 95% is concentrated in three countries, i.e., India, Pakistan, and Bangladesh. Since these countries are low- or middle-income, they share several geopolitical and economic characteristics. This area is prone to violence and natural disasters, which climate change exacerbates, making residents even more vulnerable (Arafat & Kar, 2024).

Tobacco and alcohol use are major risk factors for preventable deaths from non-communicable illnesses in the region. Pharmaceutical opioids and stimulants like methamphetamines are the most common synthetic drugs used in the region. This is also reflected in data from addiction treatment clinics, where opioids form the largest group at about 42.68% of the population, followed by amphetamine-type stimulants (ATS) at 27.15% and cannabis at 26.08%, among illicit drugs (Fig. 10.1), whereas other substances such as cocaine, solvents, and sedative and tranquilizer use comprise less than 5% of the treatment-seeking population. The substance use disorders are further associated with medical as well as psychiatric co-morbidities increasing demand on limited treatment services for substance use disorders in the region (Bhad & Shukla, 2024). The treatment gap is huge in Asia, with only 5.1% of people with drug use disorders in treatment in 2022—1.9% for women and 10.5% for men. The most common pathway of referral is the criminal justice system for treatment in Asia (Choudhury et al., 2024; Jha et al., 2024; World Drug Report 2024 -Drug Market Patterns and Trends).

This region is also home to two significant areas: the "Golden Crescent" (Iran, Pakistan, and Afghanistan) and the neighboring "Golden Triangle" (Thailand, Laos, and Myanmar). These regions rank among the top illicit opioid producers in the world. A key facilitator of increasing drug availability appears to be globalization in the operational methods used by organized crime groups. Beyond drug trafficking, armed organizations in the Golden Triangle and Latin America have branched out into cybercrime and scamming, trafficking in persons for forced criminality, and crimes that affect the environment.

The views and policies towards drugs in South Asian countries have taken a transition in line with the Western libertarian approaches to the drug problem to medical and criminal views of the problem, policies framed accordingly. This chapter will cover four aspects of substance use and legal interface—namely, the sale, production, and consumption of illicit substances; legal approaches to substance use in the region; substance use in prison settings; and offences under intoxication and capacity assessment under those circumstances.

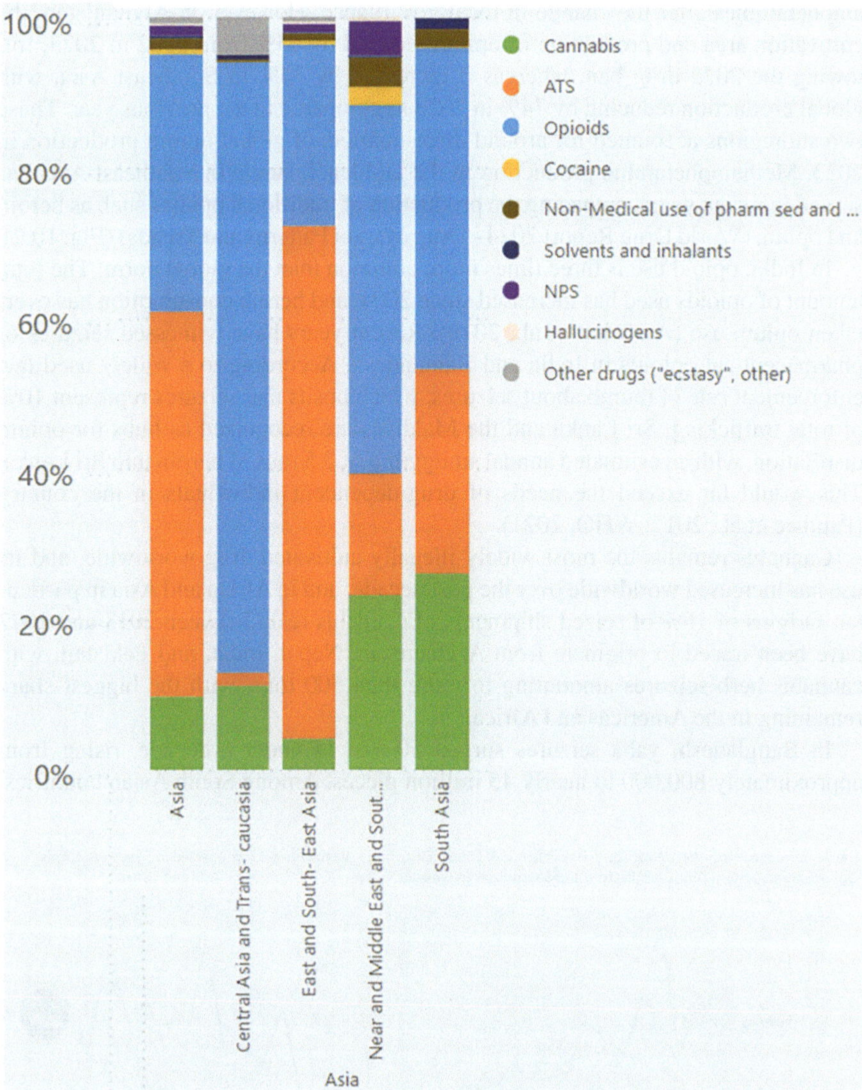

Fig. 10.1 Proportion of people in drug-related treatment according to primary drug of concern, 2022, in Asia (World Drug Report 2024 - Drug Market Patterns and Trends)

2 Illicit Drug Trade Status in the Region

An international drug control issue is the narcotics trade, which begins in Afghanistan and Pakistan and travels via India to other South Asian countries, Europe, and the United States. The world's largest illicit opium grower used to be Afghanistan, and the country has seen a rise in the production and trade of stimulants related to amphetamines after the change in local governance. However, in Afghanistan, the cultivation area and production of opium reduced by 95% from 2022 to 2023, following the 2022 drug ban, whereas it increased by 34% in Southeast Asia, with global production reducing by 74% in 2023 as compared to the previous year. These two subregions accounted for around three-quarters of global opium production in 2023. Methamphetamine production in the Golden Triangle in Southeast Asia has surged in recent years, outpacing the production of traditional opiates such as heroin and opium (World Drug Report 2024 - Drug Market Patterns and Trends) (Fig. 10.2).

In India, opioid use is three times more common than the global norm. The total amount of opioids used has increased since 2004, and heroin consumption has overtaken opium use (Ambekar et al., 2019). Recent years have witnessed seizures of pharmaceutical opioids in India and Bangladesh. According to a widely used law enforcement rule of thumb about seizures, which posits that seizures represent 10% of total trafficking, Sri Lanka and the Maldives are recognized as hubs for opium distillation, with an estimated annual smuggling of 3.5 tons of heroin into Sri Lanka. This would far exceed the needs of drug-dependent individuals in the country (Panthee et al., 2017; WHO, 2021).

Cannabis remains the most widely illegally cultivated drug worldwide, and its use has increased worldwide over the past decade, and in Africa and Asia in particular. Origins of 16% of seized shipments of cannabis resin between 2018 and 2022 have been traced to originate from Afghanistan, Nepal, India, and Pakistan, with cannabis herb seizures amounting to more than 500 tons, with the biggest share remaining in the Americas and Africa.

In Bangladesh, yaba seizures surged 50-fold in under a decade, rising from approximately 800,000 to nearly 45 million pieces. Among South Asian countries,

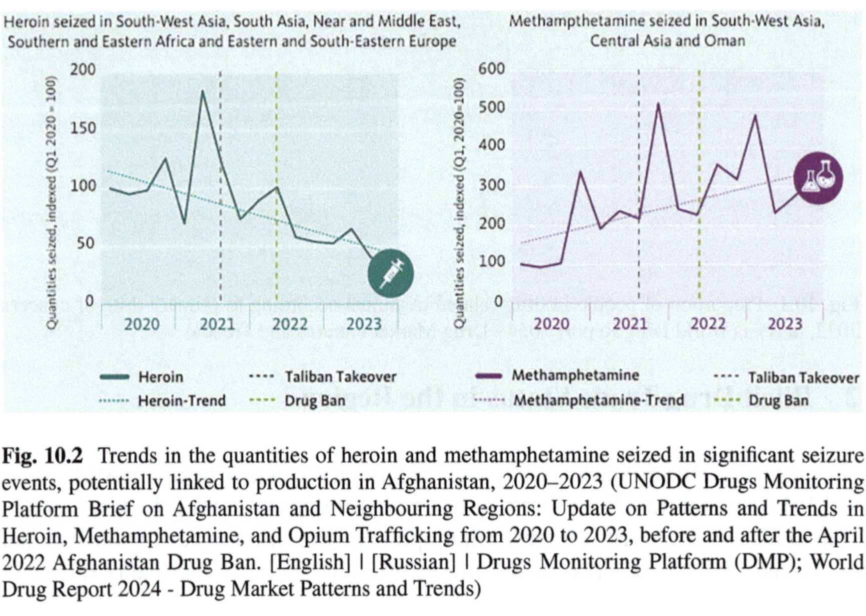

Fig. 10.2 Trends in the quantities of heroin and methamphetamine seized in significant seizure events, potentially linked to production in Afghanistan, 2020–2023 (UNODC Drugs Monitoring Platform Brief on Afghanistan and Neighbouring Regions: Update on Patterns and Trends in Heroin, Methamphetamine, and Opium Trafficking from 2020 to 2023, before and after the April 2022 Afghanistan Drug Ban. [English] I [Russian] I Drugs Monitoring Platform (DMP); World Drug Report 2024 - Drug Market Patterns and Trends)

India is currently the dominant source of synthetic cathinones. Most seized ketamine in Europe is also believed to originate from India; however, there is also evidence of its origins in Pakistan and China. However, Europe is also producing more cathinones locally (European Union Drugs Agency, 2024).

3 Legal Approaches to Substance Use in South Asia

The WHO Global Alcohol Action Plan has established a strategic framework for national harm reduction policies, with the exception of Bhutan, Sri Lanka, and Nepal; other countries lack a nationally structured policy on alcohol consumption in accordance with the WHO strategic plan. Consequently, policies are being assessed through the framework of the SAFER alcohol control plan introduced by the WHO.

Countries' tobacco policies have predominantly been based on the Framework Convention on Tobacco Control (FCTC) brought in by WHO. Countries ratified it at various times from 2003 to 2006 (Geneva, 2003).

South Asian countries predominantly favor a criminal justice system approach to drug control rather than a public health strategy. The current regulatory framework for narcotic and psychotropic substances is primarily governed by three United Nations conventions: the Single Convention on Narcotic Drugs, 1961, as amended by the 1972 Protocol; the Convention on Psychotropic Substances, 1971; and the Convention Against Illicit Traffic in Narcotic Drugs and Psychotropic Substances, 1988. The majority of countries have ratified UN agreements on drug control and have developed national drug control policies or action plans. However, an increasing number of countries are deviating from these regulations by legalizing cannabis, none in South Asia so far. Recently, in the year 2020, India supported the resolution to remove cannabis and cannabis resins from Schedule IV, whereas Afghanistan and Pakistan voted against it. India, however, voted against the resolution to add delta-9-THC (tetrahydrocannabinol) and delete the extracts and tincture of cannabis from Schedule I of the 1961 single convention. India also opposed the resolution that would have put the preparations containing predominantly CBD and not >0.2% of delta-9-THC out of international control (Riboulet-Zemouli & Krawitz, 2022).

All South Asian nations enforce criminal and administrative sanctions for drug usage. Concurrently, there exist specific exceptions. Indian legislation outlaws the consumption of all cannabis products, with the exception of Bhang, which is derived from cannabis leaves (Parmar et al., 2024). Capital punishment for drug-related crimes is implemented in South Asian nations such as Bangladesh and India (Girelli et al., 2022). This criminalization stigmatizes drug users and exacerbates the stigma around drug use, discouraging them from pursuing assistance and treatment. Individuals who use drugs (PWUD) describe experiencing many forms of abuse, including oppressive law enforcement activities, coercive treatment, and discriminatory access to healthcare, occasionally resulting in the denial of health treatments. In South Asian nations such as Sri Lanka and Bangladesh, large arrests and human rights violations against people who use drugs (PWUD) have been documented as measures to regulate drug consumption. Prior observations indicate that punitive legislation and actions targeting people who use drugs hinder initiatives aimed at delivering harm reduction and demand reduction strategies, such as opioid agonist therapy (Murphy & Cliff, 2021).

Policy formulations of each nation pertain to initiatives aimed at reducing supply and demand. The importance of demand reduction initiatives has recently been evident with the gradual and consistent transition from supply reduction to demand reduction. Actions to diminish supply necessitate legal intervention. In contrast, primary prevention, treatment, and societal reintegration constitute several demand reduction strategies. The details of drug programs in South Asian countries are elaborated in a chapter titled "Policy, Legalisation, and Programs Related to Substance Use Disorders in South Asia" (Bojappen & Chand, 2024).

3.1 India

3.1.1 Alcohol

Alcohol continues to be regulated under state excise laws, which regulate the manufacturing, distribution, sales, taxation, legal age of drinking, fines, etc., at the state levels. India lacks a uniform national alcohol policy. The legal age of drinking varies from 18 to 25 years across India. Apart from these, some states have also set some other days as dry days, while some states like Bihar (since 2016), Gujarat, Nagaland, and Mizoram have completely banned alcohol, and drinking alcohol in these states is punishable with restricted use and sale of alcohol in Lakshadweep since the law changed in 2021.

3.1.2 Tobacco

Tobacco is controlled under the National Laws of Cigarettes and Other Tobacco Products (Prohibition of Advertisement and Regulation of Trade and Commerce, Production, Supply, and Distribution) Act, 2003 [COTPA, 2003] and Related Rules (Kaur & Jain, 2011). This regulates the consumption, production, supply, and distribution of tobacco products by imposing restrictions on the advertisement, promotion, and sponsorship of tobacco products. The production, sale, storage, and distribution of food products containing tobacco or nicotine, such as Gutkha, have been prohibited under The Food Safety and Standards (Prohibition and Restrictions on Sales) Regulations, 2011, dated 1st August 2011, notified under the Food Safety and Standards Act, 2006. The Drugs and Cosmetics Act of 1940, amended in 1992, banned the sale of toothpaste and tooth powders containing tobacco. Electronic cigarettes and electronic nicotine delivery systems (ENDS) have also been banned from sale in India since 2019.

3.1.3 Narcotics and Psychotropics

Drug regulation in India has had a complex and lengthy trajectory, closely linked to historical legacies, international treaties, and domestic imperatives. During the colonial era, the Opium Acts (1867 and 1878) were passed to control the cultivation and manufacture (not consumption) of opium and to bring them under government regulation. During the 1920s, due to the pressure of the growing nationalist movements, many provincial governments enacted laws to control the consumption of opium. The Dangerous Drugs Act was passed in 1930. The Act primarily applied to the drugs derived from plants such as poppy, hemp, and coca and had no offenses attached to the consumption of drugs/cannabis. The control was primarily through licensing and penalizing unlicensed activities. These laws reflected the imperial interests of the British Empire, which sought to maintain control over lucrative commodities like opium while exerting authority over colonial territories. India is a signatory to the UN conventions on narcotic drugs and psychotropic substances. India passed and implemented the NDPS Act in 1985 to give effect to its obligations under these conventions. It replaced the Opium Acts and the Dangerous Drugs Act of 1930. However, the DCA of 1940 continues to apply (Parmar et al., 2024). Prior to 1985, there was no legislation governing cannabis, and its products were sold legally. India initially resisted the Western position on prohibiting cannabis under international treaties but later acquiesced to banning its use and trade under the NDPS in 1985.

The Narcotic Drugs and Psychotropic Substances Act of India (NDPS Act of 1985, with amendments over the years) covers three broad categories of drugs and substances: (1) narcotic drugs (as defined in the 1961 Convention), (2) psychotropic substances (as defined in the 1971 Convention or the drugs notified by the government as such), and (3) controlled substances that are used to manufacture these substances, including precursor chemicals such as ephedrine and pseudoephedrine. The cannabis-leaf product known as *bhang* in India is excluded from the Act (as per the 1961 Convention) and is primarily regulated through respective state governments' excise laws. The NDPS Act prohibits the cultivation, production, sale, purchase, trade, import, export, use, and consumption of psychotropics and narcotics except for scientific and medical purposes. The Act is primarily punitive. However, it also empowers the government to allow drug-related activities under "medicinal or scientific use." The NDPS Act has been amended three times to date, in 1989, 2001, and 2014. It provides quantity-based sentencing (i.e., graded punishment based on "small," "intermediate," and "commercial" quantity). It regulates certain essential narcotics in a unified manner across the country using terms like "management" and "recognition and approval" of treatment centers to establish evidence-based treatment approaches under Section 71. Some major criticisms of the act are criminalizing drug use and consumption, quantity-based sentencing (thus making motives and the role of the offender irrelevant), restricting access to essential medicines, including buprenorphine (not being part of essential narcotic drugs and continuing to be a psychotropic), uneven coordination among governmental agencies, and lack of implementation of sections like 64A, which offers treatment instead of imprisonment for those found in possession of a substance for personal use.

3.2 *Nepal*

Alcohol and tobacco are sold and consumed legally. The Liquor Act 1974 is the main law that regulates liquor and alcoholic beverages. It is a moderate and flexible law that aims to regulate and control liquor and alcoholic beverages in Nepal. It also seeks to protect public decency, health, convenience, and economic interest from the negative effects of liquor. The Drugs Act 1978 is the principal law that regulates the drugs and pharmaceutical substances in Nepal, under which individuals engaged in the cultivation, production, preparation, purchase, sale, distribution, exports, imports, storage, or consumption of any narcotic drug are subject to fines and a maximum penalty of life imprisonment (Nepal Law Commission, 1976). The Drugs Act 1978 also establishes a Drugs Advisory Committee, a Department of Drug Administration (DDA), and a Drugs Court to oversee and enforce the law. The non-physician-prescribed use of narcotic substances is a criminal violation; nonetheless, the Act provides for the prevention and treatment of drug users. The prevailing theme has been the recognition of substance use disorder as a criminal matter but neglecting to recognize it as a health issue requiring intervention. The Penal Code 2017 is the general law that defines and penalizes various offenses related to drugs and alcohol in Nepal. Under this, possession/consumption or trafficking of narcotics or psychotropics without authorization can lead to a penalty that ranges from a fine of up to 500,000 rupees to imprisonment for life, depending on the quantity and type of the drug or substance.

3.3 *Bhutan*

3.3.1 Alcohol

The National Policy and Strategic Framework to Reduce Harmful Use of Alcohol 2015–2020, approved by the 90th session of the Lhengye Zhungtshog, sets the permissible age for alcohol consumption at 18 years, restricts sales in bars before 1 pm and after 10 pm, and permits foreigners to carry a maximum of 1 L of alcohol, with prohibition at religious sites and monasteries. Strict penalties are in place with enforcement of BAC levels (RBT, sobriety checkpoints) and offender management alcohol ignition interlocks, alcohol rehabilitation, and/or treatment programs (Dolkar, 2016).

3.3.2 Tobacco

Bhutan has been working towards a tobacco-free society since ratifying the WHO Framework Convention on Tobacco Control in 2004. The Tobacco Control Act of 2010 imposed a comprehensive ban on tobacco products, but tobacco consumption was not banned. Importing tobacco products for personal consumption was permitted but taxed at 100%. Despite a robust legal and regulatory framework, smuggling and a black market for tobacco persisted, especially during COVID-19. There were a whopping 26 million tobacco users who had been smuggling tobacco all along. In July 2021, the government amended the Act, lifting the decade-long ban and allowing tobacco sales in grocery and pan shops. However, the country still bans the production and manufacturing of tobacco products, prohibits sale to minors with strict identification and proof of age from buyers, and does not permit sale near schools, monasteries, hospitals, clinics, and heritage sites. Bhutan lacks regulations specific to newer tobacco products such as ENDS, and evidence suggests that electronic cigarettes are particularly appealing to the youth and Act as an initiation product. Claims by the Bhutanese government suggest that the overhaul of the ban on tobacco and tobacco products in the country is a temporary measure. The tobacco control framework has shifted from a ban to regulation, raising concerns about the inadequacy of legal and policy infrastructure to support such regulation, including labeling measures and the taxation regime (Evans-Reeves, 2023).

3.3.3 Narcotics and Psychotropics

In Bhutan, the Bhutan Narcotic Control Agency (BNCA) was established in 2006 following the enactment of the Narcotic Drugs, Psychotropic Substances, and Substance Abuse (NDPSSA) Act in 2005. The NDPSSA Act of Bhutan was revised in 2015 and again amended in 2018. BNCA functions as the secretariat to the Narcotic Control Board and is the nodal agency of the government for all matters related to narcotic drugs, psychotropic substances, and substance abuse. Key highlights of the Act include: consideration of substance users as patients, classification of drugs based on quantity with grading of penalty, asset forfeiture for trafficking, with punishment for drug trafficking not including the death penalty (Bojappen & Chand, 2024).

In addition, the Cannabis Framework for Medicine, Research, and Export outlines the controlled use of cannabis for medical purposes and research while also regulating its cultivation to prevent misuse. The government has also formed the National Drugs Task Force, recognizing the need for coordinated action. This dedicated task force is responsible for managing substance-related issues and overseeing the implementation of interventions across multiple sectors.

3.4 *The Maldives*

The first drug law of the Maldives, 1977—Law on Narcotic Drugs and Psychotropic Substances, criminalized drug use, filling our jails beyond capacity and disrupting many lives in the process. It was prohibitionist and focused on supply control aspects. Tobacco is the only drug that can be sold legally.

In 2020, the Maldives Drug Act was enforced, which stipulates penalties for drug traffickers. At the same time, it establishes a mechanism for the rehabilitation of drug-dependent persons, believing that drug-dependent persons are not just criminals but those in need of rehabilitation, and aims to identify those who are in the early stages of drug dependency and to assist them in obtaining measures which will enable them to overcome their dependency on drugs. It also proposes to establish a specialist "drug court" to hear criminal cases of drug-dependent persons and subject such persons to mandatory treatment and rehabilitation programs to reduce or eliminate their dependency on drugs and thus increase their chances of reintegration into the community as responsible citizens. It recognizes that some peddlers may be drug dependent and, therefore, engaging in peddling, and aims to prevent peddlers from dealing in drugs to sustain their drug dependency and to reduce the level of criminal activity associated with their drug dependence.

The National Drug Agency is required to establish under this Act or those that are licensed by the Agency under this Act. The National Drug Control Council provides advice on the policies on combatting drug trafficking in the Maldives, the prevention of the use of drugs, and policies relating to the rehabilitation of drug-dependence persons (2020 Drugs Act of the Maldives | International Society of Substance Use Professionals, 2020).

3.5 *Sri Lanka*

The National Dangerous Drug Control Board (NDDCB) in Sri Lanka was established in 1984 to formulate and review national policies on drug abuse prevention and control and the treatment and rehabilitation of drug users (National Dangerous Drug Control Board (NDDCB), Sri Lanka, 2018). It is currently governed by the Ministry of Public Security. The National Authority on Tobacco and Alcohol (NATA) was established in 2006 to regulate tobacco and alcohol in Sri Lanka. ADIC (Alcohol drug and information center) is a resource center that promotes demand reduction and effective control policies, providing technical help and resources (National Authority on Tobacco and Alcohol Act, No. 27 of 2006). Sri Lanka has also enacted the National Policy for Prevention and Control of Drugs of Abuse, 1984, which is also prohibitionist and focuses on supply control aspects.

3.6 Afghanistan

Afghanistan is the latest country in the region to formulate the National Drug Demand Reduction Policy in 2012–16. The country has experienced decades of war, is one of the highest illicit opium-cultivating countries, and has a higher prevalence of opioid use disorders in the region. Current policy focuses on drug bans, including alcohol bans, with a reduction in opium production (Noroozi et al., 2024).

Afghanistan is home to an estimated 3.5 million substance users, nearly 10% of the population. The United States Department of State's Bureau of International Narcotics and Law Enforcement Affairs (INL) reported that by 2020, it had established a network of 103 drug treatment centers providing residential, outpatient, and home-based treatment services in partnership with the Colombo Plan Drug Advisory Programme (CPDAP). Several dozen drug treatment centers of various types (residential and non-residential) were also established by organizations partnering with the United Nations Office on Drugs and Crime (UNODC), with others such as Médecins du Monde (MDM) also running some of their own. Over the years, a number of these centers were handed over to the Afghan government. The Ministry of Public Health (MoPH), for example, reported that it ran 50 treatment centers in 2019. In December 2023, the Lancet reported that only 10% of treatment centers were still active (Bjelica, 2024).

3.7 Bangladesh

In Bangladesh, the Narcotics Control Act of 2018 is the principal counter-narcotics legislation (Maruf et al., 2024). Bangladesh‘s current policy follows more stringent supply reduction measures, “The War on Drugs,” with limited success.

3.8 Pakistan

In Pakistan, the stricter anti-narcotic laws against drug use have failed to keep a check on the use of controlled drugs and other narcotic substances, and drug addiction, which is a constantly growing problem in Pakistan. The key laws and policies are the Prohibition of (Enforcement of Hadd) Order of 1979, the Control of Narcotics Substances Act (CNSA), 1997, and the National Anti-Narcotics Policy, 2019. Reason for the anti-narcotics legal regime to contain the growing problem of drug use and addiction for various reasons, including, but not limited to, the unwillingness of Pakistani society to respect these laws, misuse of the existing laws by police against the poor and addicts, and the government's lack of interest in treatment and rehabilitation of people with substance use problem (Uddin & Rahman, 2021).

The **2022 Amendment to the Control of Narcotics Substances Act (CNSA),** which aimed to streamline sentencing for drug offences, introduced harsher penalties for wider quantity thresholds and eliminated the possibility of remissions, parole, and probation for drug offenders except for women and juveniles. The rigid sentencing guidelines have eliminated alternatives to incarceration and directly led to disproportionate penalties, exacerbating the issue of over-incarceration. Despite the Control of Narcotics Substances (Amendment) Act 2023, which abolished the death penalty for drug-related offences, such offences remain a significant category for which death sentences are imposed. In Sindh alone, at least three death sentences for drug-related crimes were handed down in 2024, raising concerns about the inconsistent application of the amended law by the judiciary (Prison Reforms | JPP, 2024).

4 Substance Use and Criminal Behavior

Research has consistently found increased violence risk in drug use disorders; individual studies have shown that the magnitude of this increased risk varies depending on the drug category. Furthermore, it has been suggested that certain types of stimulants, such as crack cocaine, that are associated with irritability and aggressiveness, might have a higher risk of criminal behavior than others, including less strong forms of cannabis that might reduce risks due to sedative and calming effects. The link between drug use and violent outcomes is complex; a wide range of factors—such as experiences of violence, including both as victim and perpetrator, the comorbidity of other mental disorders, and social determinants, such as sex, ethnicity, and poverty—might moderate and mediate this link. For instance, previous violence victimization might trigger the development of drug use disorders, which might, in turn, lead to later perpetration of violence. Moreover, structural causes of drug use problems are relevant, given that they have been linked to criminalization, as well as factors such as poverty, poor mental health, treatment availability, and homelessness. In addition, the physical and psychological effects of drugs can lead to agitation, aggression, and cognitive impairment that might, in turn, heighten the risk of violence. Individuals with drug use disorders might also turn to violence to finance their drug use, and disputes within illegal drug markets might be associated with violence.

A systematic review found that individuals with a diagnosed drug use disorder have a 4- to 10-fold higher risk of perpetrating violence compared with the general population or individuals without the drug use disorder being studied. All of the examined categories of drug use disorders—including cannabis, hallucinogens, stimulants, opioids, and sedatives—are associated with elevated violence risks (Zhong et al., 2020).

Substance is also found to co-occur in 40–60% of IPV (intimate partner violence) incidents across various studies (Intimate Partner Violence and Co-Occurring Substance Abuse/Addiction, 2021). Alcohol is arguably the most commonly used psychoactive substance among IPV, unsurprising as it is also the most commonly used psychoactive substance in the world. IPV-exposed women are also at higher risk of substance use and progression to SUD. IPV can also result in psychological trauma or other mental health outcomes that lead to substance use as a coping mechanism. In South Asia, physical and/or sexual IPV varies from 5.5% in the Maldives to 46.0% in Afghanistan (Coll et al., 2020). Around 24%–75% of women report lifetime IPV exposure at SUD treatment intake (Mehr et al., 2023). This necessitates screening women with SUD for IPV and vice versa.

There are studies that demonstrate reduced crime after drug treatment (e.g., opioid maintenance treatment, methadone, buprenorphine, and naltrexone) and non-medical treatment (e.g., therapeutic communities, drug courts) among individuals using cocaine and opioids, as well as with general drug use disorders. Moreover, prison-based interventions—such as therapeutic communities, opiate maintenance treatment, and pharmacotherapies for drug use disorders—are effective in reducing recidivism in prisoners (de Andrade et al., 2018; Mitchell et al., 2012; Perry et al., 2016; Vorma et al., 2013).

5 Capacity Assessment in Substance Use in Forensic Settings

Capacity assessment in forensic settings determines an individual's mental competence, criminal responsibility, and ability to stand trial. Substance use disorders (SUDs) can impact cognitive functioning, decision-making abilities, and legal culpability. Key domains include fitness to stand trial, criminal responsibility, and capacity for decision-making and giving consent.

For assessing mental competence (fitness to stand trial), evaluation is done to see whether the accused can understand court proceedings, communicate with legal counsel, and participate in their defense. Acute intoxication can impair attention and concentration, memory, and critical thinking skills. Chronic substance use, especially alcohol, withdrawal symptoms, or substance-induced psychosis or depression, may also impair competency.

For assessing criminal responsibility (Insanity Defense and Diminished Responsibility), it has to be determined if an individual was aware of their actions and could distinguish right from wrong at the time of the crime.

Some legal systems consider voluntary intoxication as no defense, while others allow mitigation in cases of severe substance-induced mental disorders. For example, in India, illegal acts done under voluntary intoxication are considered to be voluntary acts under "Mens rea" or insanity defense under Section 84 of IPC in India. Under involuntary intoxication or substance-induced mental disorder, punishment may be mitigated or reduced. In India, driving or attempting to drive a motor vehicle under the influence of a drug to the extent that the drug makes the person incapable of exercising proper control over the vehicle is prohibited and punishable under the Motor Vehicle Act, 1988, as amended in 2019. Alcohol consumption is banned in Afghanistan, Maldives, and Bangladesh. Other countries have different

BAC limits while driving or attempting to drive a motor vehicle under the influence of alcohol, concentration ranging from 0.08% in Bhutan to 0.03% in India, with different penalties ranging from imprisonment in Pakistan to monetary fines in India. Also, the police are authorized to conduct a breath alcohol test by law in India. Enforcement of BAC levels (RBT, sobriety checkpoints) is done in Bhutan and India (Bojappen & Chand, 2024).

Capacity for decision-making and consent involves evaluating whether individuals with SUDs can make informed decisions regarding medical treatment, legal matters, and contractual obligations. Cases can include substance-dependent individuals consenting to plea deals, signing legal documents, or participating in their defense or medical treatment. The Mental Healthcare Act (MHCA) 2017 in India includes substance use disorders under the category of mental illness. The inclusion emphasizes that substance use disorders are health issues rather than solely matters of law enforcement, which has been praised for taking a rights-based approach towards SUDs. Notwithstanding these favorable modifications, there are still disadvantages in the MHCA pertaining to SUDs. Substance Use Disorders (SUDs) are not defined clearly enough to make a distinction if harmful use can also be subsumed under SUD as per MHCA. This is especially important as MHCA allows for involuntary admission. In the case of SUD, impaired judgment can be present during an intoxicated state or withdrawal state. Can it be used to get someone into a treatment facility against their will, as per MHCA, undersupported admission? This is crucial, given that inhumane treatment and abuses of human rights are frequently recorded in the context of substance use disorder treatment. Also, most states still do not have a state mental authority that is supposed to have regulatory oversight over the functioning of the mental health centers even after 8 years of MHCA (Rao et al., 2019). There is a lack of standardized forensic psychiatric protocols across South Asian countries with limited access to trained forensic psychiatrists and neuropsychological testing facilities in many regions. Capacity assessment in forensic settings is crucial to ensuring fair legal proceedings, appropriate sentencing, and access to rehabilitation for individuals with substance use disorders, balancing public safety with human rights.

6 Substance Use in Prison Settings

Drug users are vastly overrepresented in prison populations. Internationally, alcohol use disorder is highly prevalent in prisoners, with a pooled estimate of 24% (95% CI 21–27). In men, the lowest estimate suggests one in six (or 16%) met the threshold for alcohol use disorder on arrival into prison, and in women it was one in ten. Drug use disorder (based on the past one year of use) was as high as the alcohol estimates, being 30% in male prisoners (95% CI 22–38), and possibly higher in female prisoners with a pooled estimate of 51% (95% CI 43–58) (Fazel et al., 2017). All South Asian countries have criminalized drug use except for tobacco and alcohol, with alcohol too being criminalized in Maldives, Pakistan, and Afghanistan.

Criminalization of the consumption of psychoactive substances has negative health, security, and human rights consequences (Favril, 2023). The arrests made for possession of psychoactive substances for personal use are an impediment to accessing the health services that these people are in need of. The lack of appropriate, evidence-based interventions in prison settings translates into poor or no interventions for the underlying substance use disorders, which may be at the core of substance use (Emerson & Haden, 2018). For those who are "using" substances and have not yet developed a substance use disorder, the arrests and subsequent incarceration can be argued as an even more disproportionate and inappropriate response, as this adversely impacts their chances for education and employment and may lead to social alienation.

Rates of re-incarceration are especially high for inmates with a drug problem. Drug-dependent offenders are much more likely to return to prison than other offenders. Many drug users stop using and injecting drugs when imprisoned. For other prisoners, though, some will commence drug use or switch the route of drug administration if their preferred drug is unavailable. A history of injecting drug use is substantially higher among prisoners than among the general population. Needles and syringes are scarce in the prison setting. With few needles and syringes circulating among many drug-injecting inmates, sharing is inevitable. Up to 15 or 20 individuals may inject with the same equipment, which increases the risk of HIV, HCV, and HBV transmission. Prison overcrowding has emerged as a critical issue in Bangladesh, India, Sri Lanka, and Pakistan; a primary contributor to inadequate prison conditions, it may yield possibly lethal consequences.

The primary goal has to be the reduction of drug injecting in prison. One way to achieve this is to reduce the number of drug injectors who are sent to prison. There is abundant evidence that community-based methadone treatment reduces injecting, crime, and the subsequent incarceration of drug users. Another way is to target pre-trial detainees. International standards clearly state that pre-trial detention should be an exceptional measure used sparingly. Therefore, programs providing safe alternatives to pre-trial detention for persons accused of low-level crimes should be implemented. A third way to reduce the level of drug injecting in prison is to provide opioid agonist treatment (OAT) during incarceration. The most controversial strategy has been prison-based needle and syringe exchange programs (NSEP). These programs have been implemented in 70 different prisons in over a dozen countries. Imprisoned drug offenders need treatment to reduce their risk of relapse and re-incarceration. Minor drug offenders need treatment, not incarceration. Advocacy is required to reorientate the focus of prison policies to implement drug treatment and harm reduction programs in order to protect the health of inmates and the general public (Dolan et al., 2015).

Harm Reduction International reports that opioid agonist treatment (OAT) is available in India, Bangladesh, Maldives, and Bhutan, while the rest do not have operational OST services. All South Asian countries have NSEP except Maldives and Sri Lanka. Pakistan has an OAT pilot, and Bhutan‘s national policy also supports OAT, but it is not yet available in these countries. In Nepal, OAT has been included in the national program and is being provided by government hospitals and

NGOs. However, apart from a few prisons in India, OAT is not available in any South Asian prison setting. NSEP is not available in any prison in South Asia. Major barriers for OAT services in prison include expenses, waiting periods, and adverse public perceptions of therapy. Key facilitators include OAT education and flexible treatment modalities, including telehealth-based OAT. In correctional facilities, inadequate assistance with treatment referrals posed an obstacle. The fear of judgment posed a challenge for pregnant individuals (Power et al., 2024).

6.1 India

A study done in the Tihar Prison, New Delhi (the largest prison in India with more than 11,000 inmates), found that 8% of the new admissions to the prisons were substance dependent, with a majority (76%–82%) reporting heroin as the primary drug of use during the years 1997–2000 (Sethi, 2002). Another report based on a study among 466 inmates in Delhi, Mumbai, and Punjab found that 63% of those included in the study had used illicit drugs at least once in their lifetime (UNODC, 2014). According to media reports, nearly 47% of inmates in 25 jails of Punjab were found to be "addicted to drugs" in a special drive aimed at "screening of the prisoners for drug use" in the year 2022 (The New Indian Express, 2022). A high rate of engagement with the criminal justice system among people with opioid use disorders seeking treatment has been reported (Sarkar et al., 2021).

India criminalizes all drug use except tobacco, alcohol, and bhang under the NDPS Act. There exists a wide variation in the rate of offences under the NDPS Act (per lakh population). This ranged from a low of 0.7 in Gujarat to a high of 32.8 in Punjab in the year 2021 (Balhara et al., 2024). There is a provision Under the NDPS Act, 1985, Section 64A, "Immunity from prosecution to addicts volunteering for treatment," implies that a person who is found in possession of small quantities can plead guilty, and a judge may choose to send the person for mandatory treatment. However, section 64A is one of the rarely utilized legal provisions. A key critique is that it requires a substance user to plead guilty to possession of the illicit drug, because of which it remains underutilized.

The Mental Health Care Act (MHCA) of 2017 also includes mental ailments occurring due to substances and drugs under the ambit of "mental illness." The MHCA section 103 lays out provisions for treatment of prisoners with mental illnesses, which can be alternately used for patients with substance use disorders as well; however, it has been underutilized till now.

In 2012, the Government of India implemented a national policy on NDPS for the first time. The aim was to direct many ministries, state governments, international organizations, and NGOs while reaffirming India's dedication to addressing the drug crisis comprehensively. The policy, among other things, delineates the government's involvement in the treatment, rehabilitation, and social reintegration of drug "addicts." The policy has adopted a contradictory stance compared to the prevailing international policies (Ambekar et al., 2013). It advocated mandatory drug testing and categorically disallowing harm reduction in prisons, leading to discontinuation of OAT in one of the largest prisons in Delhi. Currently, there is no centralized record of how many prisons in the country offer interventions for substance use and SUD. A report published in 2022 found that nine out of the 24 prisons in the state of Punjab (the state with the highest crime rate for NDPS Act–related offences) had provision for outpatient opioid-assisted treatment (OOAT) and de-addiction centers (Commonwealth Human Rights Initiative, 2022). In addition, a significant shortage of medical staff (up to 84% in one of the states) was reported across the prisons in the country (National Crimes Record Bureau, Ministry of Home Affairs. Prison Statistics India, 2021).

6.2 *Nepal*

Nepal criminalizes drug dependence itself—a medical condition. The magnitude of the criminalization of substance use disorder is evident in that one in two drug users has a history of police arrest. Ministry of Home Affairs statistics indicate that there are 130,424 drug users in the nation. As of April 2023, law enforcement apprehended 4,220 individuals for drug-related offenses, constituting 20.73% of all criminal cases. Approximately 5,911 individuals are incarcerated for drug offenses, while approximately 5,000 drug users are receiving rehabilitation. Over 54% of women who use drugs have faced arrest, compared to 45.2% of men. Women are often searched by male police officers and are verbally and physically abused in detention. Women are disproportionately detained for drug offences and are incarcerated in alarming conditions, especially in relation to nutrition and sexual and reproductive healthcare (IDPC, 2021). Nepal has reported that 19% of inmates in five prisons had a history of injecting drugs (Dolan & Larney, 2009).

The Drugs Act has provisions for avoiding imprisonment of patients with substance use disorders by submitting to a drug treatment facility. There has been an increase in drug treatment facilities over the years in Nepal. A scoping mission to Nepal was conducted by UNODC in 2018 to identify and validate prison rehabilitation opportunities. The mission involved visits to three facilities, debriefings, and stakeholder consultations. The findings were to be used to develop a nation-specific plan; however, its current status is unclear (Nepal: Prison-Based Rehabilitation, 2018).

6.3 *Bhutan*

Drug offenses now account for 36.5% of the prison population, highlighting the urgent need for effective interventions. Between 2018 and 2023, Bhutan recorded 4,721 drug-related incidents, leading to the arrest of 9,552 individuals, a bigger portion of whom were youth (Sharma, 2024). To address the issue of recidivism among drug offenders, the government has introduced prison-based SUD treatment and care services. This initiative aims to reduce repeat offenses by offering inmates the necessary resources and support to overcome their addictions. Prison-based SUD Treatment and Care Services was first launched at the Chamgang Central Prison in Chamgang on November 11, 2023. Since the launch, 209 inmates have successfully completed the 1st Phase (Orientation Phase) and advanced to the 2nd Phase (Intensive Phase) of the Prison-Based SUD treatment and care. Another 200 inmates (150 male and 50 female) with SUD issues at Chamgang Central Prison are expected to be inducted into the treatment program (Thepema_Web_Admin, 2024).

Bhutan has a Compulsory Treatment Facility which serves persons with substance use disorders and legal issues. Clients are primarily referred to the center following a thorough evaluation process conducted by a treatment assessment team that includes mental health specialists, the Royal Bhutan Police, and legal officers. Originally founded by the BNCA, it is currently administered by the Pema Secretariat. Counseling is offered to those recognized as peddlers and traffickers with substance use disorders in prison environments, currently accessible solely in Thimphu.

6.4 *The Maldives*

A recent prison-based study conducted in the Maldives showed that the third most common illicit substance consumed was alcohol (UNDP, 2011). The prison-based study also found that the majority of the inmates were serving a sentence for a drug-related offence, of which, 70% were sentenced for drug use. Among this group, the majority of them had used heroin (69.1%) and cannabis (63.3%), followed by alcohol (47.9%). The Maldives Correctional Service (MCS) reported that 55% of individuals sentenced to prison last month were incarcerated for drug-related offenses. There are news reports of drug use within the prison, with jail officials being involved in peddling.

The Maldives Drugs Act, 2020, has empowered the National Drug Agency, in collaboration with the prison authority, to facilitate the treatment in prison of persons who are sentenced to imprisonment under Section 69(a) of this Act.

6.5 *Sri Lanka*

In Sri Lanka, 152,979 individuals were apprehended for drug-related offenses in 2022, indicating a 36% increase compared to the prior year. The incidence of drug-related arrests in 2022 was 751 individuals per 100,000 population. Additionally, the total number of incarcerations documented for drug-related offenses was 30,331, of which 63% pertained to narcotic drug offenses.

In a study evaluating substance use patterns in 278 drug users in three prisons, it was found that the majority of interviewees aged 25–45, with low education and childhood delinquency, experienced drug use from early adolescence. Family history of abuse was high (25–35%), with heroin (98%) and cannabis (54%) being the main drugs of abuse in the past 30 days. Tobacco and alcohol use were widespread, with higher intravenous drug use than officially reported (15.8% vs. 1%) (Dissabandara et al., 2009).

NDDCB is the agency that monitors and assists designated drug treatment centers in prisons and private treatment centers. NDDCB also provides rehabilitation and treatment for patients who come through court orders and community rehabilitation orders. Individuals may obtain psychiatric services as inpatients or outpatients and, thereafter, be monitored by prison hospitals. At least ten of the 129 prisons possess designated substance treatment centers, and the majority of these facilities include prison hospitals and medical officers. Two established forensic psychiatry services are accessible in the Colombo and Kandy areas. In several areas, hospital psychiatrists oversee mental health clinics within prisons and oversee substance use treatment services provided in prison hospitals. Offenders with addiction issues who are not required to serve prison terms are assigned to one of the two drug rehabilitation centers for a treatment and rehabilitation period of up to one year. At other times, they are also placed in the NDDCB rehabilitation centers alongside volunteer patients. In the year 2022, a total of 1,996 reported drug users received treatment services, out of which 3.4% were treated at the prison drug treatment rehabilitation program.

The Kandakadu drug treatment and rehabilitation center was established by the Ministry of Rehabilitation and Prison Reforms as a facility for those with drug addiction referred by the courts. Individuals receive treatment through counseling, sports, religious and aesthetic activities, as well as educational and vocational training. The Senapurareha Rehabilitation Centre, situated in the Polonnaruwa area, functions as a drug rehabilitation facility for criminals. Drug rehabilitation centers have faced criticism from human rights organizations due to the militaristic nature of their programs (Satkunanathan, 2021).

6.6 Afghanistan

The news reports suggest that they are taking a moralistic approach to tackling drug use, with some news reporting Taliban fighters taking large numbers of addicts from the streets, often using whips and the barrel of a gun to force them into rehab. Some are forcibly taken to overcrowded clinics that often resemble prisons. Others were sent to actual penitentiaries that have been largely cleared of Taliban fighters imprisoned by the previous government. Once incarcerated, shaven-headed substance users are forced into withdrawal without the aid of treatments such as counseling and methadone, a drug commonly used for opioid use disorder treatment (BBC, 2023).

6.7 Bangladesh

There was a significant rise in arrests in Bangladesh due to drug-related crimes, increasing from 11,380 to 18,346 between 2015 and 2019. Recent data showed that over one-third (35.97%) of inmates have been imprisoned due to drug-related charges. Bangladesh prisons have 77,124 prisoners in 68 jails throughout the country, even though their official housing capacity is 36,614 prisoners. Among the total number of prisoners, drug-related inmates stood at 27,764 (Dhaka Tribune, 2018). There have been news reports of people among jail authorities smuggling drugs into prisons. The criminalization of substance abuse has led to overcrowded prisons with minimal to no medical help and an overwhelmed justice system.

The Department of Narcotics has recently initiated a comprehensive action plan (Annual Drug Report, 2020; Department of Narcotics Control, Bangladesh, 2020; Ray, 2018) to conduct workshops with relevant prisons for the implementation of the aforementioned activities and to monitor progress through applications. This plan includes anti-drug awareness meetings, the distribution of posters and souvenirs, discussions on drug prevention within prisons, anti-drug campaigns in television and print media, the establishment of mentorship programs in educational institutions, lectures on narcotics, and the formation of narcotics committees in schools and colleges. However, proper addiction treatment within prison settings is still lacking.

6.8 Pakistan

The 2022 Amendment to the Control of Narcotics Substances Act (CNSA) has introduced harsher penalties for wider quantity thresholds, leading to overcrowding of prisons with a rise in the prison population by 18.98%, from 19,636 individuals in 2023 to 23,367 in 2024 under the CNSA, which accounts for 23.21% of the total prison population of Pakistan. Among the provinces, Punjab leads with the highest number of incarcerations for drug offences, with 13,331 cases accounting for 68.34% of the national total (Prison Reforms I JPP, 2024).

A cross-sectional survey of 600 male prisoners in Karachi revealed that about 97% of prisoners had a lifetime history of substance abuse. For tobacco, 80.5% of prisoners were at moderate risk of use. For opioids, 13% were at high risk; 12.7% and 9.5% of prisoners were at high risk for using cannabis and tobacco, respectively (Jamal et al., 2022). In Pakistan, 80% of PWID had been to jail, where reports of injecting ranged from 22% to 70%, and syringe sharing was 56% (Nai Zindagi, 2009).

The prisoners who are addicted to drugs are allocated barracks that are called recovery centers across Pakistani jails. To ensure the treatment of such prisoners, psychologists have been appointed. At the Lahore Central Jail and Rawalpindi's Adiala Jail, 20-bed detoxification centers have been established. According to the report, during the past five years, 32,227 drug-addict prisoners have been detoxified (Shabbir Hussain, 2019) (Table 10.1).

Table 10.1 Prison treatment services and guiding policies in South Asia

S. no	Country	Treatment for substance use in at least one prison	At least one OAT available in prison	At least one NSP in prison	National policy
1.	Afghanistan	No	No	No	National Drug demand reduction Policy 2012–16
2.	Bangladesh	No	No	No	National Drug Policy, 1982; Narcotic Control Act, 1990
3.	Bhutan	Yes	No	No	Narcotic Drugs, Psychotropic Substances and Substance Abuse (NDPSSA) Act, 2005
4.	India	Yes	Yes	No	The Narcotic Drugs and Psychotropic Substances (NDPS) Act, 1985 National Action Plan for Drug Demand Reduction (NAPDDR) 2018–2025
5.	Maldives	Provision present in law	No	No	The Law on Narcotics Drugs, 1977
6.	Nepal	unclear	No	No	The 1976 Narcotic Drugs (Control) Act
7.	Pakistan	Yes	No	No	National Anti-Narcotics Policy 2019
8.	Sri-Lanka	Yes	No	No	National Policy for Prevention and Control of Drugs of Abuse, 1984

7 SAARC Convention on Narcotic Drugs and Psychotropic Substances

The SAARC Convention on Narcotic Drugs and Psychotropic Substances, which was signed in Malé during the Fifth SAARC Summit in November 1990, came into force on 15 September 1993, following ratification by all member states (South Asian Association for Regional Cooperation (SAARC), 2025).

The Convention seeks to reinforce and supplement at the regional level the relevant international conventions and promote regional cooperation among member states in both law enforcement and demand reduction. Incorporating the generally accepted principle of extradition or prosecution consistent with the respective national legislative regimes, the Convention envisages the widest measures for mutual legal assistance among member states in investigation, prosecution, and judicial proceedings in respect of drug offences.

The SAARC Drug Offences Monitoring Desk (SDOMD) has been established in Colombo to collate, analyse and disseminate information on drug-related offences in member countries. The SAARC Convention implementation is monitored by the

Technical Committee on Prevention of Drug Trafficking and Drug Abuse during its annual meetings SAARC Convention on Narcotic Drugs and Psychotropic Substances.

SAARC signed the MOU with UNDP in August 1995 to coordinate efforts in combating drug trafficking and drug abuse in the region. The Memorandum envisages mutual consultation and exchange of information between the two organizations; development and implementation of such activities as human resource development; improving regional cooperation on drug intelligence through the SAARC Drug Offences Monitoring Desk; legislation; financial investigation; money laundering; precursor control; and the establishment of a networking arrangement among existing institutions in drug abuse prevention, etc. A UNDCP-SAARC Workshop for policymakers of the member states on Drug Trafficking and Drug Abuse was held in Colombo in 1996.

Nonetheless, despite a common ethnic origin, there is limited information exchange among South Asian nations, as emphasized by UNODC (Regional Programme for South Asia (2018–2021) Background and Context 2021). Nations must establish transnational and transcontinental collaboration to enhance international cooperation and mutual legal assistance frameworks for more effective control of organized crime.

8 Conclusion

It has been estimated that 2.2 million people worldwide are in prison for drug offences, of which 22% have been imprisoned for drug possession for personal use. South Asian countries have traditionally taken a prohibitory approach to substance use, with more humane approaches being adopted recently. Prisons in these countries face overcrowding with disproportionately high number of inmates attributable to drug-related offences. South Asian countries exhibit diverse approaches to handling substance use and crime, ranging from punitive incarceration to treatment-oriented rehabilitation. Gaps remain in prison-based care, post-release support, and community reintegration models. There is a need to strengthen the health sector response for those in contact with the law enforcement and criminal justice systems in the SAARC nations. A shift toward evidence-based treatment, harm reduction, and legal reforms is essential to improve outcomes for individuals with substance use disorders within the criminal justice system. In addition, a wide array of services that are targeted at persons with different patterns of use may be made available. This can include prevention, screening, brief interventions, treatment (short-term and long-term), and rehabilitation-oriented services. There is a need to strengthen coordination regarding supply reduction as well as demand reduction efforts in the South Asian countries in order to improve the drug situation in the region.

References

2020 Drugs Act of the Maldives | International Society of Substance Use Professionals. (2020). Retrieved February 15, 2025, from https://www.issup.net/knowledge-share/resources/2020-08/2020-drugs-act-maldives

Ambekar, A., Rao, R., & Agrawal, A. (2013). India's National Narcotic Drugs and Psychotropic Substances policy, 2012: A 20th century document in the 21st century. *The International Journal on Drug Policy, 24*(4), 374–375. https://doi.org/10.1016/j.drugpo.2013.01.001

Ambekar, A., Agrawal, A., Rao, R., Mishra, A. K., Khandelwal, S. K., Chadda, R. K., & on behalf of the group of investigators for the National Survey on Extent and Pattern of Substance Use in India. (2019). *Magnitude of substance use in India*. Ministry of Social Justice and Empowerment, Government of India.

Arafat, S. M. Y., & Kar, S. K. (2024). Epidemiology of psychiatric disorders and overview of access to mental health care in South Asia. In S. M. Y. Arafat & S. K. Kar (Eds.), *Access to mental health care in South Asia*. Springer. https://doi.org/10.1007/978-981-99-9153-2_1

Bhad, R., Shukla, S. (2024). Understanding Substance Use Disorder and Comorbidities: Insights from South Asia. In: Arafat, S.M.Y., Kar, S.K. (eds) Current Perspectives on Substance Use Disorders in South Asia. Springer, Singapore. https://doi.org/10.1007/978-981-97-6619-2_12

Balhara, Y. P. S., Sarkar, S., & Rajguru, A. J. (2024). Drug-related offences in India: Observations and insights from the secondary analysis of the data from the National Crimes Record Bureau. *Indian Journal of Psychological Medicine, 46*(6), 527–534. https://doi.org/10.1177/02537176241228415

BBC. (2023). *Afghanistan: Rounded up from the streets into Taliban drug rehab*. Retrieved February 15, 2025, from https://www.bbc.com/news/world-asia-65138423

Bjelica, J. (2024, August 25). *Treating drug users in Afghanistan: How to respond to a massive problem?* Afghanistan Analysts Network - English. https://www.afghanistan-analysts.org/en/reports/rights-freedom/treating-drug-users-in-afghanistan-how-to-respond-to-a-massive-problem/

Bojappen, N., & Chand, P. (2024). Policy, legalisation and programs related to substance use disorders in South Asia. In S. M. Y. Arafat & S. K. Kar (Eds.), *Current perspectives on substance use disorders in South Asia*. Springer. https://doi.org/10.1007/978-981-97-6619-2_10

Choudhury, S., Joshi, T., & Ghosh, A. (2024). Overview of substance use disorder in South Asia. In S. M. Y. Arafat & S. K. Kar (Eds.), *Current perspectives on substance use disorders in South Asia*. Springer. https://doi.org/10.1007/978-981-97-6619-2_1

Coll, C. V. N., Ewerling, F., García-Moreno, C., Hellwig, F., & Barros, A. J. D. (2020). Intimate partner violence in 46 low-income and middle-income countries: An appraisal of the most vulnerable groups of women using national health surveys. *BMJ Global Health, 5*(1), e002208. https://doi.org/10.1136/bmjgh-2019-002208

Commonwealth Human Rights Initiative. (2022). *Inside Punjab prisons: A study on prison conditions*. https://pulsa.punjab.gov.in/sites/default/files/Final_Punjab%20Report_Part%20A_Print_0.pdf

de Andrade, D., Ritchie, J., Rowlands, M., Mann, E., & Hides, L. (2018). Substance use and recidivism outcomes for prison-based drug and alcohol interventions. *Epidemiologic Reviews, 40*(1), 121–133. https://doi.org/10.1093/epirev/mxy004

Dhaka Tribune. (2018). *Is it time to decriminalize drug use in Bangladesh?* Retrieved February 15, 2025, from https://www.dhakatribune.com/bangladesh/bangladesh-others/142403/is-it-time-to-decriminalize-drug-use-in

Dissabandara, L. O., Dias, S. R., Dodd, P. R., & Stadlin, A. (2009). Patterns of substance use in male incarcerated drug users in Sri Lanka. *Drug and Alcohol Review, 28*(6), 600–607. https://doi.org/10.1111/j.1465-3362.2009.00062.x

Dolan, K., & Larney, S. (2009). A review of HIV in prisons in Nepal. *Kathmandu University Medical Journal (KUMJ), 7*(28), 351–354. https://doi.org/10.3126/kumj.v7i4.2753

Dolan, K., Moazen, B., Noori, A., Rahimzadeh, S., Farzadfar, F., & Hariga, F. (2015). People who inject drugs in prison: HIV prevalence, transmission and prevention. *The International Journal on Drug Policy, 26*(Suppl 1), S12–S15. https://doi.org/10.1016/j.drugpo.2014.10.012

Dolkar, T. (2016). Prevention of Illegal Substance Use and Abuse in Bhutan. In: Israelashvili M, Romano JL, eds. The Cambridge Handbook of International Prevention Science. *Cambridge Handbooks in Psychology*. Cambridge University Press, 597–605.

Emerson, B., & Haden, M. (2018). Public health and the harm reduction approach to illegal psychoactive substances. In *Reference module in biomedical sciences*. Elsevier. https://doi.org/10.1016/B978-0-12-801238-3.66208-6

European Union Drugs Agency. (2024). *European drug report 2024*. Publications Office. https://data.europa.eu/doi/10.2810/91693

Evans-Reeves, K. (2023, February 1). *Bhutan reverses sales ban on tobacco*. Blog - Tobacco Control. https://blogs.bmj.com/tc/?p=1667

Favril, L. (2023). Drug use before and during imprisonment: Drivers of continuation. *International Journal of Drug Policy, 115*, 104027. https://doi.org/10.1016/j.drugpo.2023.104027

Fazel, S., Yoon, I. A., & Hayes, A. J. (2017). Substance use disorders in prisoners: An updated systematic review and meta-regression analysis in recently incarcerated men and women. *Addiction (Abingdon, England), 112*(10), 1725–1739. https://doi.org/10.1111/add.13877

Geneva. (2003). *4. Who framework convention on tobacco control.*

Girelli, G., Jofré, M., & Larasati, A. (2022). *The death penalty for drug offences: Global overview 2022.*

IDPC. (2021). *Human rights and drug policies in Nepal*. https://idpc.net/publications/2021/12/human-rights-and-drug-policies-in-nepal

Intimate Partner Violence and Co-Occurring Substance Abuse/Addiction. (2021). Retrieved February 15, 2025, from https://www.asam.org/blog-details/article/2021/08/09/intimate-partner-violence-and-co-occurring-substance-abuse-addiction

Jamal, M., Waheed, S., & Shakoor, A. (2022). The prevalence of substance abuse and associated factors among male prisoners in Karachi jails, Pakistan. *Journal of Taibah University Medical Sciences, 17*(6), 929–935. https://doi.org/10.1016/j.jtumed.2022.05.001

Jha, A., Sharma, A. K., & Mahadevan, J. (2024). Addiction research in South Asia. In S. M. Y. Arafat & S. K. Kar (Eds.), *Current perspectives on substance use disorders in South Asia*. Springer. https://doi.org/10.1007/978-981-97-6619-2_13

Kaur, J., & Jain, D. C. (2011). Tobacco control policies in India: Implementation and challenges. *Indian Journal of Public Health, 55*(3), 220–227. https://doi.org/10.4103/0019-557X.89941

Maruf, M. M., Chowdhury, A., & Islam, M. R. (2024). Substance use and mental health conditions: Co-existence of dual problems in Bangladesh. In S. M. Y. Arafat (Ed.), *Mental health in Bangladesh*. Springer. https://doi.org/10.1007/978-981-97-0610-5_7

Mehr, J. B., Bennett, E. R., Price, J. L., de Souza, N. L., Buckman, J. F., Wilde, E. A., Tate, D. F., Marshall, A. D., Dams-O'Connor, K., & Esopenko, C. (2023). Intimate partner violence, substance use, and health comorbidities among women: A narrative review. *Frontiers in Psychology, 13*, 1028375. https://doi.org/10.3389/fpsyg.2022.1028375

Mitchell, O., Wilson, D. B., & MacKenzie, D. L. (2012). The effectiveness of incarceration-based drug treatment on criminal behavior: A systematic review. *Campbell Systematic Reviews, 8*(1), i–76. https://doi.org/10.4073/csr.2012.18

Murphy, E., & Cliff, V. (Eds.). (2021). *Legal and policy trends impacting people living with HIV and key populations in Asia and the Pacific 2014–2019*. UNAIDS.

Nai Zindagi. (2009). *Rapid situation assessments of HIV prevalence and risk factors among people injecting drugs in four cities of the Punjab*. Islamabad

Narcotic Drugs Estimates. (2025). Retrieved January 18, 2025, from https://www.incb.org/incb/en/narcoticdrugs/estimates/narcotic-drugs-estimates.html

National Authority on Tobacco and Alcohol Act, No. 27 of 2006. https://www.nddcb.gov.lk/Docs/acts/NATA%20Act%20English.pdf

National Crimes Record Bureau, Ministry of Home Affairs. Prison Statistics India, 2021; 2022. https://ncrb.gov.in/sites/default/files/PSI-2021/Executive_ncrb_Summary-2021.pdf

National Dangerous Drug Control Board (NDDCB), Sri Lanka. (2018). https://www.nddcb.gov.lk/index.php

Nepal Law Commission. (1976). *Narcotic Drugs (Control) Act, 2033 (1976)*. https://lawcommission.gov.np/en/?cat=407

Nepal: Prison-Based Rehabilitation. (2018). Retrieved February 15, 2025, from https://www.unodc.org/southasia/en/frontpage/2018/March/nepal_-prison-based-rehabilitation.html

Noroozi, A., De Lara, M., & Abouzeid, A. (2024). Drug policies and responses in Afghanistan. *The Lancet. Psychiatry, 11*(2), 90–91. https://doi.org/10.1016/S2215-0366(23)00390-5

Panthee, B., Panthee, S., Gyawali, S., & Kawakami, N. (2017). Prevalence and correlates of substance use among health care students in Nepal: A cross sectional study. *BMC Public Health, 17*(1). https://doi.org/10.1186/s12889-017-4980-6

Parmar, A., Narasimha, V. L., & Nath, S. (2024). National Drug Laws, policies, and programs in India: A narrative review. *Indian Journal of Psychological Medicine, 46*(1), 5–13. https://doi.org/10.1177/02537176231170534

Perry, A. E., Woodhouse, R., Neilson, M., St James, M. M., Glanville, J., Hewitt, C., & Trépel, D. (2016). Are non-pharmacological interventions effective in reducing drug use and criminality? A systematic and meta-analytical review with an economic appraisal of these interventions. *International Journal of Environmental Research and Public Health, 13*(10), 966. https://doi.org/10.3390/ijerph13100966

Power, N., Archambault, L., & Perreault, M. (2024). New challenges and opportunities for opioid agonist treatment access and retention: A scoping review. *Journal of Drug Issues*. https://doi.org/10.1177/00220426241269828

Prison Reforms | JPP. (2024). Retrieved February 15, 2025, from https://jppprisonreforms.com/

Rao, R., Varshney, M., Singh, S., Agrawal, A., & Ambekar, A. (2019). Mental healthcare act, 2017, and addiction treatment: Potential pitfalls and trepidations. *Indian Journal of Psychiatry, 61*(2), 208. https://doi.org/10.4103/psychiatry.IndianJPsychiatry_463_18

Regional Programme for South Asia (2018–2021) Background and Context. (2021). *South Asia: The emerging threat of synthetic drugs*. Retrieved February 7, 2024, from https://www.unodc.org/southasia/frontpage/2011/january/emerging-threat-of-synthetic-drugs-in-south-asia.html

Riboulet-Zemouli, K., & Krawitz, M. A. (2022). WHO's first scientific review of medicinal Cannabis: From global struggle to patient implications. *Drugs, Habits and Social Policy, 23*(1), 5–21. https://doi.org/10.1108/DHS-11-2021-0060

Sarkar, S., Majumder, P., Gupta, R., Das, N., Narnoli, S., & Balhara, Y. P. S. (2021). Prevalence and socio-demographic correlates of law enforcement involvement among treatment-seeking adult males with opioid use disorder. *International Journal of Law and Psychiatry, 74*, 101653. https://doi.org/10.1016/j.ijlp.2020.101653

Satkunanathan, A. (2021). *A broken system: Drug control, detention and treatment of people who use drugs in Sri Lanka*. https://www.hri.global/files/2021/08/03/HRI_Report_-_Sri_Lanka_Drug_Control.pdf

Sethi, H. S. (2002). *Drug abuse among prison population: A case study of Tihar Jail*. Ministry of Social Justice and Empowerment, Government of India/UNDCP Regional Office for South Asia.

Shabbir Hussain. (2019, August 18). *Drug addicts, AIDS patients being treated in jails across Pakistan*. The Express Tribune. https://tribune.com.pk/story/2036804/drug-addicts-aids-patients-treated-jails-across-pakistan

Sharma, K. P. (2024). *Bhutan intensifies battle against drug cases*. Retrieved February 15, 2025, from https://asianews.network/bhutan-intensifies-battle-against-drug-cases/

South Asian Association for Regional Cooperation (SAARC). (2025). Retrieved January 25, 2025, from https://training.itcilo.org/actrav_cdrom1/english/global/blokit/saarc.htm

The New Indian Express. (2022). *47 per cent inmates in Punjab jails addicted to drugs.* https://www.newindianexpress.com/thesundaystandard/2022/aug/07/47-per-cent-inmates-in-punjab-jails-addicted-to-drugs-2484827.html

Thepema_Web_Admin. (2024, February 23). *Launch of the prison-based SUD treatment and care services in Lungzor District Prison.* The PEMA. https://thepema.gov.bt/launch-of-the-prison-based-sud-treatment-and-care-services-in-lungzor-district-prison/

Uddin, S., & Rahman, S. (2021). Pakistani laws on drug use and addiction: Need for reform, *4*, 105. https://doi.org/10.1016/j.puhe.2018.10.020

UNDP. (2011). *Prison assessment and proposed rehabilitation and reintegration of offenders report.* Government of Maldives and the United Nations Development Programme.

UNODC drugs monitoring platform brief on Afghanistan and neighbouring regions: Update on patterns and trends in heroin, methamphetamine and opium trafficking from 2020 to 2023, before and after the April 2022 Afghanistan Drug Ban. [English] | [Russian] | Drugs Monitoring Platform (DMP). Retrieved January 17, 2025, from https://dmp.unodc.org/brief6-public

UNODC. (2014). *Prevention of spread of HIV amongst vulnerable groups in South Asia.*

Vorma, H., Sokero, P., Aaltonen, M., Turtiainen, S., Hughes, L. A., & Savolainen, J. (2013). Participation in opioid substitution treatment reduces the rate of criminal convictions: Evidence from a community study. *Addictive Behaviors, 38*(7), 2313–2316. https://doi.org/10.1016/j.addbeh.2013.03.009

World Health Organization. (2021). Situational Analysis of Drugs in the Maldives 2021. (United Nations publication).

World Drug Report 2024—Drug market patterns and trends. United Nations: Office on Drugs and Crime. Retrieved January 17, 2025, from www.unodc.org/unodc/en/data-and-analysis/wdr2024-drug-market-trends.html

Zhong, S., Yu, R., & Fazel, S. (2020). Drug use disorders and violence: Associations with individual drug categories. *Epidemiologic Reviews, 42*(1), 103–116. https://doi.org/10.1093/epirev/mxaa006

Chapter 11
Forensic Psychiatric Aspects of Child Sexual Abuse in South Asia

Dheeraj Kattula, Dhandapani Nandakumar, and Rachna George Joseph

Abstract This chapter addresses childhood sexual abuse (CSA) in South Asia, home to 36% of the world's children. CSA is alarmingly prevalent, with underreporting due to stigma, fear, and lack of awareness. Risk factors include individual (e.g., age, trauma), family (e.g., poverty, substance abuse), and societal determinants (e.g., patriarchal norms, weak law enforcement). Theoretical models like Finkelhor's Precondition Model and Ward and Siegert's Pathways Model explain CSA's etiology. Clinical identification involves recognizing behavioral changes, physical symptoms, and indirect disclosures. Ethical challenges in reporting, such as confidentiality and child safety, are discussed. Legislative frameworks across South Asia are discussed, with countries like India and Nepal having robust laws, while others like Afghanistan and Bhutan lag due to systemic issues. Challenges include underreporting, judicial delays, and cultural barriers. The chapter calls for stronger enforcement, victim-friendly legal processes, and increased awareness to combat CSA and ensure justice for survivors.

Keywords Childhood sexual abuse · Sexual violence · Child abuse · Child protection laws

1 Introduction

Children from South Asian countries like Afghanistan, Bhutan, Bangladesh, India, Maldives, Nepal, Pakistan, and Sri Lanka account for 36% of the world's population of children. It translates to one out of every three children in the world living in this

D. Kattula (✉)
Department of Psychiatry, Christian Medical College, Vellore, India

D. Nandakumar · R. G. Joseph
Department of Child and Adolescent Psychiatry, Christian Medical College, Vellore, India

A. Parmar et al. (eds.), *Forensic Psychiatry and Prison Mental Health in South Asia*, South Asian Perspectives in Mental Health and Psychology,
https://doi.org/10.1007/978-981-96-7206-6_11

region. It is home to 616 million children under the age of 18 years (Rai, 2016). Children are a vulnerable group, and childhood sexual abuse (CSA) is alarming and recognized to have long-term complications. In this chapter, we introduce concepts related to CSA, such as its definition, determinants, theoretical models, clinical approach to a case, and ethical challenges in reporting, followed by an examination of the evolution of current legislation and perceived gaps in laws in various South Asian countries.

2 Definition

According to the World Health Organization (WHO), CSA is defined as "the involvement of a child in sexual activity that he or she does not fully comprehend, is unable to give informed consent to, or for which the child is not developmentally prepared and cannot give consent, or that violates the laws or social taboos of society." This definition does factor multidimensionality into the concept by including the developmental age of the child, consent, and societal law/norms. CSA encompasses acts of "penetrative intercourse, attempted intercourse, non-penetrative sexual behaviors like oro-genital contact, touching of genitals with or without clothes, exhibitionism, and exposing or using the child for pornographic activity/prostitution (Selengia et al., 2020)."

3 Magnitude of the CSA in South Asia

The prevalence of CSA is high in South Asian regions. The prevalence in Asia varies significantly, ranging from 4.1% to 60% for males and 3.3% to 42.7% for females, depending on the region (Selengia et al., 2020). The prevalence of CSA among girls is higher than among boys, but the difference is small. A lack of consensus on the definition of CSA has led to the reporting of wide differences in prevalence statistics (Solehati et al., 2021). Even though prevalence in India, Sri Lanka, and Pakistan is reported to be up to 44%, there is sparse literature on country-specific data (Rahim et al., 2021). Incidence in South Asian countries is reported to be higher than in developed countries. Factors like social stigma, lack of awareness, fear of perpetrators, etc., lead to underreporting of CSA. Teachers, relatives, and family members were the commonest perpetrators (Solehati et al., 2021). More than half of the children (53%) faced sexual abuse of at least one form before they turned 12 years old (Chacko et al., 2022). There is a wide gap in national-level data related to CSA in this region.

4 Determinants of CSA

There are societal, family-related, and individual risk factors for CSA (Choudhry et al., 2018)

1. Individual factors: age of the child, exposure to sexual trauma, gender non-conformity, intellectual capacity, attachment with caregiver
2. Family factors: socioeconomic status, number of children, substance use in family members, occupation of parents, non-availability of caregivers, poverty
3. Societal and community factors: patriarchal norms, lack of safety for women, poor law enforcement, war-prone regions, crime rate in the locality

5 Theoretical Models of CSA

According to Marshall and Barbaree's theory, sexual offenses occur as a result of the fusion of an individual's drives of sex and aggression. Sexual offenders have vulnerabilities due to extreme conditions during their childhood and often satisfy their sexual and emotional needs inappropriately in deviant ways (Marshall & Barbaree, 1990).

1. Hall and Hirschman's Quadripartite Model

   Quadripartite model of Hall and Hirschman was initially developed to explain rape but was later applied to CSA. It suggests that CSA occurs due to four vulnerability factors: physiological sexual arousal, distorted cognition justifying sexual aggression, affective dyscontrol, and problems in personality, along with the presence of opportunity. Offenses occur when these factors cross a certain threshold (Hall & Hirschman, 1992).
2. Precondition Model of CSA.

   The Four Preconditions Model by David Finkelhor suggests that four preconditions are to be met for CSA to occur (Finkelhor, 1984)

   1. An offender with a predisposition to sexually abusing a child
   2. The ability to overcome any internal inhibitions against acting on that predisposition
   3. The ability to overcome external barriers, such as lack of access to the child or supervision of the child by others
   4. The ability to overcome any resistance or reluctance on the part of the child

3. Ward and Siegert's Pathways Model

   Ward and Siegert's model suggests that any dysfunction or deviation in one or more psychological mechanisms, like difficulty in the regulation of emotions, deficits in intimacy, cognitive distortions, and deviant sexual scripts for arousal, would lead to CSA. Most of the time, some degree of every aspect is present in the offender, along with the opportunity to commit the offense (Ward & Siegert, 2002).

6 When to Suspect CSA

Children may not disclose sexual abuse for various reasons. They might believe it is their fault, or their abuser may have convinced them it is normal or framed it as a "special secret."

Abusers may also use bribes or threats to silence the child or tell them no one will believe them. Additionally, a CSA victim might feel a bond with their abuser and worry about causing them trouble.

Here are some signs that may indicate a child may be a victim of CSA (Jiloha et al., 2019):

1. **Behavioral changes**: The child may become aggressive, withdrawn, or clingy. They might struggle with sleep, have recurring nightmares, or start bed-wetting.
2. **Avoidance of the abuser**: Such children might appear fearful of or express a strong dislike for a specific person, avoiding time alone with them.
3. **Sexually inappropriate behavior**: They may exhibit behavior that is sexually inappropriate for their age or use sexually explicit language.
4. **Physical issues**: The child might experience health problems like soreness in the anal or genital region, pregnancy, or sexually transmitted diseases.
5. **Academic difficulties**: They may have trouble concentrating or learning or notice a decline in their grades.
6. **Subtle clues**: The child may drop hints or indirectly indicate that abuse is occurring without explicitly stating it.

7 Interviewing Techniques in CSA

The interviewer should consider four important aspects while interviewing a child with sexual abuse: sensitivity to the child's developmental age, flexibility, objectivity, and empathy. Interviewer should also be mindful of the following aspects while interviewing the victim of CSA (Fernandes et al., 2024):

1. Phrase the question so the child understands
2. Talk about what children understand about the event
3. Help the children deal with questions they don't understand
4. Be objective and avoid suggesting answers
5. Provide a non-judgmental atmosphere
6. Begin the interview with open-ended questions
7. Avoid leading questions whenever possible
8. Use specific questions where necessary
9. Help the child overcome their anxiety
10. Let the child know the limits of confidentiality
11. Understand child's emotional reaction

12. Using anatomical dolls and drawing where necessary

The interview could be phased for the convenience of the interviewer. The following steps could be taken to conduct the interview:

Step 1: Preparation
Step 2: Setting and context
Step 3: Rapport building and developmental observations
Step 4: Information exchange
Step 5: Closure

8 Handling of Children with CSA

Here is a list of steps to follow while handling children with CSA (Jiloha et al., 2019):

1. Trust the child. The most crucial step is to believe them. Children seldom fabricate stories about abuse; it's more common for them to deny abuse even when it has occurred. Assure the child that you believe them.
2. Stay calm and composed while speaking with the child. Avoid displaying overwhelming emotions.
3. Refrain from interrogating the child, as repeatedly recounting their experience can be traumatic. Allow legal and law enforcement professionals to handle detailed questioning.
4. Reassure the victim that being abused was not their fault and facilitate speaking up. Emphasize that what happened is not due to anything they did or didn't do, especially if the perpetrator is a family member. Assure the victim that steps will be taken promptly to ensure their safety and stop the abuse.
5. Do not make promises you cannot keep.
6. Ask if the child has shared this information with anyone else and what their response was.
7. Ensure the child's safety by determining if the abuse is ongoing and addressing any immediate concerns.
8. At an appropriate time, considering the child's emotional state, provide education on "good touch" and "bad touch," emotions, cognitions, behaviors, and safer coping strategies.
9. Clarify the limits of confidentiality, explaining that the next step involves informing the parents and relevant authorities.
10. It is essential to understand the stages of Child Sexual Abuse Accommodation Syndrome (CSAAS). It consists of five stages (Summit, 1983):

    I. Secrecy: Victims often feel vulnerable to disclose the abuse or fears about possible manipulation by the abuser.
    II. Helplessness: Children due to their fear, feel isolated, victimized, cornered, and powerless to change their circumstances.

III. Entrapment and accommodation: Child tend to accept and adapt to the situation as normal and could be subjected to continued abuse for a long time.
IV. Delayed- unconvincing disclosure: Children happen to disclose things much later as they fear rejection, parental disbelief, or confusion.
V. Retraction: Child can renounce their statement due to distorted memory of trauma or social pressure due to family dynamics and lack of support.

9 Handling of Parents with CSA

Here is a list of steps to follow while handling parents with CSA (Jiloha et al., 2019):

1. Emotional reactions of parents:
    - Initial feelings may include denial, anger, betrayal, confusion, disbelief, self-blame, and guilt.
    - Parents may feel they failed to protect their child or missed earlier signs of abuse.
    - Confusion about why the child disclosed to someone else instead of them.
2. Physical and emotional impact:
    - Insomnia, appetite changes, and other physical complaints.
    - Conflicted emotions, especially so if the abuser is a trusted person or family member.
3. Family dynamics:
    - Divided loyalties may emerge, with some family members believing the abuse occurred and others denying it.
    - Parents may disagree on handling the situation, especially if the offender is a spouse or partner.
    - Decisions may include whether to stay with the offending partner, divorce, or manage contact between the child and the offender.
4. Impact on parent-child relationship:
    - Parents' feelings toward the offender can influence their ability to support the child.
    - Denying or minimizing the abuse or siding with the offender can severely harm the child and their recovery.
5. Child's needs:
    - Every abused child needs to be believed and assured that the abuse is not their fault.
    - Parental support and advocacy are crucial for the child's recovery.

6. Support for parents:
   - Parents should seek help and support for their emotions to positively influence their child's recovery.
   - Families play an important role in the healing process, being the vitally important resource for recovery.

10 Examination of Child with CSA

A comprehensive physical examination including inspection of the full body with special attention to the oral cavity, breasts, genitalia, perineal region, anus, and buttocks. Table 11.1 describes the findings in each region seen in cases of CSA. There is concern regarding the collection of biologic evidence, if the alleged CSA has occurred within the previous 72 hours. Serological tests and cultures for sexually transmitted infections are to be decided depending on the special circumstances of the specific case. If the victim is a girl of reproductive age, a pregnancy test should also be done (Sakelliadis et al., 2009).

11 Reporting of CSA

A report of CSA should contain the following information, if known (Jiloha et al., 2019):

1. The names of the child, the child's parents, or other persons believed to be responsible for the child's care and their home addresses

Table 11.1 Examination of a child with CSA

Labia majora and minora	Note skin lesions, unusual pigmentations, or other skin changes.
Clitoris	Note unusual size or changes of the clitoris or hood.
Urethral meatus	Note signs of inflammation, edema, or other lesions of the periurethral tissue.
Perihymenal tissue	Note fresh or healed lacerations, STI lesions, pubic lice, rashes, or other unusual findings.
Hymen	Note any signs of trauma or STI lesions. Evaluate for significant distortion of the hymenal shape, fresh tears, transections, fresh hemorrhages, abrasions, and bruises.
Posterior fourchette and fossa navicularis	Note lacerations or scars, bruises, healing abraded areas, STI lesions, or neovascularization.
Vagina	Note bleeding, discharge, STI lesions, foreign bodies, abnormal vascular patterns, petechiae, or other lesions on the walls of the vagina.
Cervix	Note bleeding, discharge, STI lesions, cervicitis, tears, or other signs of trauma.

Source: Responding to child maltreatment by WHO (*Responding to Child Maltreatment*, 2022)

2. Present whereabouts of the child
3. The age of child
4. The nature and extent of the injuries borne by the child, both current and evidence of past injuries, if any
5. The name, age, and condition of other children in the same household
6. Any other information that may be helpful in establishing the cause of the CSA
7. The name and identity of the person or people responsible for the abuse or neglect of the child, if known
8. Name and address of the one reporting

12 Outcomes of CSA

There are numerous adverse outcomes associated with CSA (Talbot et al., 2009; Talwar et al., 2024).

1. Mental health outcomes
   (a) Depression
   (b) Anxiety
   (c) Post-traumatic stress disorder
   (d) Decreased self-esteem and self-confidence
   (e) Self-guilt
   (f) Personality disorders
2. Physical health outcomes
   (a) Chronic and diffuse pain
   (b) Weight loss
   (c) Gastrointestinal problems
3. Interpersonal outcomes
   (a) Lack of attachment
   (b) Avoidance of social circle
   (c) Isolation
   (d) Marital instability
4. Behavioral outcomes
   (a) Physical aggression
   (b) Irritability
   (c) Poor frustration tolerance
   (d) Self-injurious behavior

13 General Principles and Ethical Considerations

(a) *Respect for autonomy:* To get consent to examine the child/victim
(b) *Beneficence:* To act in the best interest of the patient
(c) Non-maleficence: To avoid any harm to the patient
(d) *Non-disclosure of identity:* To avoid any disclosure of details regarding the victim

14 The Ethical Dilemma of Reporting

There are concerns related to family, profession, and child safety as described by Ramasamy et al. (2023):

Family concern: Families often grapple with a range of concerns when faced with the prospect of reporting such abuse. They refuse or hesitate to report abuse due to fear of stigmatization and victimization of the child and their future. Fear of straining or breaking family relationships, particularly when the abuser is a relative or trusted individual.

Professional concern: These concerns often stem from the ethical, legal, and practical challenges associated with mandated reporting and their responsibilities to the child and the wider community. Professionals may struggle with breaching a child's or family's trust, especially when confidentiality is a core part of their role. Other concerns include reporting an unclear or unconfirmed suspicion and its potential consequences for the child and alleged perpetrator, Fear of retaliation, criticism, or lack of support from supervisors or colleagues for making a report, and hostility or aggression from the family or community after a report is made.

Child safety concerns: Families may worry about retaliation from the abuser, especially if the perpetrator is a family member or someone close to the victim. Concerns about how the reporting process, interviews, and potential legal proceedings may affect the child's emotional well-being and recovery.

15 Legislations on Child Sexual Abuse in South Asia

CSA is a profoundly concerning child rights issue. When coupled with cultural barriers and stigma, a weak legislative framework can be detrimental to the protection of the rights of children. The United Nations Convention on the Rights of the Child (UNCRC) is a comprehensive treaty related to human rights that was ratified by every member of the UN except for the USA. The 54 articles in the treaty cover the civil, economic, political, and social rights of children. Articles 19 and 34 pertain to the responsibilities of states to protect children from all forms of sexual abuse and sexual exploitation. Towards this end, it is stated that state parties shall take appropriate measures to prevent the following (*The United Nations Convention on the Right of the Child*, 1989).

(a) The coercion or inducement of a child to engage in any illegal sexual activity
(b) The exploitation of children in commercial sex work or other illegal sexual activity
(c) The exploitation of children through pornography

The legislative framework of various countries in South Asia is examined in this context. The legislative framework in South Asian countries like Afghanistan, India, Nepal, Bhutan, Maldives, Bangladesh, Pakistan, and Sri Lanka, which account for nearly 36% of the global population of children, is diverse. These seven South Asian countries have ratified the UNCRC and have attempted to build the domestic legislative framework based on international guidelines (Adamcheck et al., 2020). However, certain countries lack a robust legal framework for addressing child sexual abuse. This creates a perpetuating loophole that fails to protect or provide justice to children facing violations of their rights.

16 Domestic Legislative Framework in South Asian Countries that Ratified the UNCRC

Afghanistan, Bangladesh, Bhutan, Sri Lanka, India, Pakistan, and Nepal are the 7 South Asian countries that ratified the UNCRC (*Ratification Status by Country or Treaty*, n.d.). We shall examine the domestic legislation in these nations before exploring the other nations in South Asia (Table 11.2).

Table 11.2 Ratification status of South Asian Nations on UNCRC and related protocols

South Asian nations	UNCRC, year of ratification	Optional Protocol to the Convention on the Rights of the Child on the sale of children, child prostitution, and child pornography, ratification status	Optional Protocol to the Convention on the Rights of the Child on a Communications Procedure (OPIC), ratification statuss
Afghanistan	1994	Ratified, 2002	Not ratified
Bangladesh	1990	Ratified, 2000	Not ratified
Bhutan	1990	Ratified, 2009	Not ratified
India	1992	Ratified, 2005	Not ratified
Maldives	1991	Ratified, 2002	Ratified, 2019
Nepal	1990	Ratified, 2006	Not ratified
Pakistan	1990	Ratified, 2011	Not ratified
Sri Lanka	1991	Ratified, 2006	Not ratified

17 Legal Framework in Different Countries

In the following section, laws related to CSA and the gaps that exist in the legislative frameworks for each South Asian country have been described.

17.1 Afghanistan

Nearly half of Afghanistan's 30 million people are below the age of 18 years. The precarious state with civil unrest has forced nearly 2.7 million to migrate (*Child Protection | UNICEF Afghanistan*, n.d.; *Submission to the UN Committee on the Rights of the Child on Afghanistan, 85th Session*, 2020). Against this background, international and domestic legislation is essential to protect children, the most vulnerable population, from abuse. Afghanistan ratified the UNCRC in 1994 (*Ratification Status by Country or Treaty*, n.d.).

The current domestic legislation framework for child abuse is concentrated in chapter 15, titled Protection of Children Against Prostitute and Sexual Activities.

Article 94 prohibits violent and illegal acts against children, including sexual misuse, and directs relevant ministries and governmental organizations to adopt necessary measures, and Article 95 prohibits the broadcasting of immoral movies for children. Article 96 deals with the prevention of exploitation and sexual misuse, directing relevant ministries and governmental organizations to prevent the same, including persuasion or coercion of a child to engage in any sexual activity, prostitution, or other illegal sexual activities or in pornography. Article 97 deals with preventing children from entering places like casinos, including online casinos and other programs that may harm the physical, psychological, and moral welfare of children. Article 98 prohibits the publication, purchase, and sale of media with pornographic content; even attempts to publish, sell, or give access to children are punishable (*Child Protection | UNICEF Afghanistan*, n.d.).

Another influential law that perhaps has taken societal and cultural changes into account and targets a prevalent cultural practice of Bacha Bazi, which is sexualizing young underage boys, is Article 99, which prohibits this practice—this shows a strong national resolve to take down a prevalent societal practice of exploiting young boys for entertainment or sexual gratification.

Legislative Gaps

The United Nations Special Rapporteur Report of Human Rights in Afghanistan 2024 has found that Children are still subjected to rape, sexual violence, and harmful practice such as Bacha Bazi. There is no national law to prevent child marriages. The situation, as per the report, is grim in rural and remote places (*Submission to the UN Committee on the Rights of the Child on Afghanistan, 85th Session*, 2020).

17.2 Bangladesh

In the year 2019, there were 1005 cases of rape reported in children. The coastal areas of Bangladesh are particularly vulnerable to poverty. Research has shown a high prevalence of child marriages and trafficking (*Global Monitoring Report on Bangladesh*, 2011; Shoji & Tsubota, 2022). Bangladesh ratified the UNCRC in 1990. It has also ratified most regional conventions, having drafted its domestic legislation congruent with the international legal framework.

The current domestic legislation which covers CSA in Bangladesh is as follows:

1. The Prevention and Suppression of Human Trafficking Act in 2012 has criminalized offenses related to child trafficking. However, the act applies to only girls and lacks protection for boys forced into prostitution or vulnerable to rape.
2. The 2012 Anti-Pornography Act criminalizes pornography. With the alarming rise of internet usage amongst children, it has been increasingly reported that children are being exposed to sexually explicit material. The Act, however, doesn't adequately address offenses like accessing, downloading, or viewing child sexual abuse material.
3. Child Marriage Restraint Act 2017 gives high child marriage rates. Early and forced marriage paves the way for the sexual exploitation of children. The act, however, contains an exemption that allows children to be married under special circumstances at the court's direction and with parental consent. Diabolically, the Act also contains punishment for children who marry and offers impunity to men who rape within the boundaries of marriage if the wife is above 13 years of age.
4. The Children's Act 2013 introduced a range of provisions which improved the child's lawful rights to access justice and remedies and established mandates for the setting of child-friendly courts and speedy expedition of justice.

Gaps

There is currently no legislation that prohibits children from being exploited in the context of tourism or travel. This poses a risk for sexual exploitation of children. The Anti-Pornography Act is alarmingly silent on grooming minors and live streaming of sexual abuse. The recent amendment lowered the marriageable age of girls to 16 years. This caused an outcry from human rights organizations that Bangladesh has not honored the international convention commitments. Recovery and reintegration services for victims of sexual abuse are not streamlined and are not covered under the purview of the legislation. Children often face delays in attaining justice and compensation, with case pendency extending often to 6 to 8 years.

17.3 Bhutan

Data on child sexual abuse is sparse from Bhutan. Even though the country enacted the Child Care Protection Act in 2011 to provide homes to children with stay facilities, implementation is still under process. A Women and Children Protection Division has also been established, but the training of police personnel remains unfulfilled. Family and child benches in courts have been established in a few places but are yet to be extended to all courts. The Ministry of Education is an important stakeholder in the prevention of child sexual abuse and violence against children. There are increasing concerns about its under-penetration in rural areas. Bhutan had ratified the UNCRC in 1990 (*Ratification Status by Country or Treaty*, n.d.).

Domestic Legislations:

1. Children's sexual exploitation in the form of prostitution is prohibited in the Child Care and Protection Act.
2. Child trafficking, pedophilia, the act of taking photographs or videos of children in a sexual act, and/or manufacturing, selling, and distributing any material that contains a depiction of a child in sexual contact are offenses punishable as per the Bhutan Penal Code.
3. Child Marriage is prohibited under the Penal Code, and any person below the age of 18 years is considered a child (*Penal Code of Bhutan*, 2004).

Gaps

There is also a lack of awareness and execution of laws in rural areas and a lack of one-step care service for children with sexual abuse to deal with psychological, social, medical, and legal issues. Lack of parenting and school awareness programs to guide and impart knowledge to children. Bhutan's domestic legislation is yet to harmonize with the committed international protocols.

17.4 India

As per the National Crime Records Bureau Statistics 2022, 64,469 child sexual abuse and 38,444 child rape cases were reported (*Crimes in India*, n.d.). Gross underreporting exists despite the existing strict mandatory reporting legislation. In India, the domestic framework consists of the Indian Constitution, Special Acts, and the Bharatiya Nyaya Sanhita (BNS), which replaced the Indian Penal Code (IPC) in 2024. The summary of the relevant legislation follows:

The Indian Constitution: The Constitution came into effect in 1950 and provides a legislative framework for governance and the rights and duties of citizens of India. Article 15 of the Constitution states that nothing shall prevent the state from making special provisions for women and children. The current Indian laws on the protection of the rights of children are framed keeping the essence of Article 15 (*Constitution of India | Legislative Department | India*, n.d.).

The Bharatiya Nyaya Sanhita (BNS): It is the new official criminal code of India, which replaced the Indian Penal Code in July 2024. The various codes under the BNS applicable to children facing sexual abuse and assault are placed under Chapter 5, Sections 63 to 73, which deal with grievous sexual offenses, including rape of females under 16 years. The maximum punishment awarded is the death penalty. The law also creates financial provisions to rehabilitate the victims of the offense and also prohibits media revelation of the identity of the victims. The law, however, is not gender-neutral. Sections 98 and 99 specifically are related to crimes of selling and procurement of children for prostitution.

Indian Special Acts

These special Acts were formulated to address specific populations and relevant concerns in the changing cultural landscape of the country.

The Protection of Children Sexual Offences Act, 2012 (POCSO).

This law was formulated based on the 2011 census report that the sexual crimes amongst vulnerable populations, especially children, had increased, and the prevalent penal laws at the time were insufficient to deliver justice. The relevant sections of the POCSO Act are:

- Penetrative sexual assault (Section 3)
- Aggravated Penetrative Sexual Assault (Section 5)
- Sexual assault (Section 7)
- Aggravated Sexual Assault (Section 9)
- Sexual harassment (Section 11)
- Using Child for Pornographic Purposes (section 13)

The Act also provides guidelines for measures that are child-friendly to be followed by the special courts, magistrates, and police. The degree of punishment varies from imprisonment to capital punishment. The recent amendments in 2019 introduced the death penalty for aggravated sexual assault. To plug loopholes in reporting, the POCSO Act also has a section on mandatory reporting by concerned authorities like schools and health professionals (Bhargavi, 2012; *The Protection of Children from Sexual Offences Act*, 2012).

The Juvenile Justice (Care and Protection of Children) Act, 2015: This Act was formulated as per the United Nations Standard Minimum Rules for Juvenile Justice. These rules are commonly called Beijing Rules. They provide guidelines for the protection and care of children below 18 years of age. It recognizes that a child can be in conflict with the law and also in need of protection and care (*The Juvenile Justice (Care and Protection of Children) Act*, 2015; *United Nations Standard Minimum Rules for the Administration of Juvenile Justice (The Beijing Rules)*, 1985).

The Commission for Protection of Child Rights Act, 2005 (CPCR), provides for the constitution of the National Commission and State Commission for the protection of child rights. The establishment of courts for children- for speedy trial of offenses (*Commissions for Protection of Child Rights Act, 2005*, n.d.).

Other relevant special acts in India that have legislative provisions to deal with CSA are the Immoral Traffic Prevention Act, 1956, which penalizes the trafficking of minors; the Prohibition of Child Marriage Act, 2003, which prohibits solemnizing marriage between underage persons; and the Information Technology Act, 2006, that attracts penalties for production, publication, and electronic media transmission of material related to explicit sexual acts involving minors (*The Immoral Traffic Prevention Act*, 2003; *The Information Technology Act*, 2000; *The Prohibition of Child Marriage Act*, 2006).

Critical Gaps in Legislation
The legislative framework in India has evolved to keep up with relevant societal changes and the UNCRC recommendations. However, there remain gaps evidenced by the high pendency of cases, sporadic incidences of abuse of children in welfare institutions, quality of care, and inadequate provisions to counter the sexual offenses children encounter (Choudhry et al., 2018; *Committee on Rights of Child Reviews Second Periodic Report on India*, 2004).

17.5 The Maldives

The Maldives enacted a special provision act to deal with child sex abuse offenders in 2009. It outlines legal procedures to deal with child sexual abuse cases and the process to investigate and detain offenders with post-trial follow-up. It provides a provision to accept low-standard evidence in the case of CSA to ensure strict enforcement of the law. The country ratified the UNCRC in 1991. The Children's Rights Protection Act, 2019, Article 11, states protection from sexual abuse, pornographic use of children, and sexual assault of children. Again, there are glaring legislative gaps between the commitments made to international protocols and the domestic legislative framework (*Children's Rights Protection Act*, 2019).

17.6 Nepal

This country is situated at the foot of the Himalayan range and is home to 2.8 million people, of whom 37.8% are below the age of 18 years. Nepal ratified the UNCRC in 1990 and is also a signatory to the Optional Protocol to the Convention on the Rights of the Child on the Sale of Children, Child Prostitution, and Child Pornography, 2000, which has prohibited the act of sale of children, child prostitution, and child pornography. The precarious geography of Nepal makes it prone to natural disasters like earthquakes, and economic sanctions by India in 2015 have impacted the lives of children already living in poverty. This has increased the risk of internal and external commercial sexual exploitation of children. Generational societal practices, like in the Bandi community, where women and young girls are pushed into prostitution, also increase the vulnerability of children(*A Report on the Scale, Scope, and Context of the Sexual Exploitation of Children in Nepal*, 2020).

The domestic legislations in Nepal are:

1. The constitutional laws and the Nepal Penal Code chapter 18, which include legislations Article 39(7) of the Constitution of Nepal, 2072; the National Civil Code, 2074 § 132(1) (b) and (c); the National Penal Code, 2074 §219(2), 219(3), and 225. The salient feature of this is that a child is defined as a person who is below 18 years; the law is gender neutral; and it criminalizes the rape and sexual exploitation of children.

   The punishments for the offense:

   If a person rapes a child below ten years, he will be imprisoned for life. If he is ten years or above and below 14, he will be imprisoned for 18 to 20 years. If the child is 14 years or above and below 16, he will be imprisoned for 12–14 years, and if the child is below 18 years and 16 years or above, he will be imprisoned for ten to 12 years.
2. In Nepal, a separate special act, i.e., "The Act Relating to Children, 2075," was instituted with the objective of protecting the best interest of the children. The act includes sexual abuse, sexual exploitation, exposure, and coercing children to be involved in pornography as offenses. The Act also prescribes punishment for child sexual abuse; the minimum punishment awarded to the person performing the act of child sexual abuse is a fine up to 75,000 and imprisonment of 3 years, and the maximum punishment is a fine of up to 150,000 and imprisonment of 15 years.

Gaps in Legislation

The review reports by international organizations like the ECPAT (End Child Prostitution and Trafficking) have shown that the sexual exploitation of children is embedded in tourism, and Nepal also has the 17th highest prevalence of child marriages in the world. The domestic legislation is not harmonized effectively with the international and optional protocols to combat child sexual abuse.

17.7 Pakistan

Pakistan is a young country, with more than half (53%) of the population being children and adolescents. The number of cases of child abuse that were reported in the year 2022 was 2123, with both genders being equally victimized. The province of Punjab in Pakistan reported the highest number of cases. Pakistan is a signatory of the UNCRC and ratified the convention in 1990 (Sahil-Six Months Cruel Numbers Report, 2023; Younus et al., 2018).

The following are the domestic legislations in Pakistan that address child sexual abuse:

The Pakistan Penal Code (PPC) sections 90, 375, 376, 377:

Section 90 invalidates consent from persons below 12 years of age. Section 375 defines the circumstances of rape, and sec 376 defines punishment for the same, with the maximum imprisonment term being 25 years. Section 377 defines the circumstances of unnatural carnal sexual offense with a woman, man, or animal. The PPC is a general law with a limited view of child sexual abuse (Ahmad, 2019; *Pakistan Penal Code*, 1860).

Societal changes and amendments:

The Kasur sex scandal that ranged between 2006 and 2014 and mounting evidence from media reports have brought in amendments to existing laws. The 18th Amendment, the Punjab Destitute and Neglected Children Act 2004, is the major law related to child protection that criminalizes the sexual abuse of children under section 40; it also mandates the establishment of a Child Protection and Welfare Bureau with child protection officers. The Criminal Law Second Amendment Act 2016 of the PPC was made to address the widely prevalent problem of sexual abuse in Pakistan. They raised the minimum of criminal responsibility from 7 years to 10 years and included sections related to pornography related to children and exposure of children to seduction (Jillani, 2018).

Legislative Gaps

The OHCHR (Office of the United Nations High Commissioner for Human Rights) report on Pakistan has shown that though Pakistan has made strides, coerced religious conversions and child marriages continue. Even the periodic report submitted by Pakistan has shown that domestic legislation has not been able to put a leash on CSA and that the laws need to be harmonized with the UNCRC recommendations (*Pakistan: UN Experts Urge Action on Coerced Religious Conversions, Forced and Child Marriage*, 2023).

17.8 Sri Lanka

Over 21 million people call Sri Lanka their home, among whom six million are under the age of 18 years. Several factors have been identified that increase the potential of sexual exploitation of children. One widely acknowledged factor is poverty. UNICEF has reported that 36% of children in Sri Lanka live below the poverty line. Sri Lanka ratified the UNCRC in 1991, also an optional protocol of the UN related to the Sale of Children, Child Prostitution, and Child Pornography (*National Child Protection Legisltation of Srilanka*, 2022).

Domestic Legislations

Penal Code

Articles 360A & B prohibit sexual contact with any person below 16 years of age. It defines a child as any person below 18 years of age. Those who solicit contact of a perpetrator with a minor are also held culpable under this section. Article 360 C prohibits the trafficking of minors. Article 363 penalizes rape with or without consent if a woman is under 16 years of age but has a clause that if 12 years and above and is legally married to the man is not considered an offense.

Marriage Registration Ordinance
Section 15: The prohibited age of marriage is below 18 years of age, and the marriage contract is invalid. However, in section 22, parents or guardians can offer consent for the marriage of a person below 18 years (*Code of Criminal Procedure Act in Sri Lanka*, n.d.)!

Mandatory Reporting Requirements
Penal Code Amendment of 2006: Article 286A prohibits obscene publication exhibitions relating to children and holds capable any person, including parents or guardians, who may be responsible for the same. Article 286B also states that any person responsible for running a computer center should ensure that the facility is not being used for the commission of an act of CSA (*Code of Criminal Procedure Act in Sri Lanka*, n.d.).

Gaps in Legislation
The concerns in domestic legislation, when examined by ECPAT (The International Non-profit "End Child Prostitution and Trafficking") that monitors child rights in South Asian and Southeast Asian nations, have found gaps in Sri Lankan domestic legislation. Sri Lanka, primarily a tourist destination, had no legal provisions to prohibit foreign nationals from leaving the country after committing offenses related to child abuse. Also, the establishment of a mandatory repository of offenders as mandated per the ratification of optional international protocols was also lacking (Sergeev, 2021).

18 Conclusion

CSA is a critical issue in South Asia, which houses over a third of the world's children. Prevalence rates are high due to underreporting because of stigma, fear, and lack of awareness. Determinants of CSA include individual factors (age, trauma exposure), family factors (poverty, substance abuse), and societal factors (patriarchal norms, weak law enforcement). Perpetrators usually include family members, teachers, and relatives. There are various theoretical models to explain CSA. Clinical approaches emphasize recognizing signs of abuse, such as behavioral changes, physical symptoms, and indirect disclosures. Ethical considerations in reporting include respecting autonomy, ensuring beneficence, and maintaining confidentiality. However, dilemmas arise due to family, professional, and child safety concerns.

Despite the presence of legal frameworks addressing CSA across South Asia, significant challenges persist in enforcement, victim protection, and social attitudes. Countries like India and Nepal have comprehensive laws, while others, such as Afghanistan and Bhutan, rely only on general criminal provisions. Weak implementation, judicial delays, and corruption undermine justice in Pakistan, Bangladesh, and Sri Lanka, while religious and cultural influences shape legal outcomes in Afghanistan and the Maldives. Widespread stigma and fear of retaliation lead to severe underreporting, particularly in Bhutan, Nepal, and Pakistan. There are inadequate legal procedures and support services that are victim-friendly in most countries except India and Nepal, which leaves survivors in a vulnerable state. Slow judicial processes and institutional inefficiencies further weaken legal responses across the region. Addressing these systemic issues requires stronger enforcement mechanisms, improved victim protection, and greater awareness to create a legal and social environment that ensures justice for survivors of CSA.

References

A report on the scale, scope and context of the sexual exploitation of children in Nepal. (2020). https://ecpat.org/wp-content/uploads/2021/05/ECPAT-Country-Overview-Report-Sexual-Exploitation-of-Children-in-Nepal-2020-ENG.pdf

Adamcheck, A., Carville, K., Cilingiroglu, S., Clements, R., Ford, S., Ingham, L., Macris, L., Peddada, Y., Pham, H., Sarmah, A., Schreur, H., Signy, K., Steval, K., Tunstall, L., Weber, I., & Wells, A. (2020). The implementation of the convention on the rights of children in seven South Asian countries. *Institutionalised Children Explorations and Beyond, 7*(1), 37.

Ahmad, R. (2019). Section 375 of the Pakistan Penal Code and the exclusion of male rape survivors. *Pakistan College of Law Student Journal of Law, III*(II) https://leappakistan.com/wp-content/uploads/2020/05/2.pdf

Bhargavi, S. (2012). *The protection of children from sexual offences- An overview*. https://cdnbbsr.s3waas.gov.in/s3ec03333cb763facc6ce398ff83845f22/uploads/2024/09/2024091190.pdf.

Chacko, A. Z., Paul, J. S. G., Vishwanath, R., Sreevathsan, S., Bennet, D., Livingstone, P. D., & John, J. (2022). A study on child sexual abuse reported by urban indian college students. *Journal of Family Medicine and Primary Care, 11*(9), 5072. https://doi.org/10.4103/jfmpc.jfmpc_1081_21

Child protection | UNICEF Afghanistan. (n.d.). Retrieved February 2, 2025, from https://www.unicef.org/afghanistan/child-protection

Children's Rights Protection Act. (2019). Retrieved February 2, from https://natlex.ilo.org/dyn/natlex2/r/natlex/fe/details?p3_isn=110452

Choudhry, V., Dayal, R., Pillai, D., Kalokhe, A. S., Beier, K., & Patel, V. (2018). Child sexual abuse in India: A systematic review. *PLoS One, 13*(10), e0205086. https://doi.org/10.1371/journal.pone.0205086

Code of Criminal Procedure Act in Sri Lanka. (n.d.). Retrieved February 2, 2025, from https://www.srilankalaw.lk/c/217-code-of-criminal-procedure-act.html

Commissions for Protection of Child Rights Act, 2005. (n.d.). Retrieved February 2, 2025, from https://www.indiacode.nic.in/bitstream/123456789/2056/1/200604.pdf

Committee on Rights of Child reviews Second Periodic Report on India. (2004, January 21). OHCHR. https://www.ohchr.org/en/press-releases/2009/10/committee-rights-child-reviews-second-periodic-report-india

Constitution of India | Legislative Department | India. (n.d.). Retrieved February 2, 2025, from https://legislative.gov.in/constitution-of-india/

Fernandes, D., Gomes, J. P., Albuquerque, P. B., & Matos, M. (2024). Forensic interview techniques in child sexual abuse cases: A scoping review. *Trauma, Violence & Abuse, 25*(2), 1382.

Finkelhor, D. (1984). *Child sexual abuse: New theory and research*. Free Press.

Global monitoring report on Bangladesh. (2011). End Child prostitution, Child pornography and trafficking of children for Sexual purposes(ECPAT) international. https://ecpat.org/wp-content/uploads/2021/08/A4A_V2_SA_BANGLADESH.pdf.

Hall, G. C. N., & Hirschman, R. (1992). Sexual aggression against children: A conceptual perspective of etiology. *Criminal Justice and Behavior, 19*(1), 8–23.

Jillani, A. (2018, December 2). *Punjab. Sexual aggression again.* DAWN.COM. https://www.dawn.com/news/1388805

Jiloha, R. C., Kukreti, P., & Kataria, D. (2019). *Forensic psychiatry: An Indian perspective*. Jaypee. https://www.jaypeedigital.com/book/9789352704989

Marshall, W. L., & Barbaree, H. E. (1990). An integrated theory of the etiology of sexual offending. In W. L. Marshall, D. R. Laws, & H. E. Barbaree (Eds.), *Handbook of sexual assault: Issues, theories, and treatment of the offender* (p. 257). Springer.

National Child protection Legisltation of SriLanka. (2022). https://cdn.icmec.org/wp-content/uploads/2022/03/Sri-Lanka_National-Legislation-FINAL-Feb.-2022.pdf

National Crime Records Bureau. (n.d.). Retrieved February 2, 2025, from https://www.ncrb.gov.in/crime-in-india-year-wise.html?year=2022&keyword

Pakistan Penal Code. (1860). https://www.pakistani.org/pakistan/legislation/1860/actXLVof1860.html

Pakistan: UN experts urge action on coerced religious conversions, forced and child marriage. (2023, January 16). OHCHR. https://www.ohchr.org/en/press-releases/2023/01/pakistan-un-experts-urge-action-coerced-religious-conversions-forced-and

Penal Code of Bhutan. (2004). https://www.rbp.gov.bt/Forms/PCB%202004.pdf

Rahim, S., Bourgaize, C., Khan, M., Matthew, L., & Barron, I. (2021). Child sexual abuse in Pakistan schools: A non-systematic narrative literature review. *Journal of Child Sexual Abuse, 30*(5), 546.

Rai, B. (2016). A research study on the situation of child sexual abuse in five South Asian countries and finding the effective programs for the prevention. In *Proceedings of International Academic Conferences 3305586*. International Institute of Social and Economic Sciences. https://econpapers.repec.org/paper/sekiacpro/3305586.htm

Ramaswamy, S., Devgun, M., Seshadri, S., & Bunders-Aelen, J. (2023). Balancing the law with children's rights to participation and decision-making: Practice guidelines for mandatory reporting processes in child sexual abuse. *Asian Journal of Psychiatry, 81*, 103464. https://doi.org/10.1016/j.ajp.2023.103464

Ratification status by Country or Treaty. (n.d.). Office of High Commissioner of Human Rights. Retrieved February 2, 2025, from https://tbinternet.ohchr.org/_layouts/15/TreatyBodyExternal/Treaty.aspx?Treaty=CRC&Lang=en

Responding to child maltreatment: A clinical handbook for health professionals. (2022, April 8). World Health Organization. https://www.who.int/publications/i/item/9789240048737

Sahil- Six months Cruel Numbers report. (2023). https://sahil.org/cruel-numbers/

Sakelliadis, E. I., Spiliopoulou, C. A., & Papadodima, S. A. (2009). Forensic investigation of child victim with sexual abuse. *Indian Pediatrics, 46*(2), 144.

Selengia, V., Thuy, H. N. T., & Mushi, D. (2020). Prevalence and patterns of child sexual abuse in selected countries of Asia and Africa: A review of literature. *Open Journal of Social Sciences, 8*(9), 9. https://doi.org/10.4236/jss.2020.89010

Sergeev, E. (2021). *Swedish International Development Cooperation Agency (SIDA) (SSRN Scholarly Paper 3991734)*. Social Science Research Network. https://doi.org/10.2139/ssrn.3991734

Shoji, M., & Tsubota, K. (2022). Sexual exploitation of trafficked children: Survey evidence from child sex workers in Bangladesh. *Journal of Comparative Economics, 50*(1), 101.

Solehati, T., Pramukti, I., Hermayanti, Y., Kosasih, C. E., & Mediani, H. S. (2021). Current of child sexual abuse in Asia: A systematic review of prevalence, impact, age of first exposure, perpetrators, and place of offence. *Open Access Macedonian Journal of Medical Sciences, 9*(T6), T6. https://doi.org/10.3889/oamjms.2021.7334

Submission to the UN Committee on the Rights of the Child on Afghanistan, 85th Session. (2020, August 8). https://allsurvivorsproject.org/submission-to-the-un-committee-on-the-rights-of-the-child-on-afghanistan/

Summit, R. C. (1983). The child sexual abuse accommodation syndrome. *Child Abuse & Neglect, 7*(2), 177.

Talbot, N. L., Chapman, B., Conwell, Y., McCollumn, K., Franus, N., Cotescu, S., & Duberstein, P. R. (2009). Childhood sexual abuse is associated with physical illness burden and functioning in psychiatric patients 50 years of age and older. *Psychosomatic Medicine, 71*(4), 417.

Talwar, S., Osorio, C., Sagar, R., Appleton, R., & Billings, J. (2024). What are the experiences of and interventions for adult survivors of childhood sexual abuse in South Asia? A systematic review and narrative synthesis. *Trauma, Violence & Abuse, 25*(4), 2957.

The Immoral Traffic Prevention Act. (2003). https://www.indiacode.nic.in/bitstream/123456789/15100/1/immoral_traffic_prevention_act_%28itpa%29_1956.pdf

The Information Technology Act. (2000). https://www.indiacode.nic.in/bitstream/123456789/13116/1/it_act_2000_updated.pdf

The Juvenile Justice (Care and Protection of Children) Act. (2015). http://indiacode.nic.in/handle/123456789/2148

The Prohibition of Child Marriage Act. (2006). https://www.indiacode.nic.in/bitstream/123456789/15943/1/the_prohibition_of_child_marriage_act%2C_2006.pdf

The Protection of Children from Sexual Offences Act. (2012). https://www.indiacode.nic.in/bitstream/123456789/2079/1/AA2012-32.pdf

The United Nations Convention on Right of the Child. (1989, November 20). UNICEF. https://www.unicef.org.uk/what-we-do/un-convention-child-rights/

United Nations Standard Minimum Rules for the Administration of Juvenile Justice (The Beijing Rules). (1985, November 29). Office of High Commissioner of Human Rights. https://www.ohchr.org/en/instruments-mechanisms/instruments/united-nations-standard-minimum-rules-administration-juvenile

Ward, T., & Siegert, R. J. (2002). Toward a comprehensive theory of child sexual abuse: A theory knitting perspective. *Psychology, Crime and Law.* https://doi.org/10.1080/10683160208401823

Younus, S., Chachar, A. S., & Mian, A. (2018). Child protection in Pakistan: Legislation & implementation. *Pakistan Journal of Neurological Sciences (PJNS), 13*(2), 12.

Index

A. Parmar et al. (eds.), *Forensic Psychiatry and Prison Mental Health in South Asia*, South Asian Perspectives in Mental Health and Psychology,
https://doi.org/10.1007/978-981-96-7206-6

MIX
Papier aus verantwortungsvollen Quellen
Paper from responsible sources
FSC® C105338
FSC
www.fsc.org

If you have any concerns about our products,
you can contact us on
ProductSafety@springernature.com

In case Publisher is established outside the EU,
the EU authorized representative is:
Springer Nature Customer Service Center GmbH
Europaplatz 3, 69115 Heidelberg, Germany

Printed by Libri Plureos GmbH
in Hamburg, Germany